World War II

World War II

TOTAL WARFARE
AROUND THE GLOBE

Robert A. Doughty
United States Military Academy

Ira D. Gruber
Rice University

Roy K. Flint
United States Military Academy

Mark Grimsley
The Ohio State University

George C. Herring
University of Kentucky

Donald D. Horward
Florida State University

John A. Lynn
University of Illinois

Williamson Murray
The Ohio State University

D. C. Heath and Company

Lexington, Massachusetts   Toronto

Address editorial correspondence to:

D. C. Heath and Company
125 Spring Street
Lexington, MA 02173

Acquisitions: *James Miller*
Development: *Pat Wakeley*
Editorial Production: *Melissa Ray*
Design: *Alwyn R. Velásquez*
Photo Research: *Picture Research Consultants, Inc./Sandi Rygiel
& Pembroke Herbert*
Art Editing: *Diane Grossman*
Production Coordination: *Richard Tonachel*

The views expressed herein are those of the authors and do not purport to reflect the position of the United States Military Academy, the Department of the Army, or the Department of Defense.

PREFACE

World War II: Total Warfare Around the Globe was first published as part of a larger history, *Warfare in the Western World*. We wrote that larger history to provide a coherent, readable, and authoritative account of the past four centuries of military operations in the West—to explain, as clearly as possible, how the waging of war has changed from one era to another since the beginning of the seventeenth century. Although we examined the underlying developments in population, agriculture, industry, technology, and politics that affected warfare, we focused on the employment of armed forces. We were most interested in operations, in the conduct of relatively large forces across a specific theater of war. We included warfare at sea and in the air as well as joint operations, but we concentrated on fighting ashore. In short, we set out to write a sound and readable history of military operations in the West since 1600, a history that would appeal to students, general readers, and anyone seeking an authoritative reference on warfare.

Like its parent, *World War II* was designed to provide a coherent, readable, and authoritative history of military operations—in this instance, of operations during the largest and most destructive of all wars. It is now published separately because its author, Williamson Murray, has done his job remarkably well and because after more than half a century, his subject remains among the most interesting and important in the history of warfare. Murray has succeeded in creating an unusually well-balanced and coherent account of operations in the various theaters of the war. He blends the great land battles of western Europe, North Africa, and Russia with the air offensives against Britain, Germany, and Japan and the naval campaigns in the North Atlantic and the central and western Pacific. He also succeeds in placing the operations of 1939–1945 in the larger history of warfare in the Western world. His analysis makes clear that while many practices begun during the First World War were continued during the Second, the opposing sides in World War II mounted operations of greater scale, complexity, and power and came closer to waging total, global war than anyone ever has.

Indeed, World War II represents the culmination of a prolonged and gradual shift toward total warfare in the Western world. That shift began during the wars of the French Revolution and Napoleon, when the French rejected professional armies and limited warfare and turned instead to armies of the people waging wars of survival and conquest. They and Napoleon soon taught Europeans a more mobile and decisive way of war and provoked in some places spontaneous and fanatical popular resistance. During their Civil War, the people of the new United States went even farther toward total war. When the North found that it could not destroy the Confederacy in conventional campaigns—that inspired citizen soldiers equipped with rifled weapons were a dangerous and resilient enemy—the United States adopted total war as an instrument of policy. Northern commanders sought not only to wear away Confederate forces in campaigns of attrition but also to exhaust the South by freeing slaves, destroying farms and factories, and breaking the will of the people. In World War I both sides—Allies and Central Powers—surpassed all previous efforts toward mobilizing their people and resources systematically for war and toward applying their forces against the enemy's armed forces, industry, and population. But neither side could gain the operational mobility to bring its power fully to bear on the enemy. Not until World War II were states able to combine comprehensive national mobilization with large-scale mobile warfare to sustain operations around the globe, to push society closer than ever to total war.

The mobile warfare that characterized World War II depended in some ways on weapons and methods developed during World War I, and in other important ways on improvements and innovations that came between the wars or after World War II began. By 1918 Western forces had many of the weapons and techniques that would be employed in World War II: machine guns, flamethrowers, rapid-fire artillery, and tanks—together with tactics that promised to break the hold of trench warfare; airplanes that could cooperate with ground forces, engage other planes, and undertake primitive strategic bombing missions; and submarines and rudimentary aircraft carriers to complement powerful surface warships. But not until tanks, planes, and ships had been significantly improved and until better methods had been devised for using and supporting these improved weapons could warfare become truly mobile.

During World War II armies employed faster, more powerful, and more durable tanks in combination with mechanized infantry, mobile artillery, airborne forces, and close air support to keep operations fluid on nearly all fronts. Similarly, air forces had the bombers and long-range escorts to make strategic bombing an important part of war, to bring the enemy's population and industry under systematic attack; and navies had the ships—especially improved aircraft carriers and submarines—that could be resupplied at sea and could project power across oceans, could engage the enemy well beyond the horizon, and could sustain amphibious forces thousands of miles from established bases. These land, air, and sea forces made operations in World War II more fluid, complex, and destructive than any in the history of warfare. Eventually, they gained a decisive victory on an unprecedented scale.

Murray's success in creating a balanced and coherent account of operations in World War II and in locating that account in the broader history of warfare in the Western world is a tribute to his knowledge of the subject and his talent for synthesis. It is also a tribute to the work of scores of other scholars. He, like the other authors of *Warfare in the Western World,* has benefitted from the writings and the comments of specialists and colleagues. We are all particularly indebted to Richard Kohn and John Shy, who read carefully an entire draft of the text and drew on their remarkable understanding of military history and sharp critical judgment to suggest ways of improving the whole. We are grateful to all who have had a part in creating *Warfare in the Western World* in general and *World War II* in particular. We do not imagine that we will have satisfied our critics; we do hope that they and other readers will continue to share their knowledge of warfare with us.

R. A. D. and I. D. G.

CONTENTS IN BRIEF

CONTENTS

MAP SYMBOLS

The symbols shown below are used on the maps in this volume. Most of the symbols suggest the organization of units in particular campaigns or battles. The reader should understand that the organization of military units has changed over time and has varied from army to army or even within armies. For example, the composition and size of Napoleon's corps varied within his own army and differed from those of his opponents; they also differed dramatically from those of armies later in the nineteenth century. The symbols thus indicate the organization of a unit at a particular time and do not indicate its precise composition or size.

Division	[X X box]
Corps	[X X X box]
Army	[X X X X box]
Army Group	[X X X X X box]
Cavalry Screen	• • •
Armor	[oval in box]
Airborne	[parachute symbol]
Fort	¤
Mine	o—o—o—o
Bridge	[bridge symbol]
Boundary between Units	——xxxxx——

LIST OF MAPS

1

GERMANY TRIUMPHANT: RESTORING MOBILITY TO WAR

World War II was the largest and most costly conflict in human history. It began with the German invasion of Poland on September 1, 1939; it ended on the decks of the battleship *Missouri* on September 2, 1945. By its conclusion the war in Europe had killed approximately 15 million military and 35 million civilians. The Nazis had exterminated 6 million Jews and countless others; 25 million Soviets were homeless; and Allied strategic bombing had wrecked every major German city. In Asia the casualty bill was equally horrendous. No one knows how many died as a result of the Sino-Japanese war; famine, military actions, disease—all combined to raise the Chinese losses to tens of millions. The firebombing of Tokyo and the dropping of the atomic bomb on Hiroshima, *each* killed well over 100,000 Japanese.

In a real sense World War II resulted from the desire of three of the major powers to overturn the legacy of the nineteenth century. Germany, Japan, and Italy had come late to the division of the world; World War I served only to exacerbate their frustrations. In the case of all three nations, ferocious ideologies emerged out of national historical experiences and economic collapse in the depression, and extreme ideological nationalism led them to wage merciless war against their enemies. Though initially hesitant to mobilize all its resources, Nazi Germany defined the terms within which it would fight World War II as a total war. In reply, the democracies had to go to equal extremes in order to survive. The cost was terrifyingly high, and if the world that emerged in 1945 was less than perfect, at least it was a world in which the three great tyrannies of Germany, Japan, and Italy no longer existed.

Perhaps the best way to understand warfare during World War II is to think of the period 1914–1945 as a single continuum, for the battlefields of 1939 to 1945 represented a continuation and an amplification of the developments that had occurred in World War I. Except for the final explosion of the atomic bomb, there was little that was revolutionary about World War II. Even the seemingly revolutionary operational employment of tanks by the Germans in 1940 represented the fruition of tactical and operational concepts the Germans had developed in the latter part of World War I. Technological developments largely followed the paths laid out by the last conflict, even though advances in communications, radar, sonar, jet power, proximity fuses, rockets, and other equipment raised technology to new levels. The mobilization of men, women, machines, and raw materials also largely followed the paths laid out in the last conflict. What was different was the harnessing of all resources to the war effort at unprecedented levels and the unparalleled destruction, particularly of civilians and their possessions, in the course of the war. It was not revolutionary tactics or exotic weapons but rather the greater industrial potential and economic strength that won the war. God, as Napoleon had suggested, was indeed on the side with the biggest battalions.

Military Developments Between the Wars

Ground War

With the end of World War I, Europe and the world settled into an uneasy period of peace lasting barely twenty years. With huge arsenals remaining from the Great War, the thinking of most armies remained constrained by the capabilities of weapons left over from the war. As weapons like the tank became more capable, most military leaders simply integrated the improved weapons into old concepts and prepared to fight tightly controlled and relatively static battles reminiscent of the Great War. The Germans, however, prepared to fight mobile battles. By carefully studying the experiences of World War I (particularly the doctrinal developments of the war's last years), they identified the most important innovations of that war and concluded that those innovations provided the conceptual framework for restoring mobility to the battlefield. They also recognized how improved tanks and airplanes could magnify the effect of infiltration tactics and make them even more dramatic. Thus the Germans adapted more successfully than their opponents, devised concepts for mobile warfare, and inflicted crushing defeats on their enemies in the early years of World War II.

Historians have often pictured development of the *Blitzkrieg* as a revolutionary step that took place in the late 1930s; it was not. Almost immediately after the Weimar Republic had settled down, the *Truppenamt* (the title of the disguised general staff) finished a doctrinal manual that crystalized the World War I experience. Completed in 1924, *Die Truppenführung* expertly distilled the tactical and operational methods of World War I and provided the basis of the German "way of war." The doctrine emphasized a number of crucial ideas: (1) the nature of the modern battlefield demands decentralized, mission-oriented orders; (2) speed and exploitation of enemy weaknesses demand that whether on the offensive or defensive, troop commanders use initiative and take advantage of developing situations without waiting for orders; (3) modern warfare demands a close integration and cooperation between combat branches; and (4) commanders must exercise leadership from the front.

The German success in preparing for the next conflict reflected personal as well as intellectual factors. The first commander-in-chief of the *Reichswehr* (the German army during the Weimar Republic), General Hans von Seeckt, was a general staff officer. When the Western Powers dictated a reduction of the German army to 5,000 officers and 100,000 men after World War I, Seeckt confronted the necessity of drastically reducing the officer corps. In so doing he insured that members of the general staff controlled all key positions. This was a crucial step because general staff officers had developed the offensive and defensive doctrine in 1917–1918 that had

Despite the constraints imposed by the Treaty of Versailles, General Hans von Seeckt prepared the German army for highly mobile, offensive operations.

altered the World War I battlefield. Seeckt also focused the army on the offensive. With only 100,000 soldiers, the Germans could not wage a long defensive campaign; instead, the army would become a powerful striking force relying on mobility and surprise, rather than enormous amounts of firepower. In essence, Seeckt shaped the army for what came to be known as the *Blitzkrieg*, and he did this before the Germans had panzer divisions.

Shortly after Adolf Hitler came to power on January 30, 1933, the German military began a massive rearmament program. Given Hitler's program for extensive conquests on the European continent, the army was the centerpiece of German rearmament. In particular, the army's commander-in-chief, Colonel General Werner von Fritsch, and the chief of the general staff, General Ludwig Beck, set the tone and direction of the army effort. They aimed at creating a modern military force and incorporating the experience of World War I in its doctrine, training, and preparation. In no sense was their approach revolutionary. The focus of the buildup emphasized traditional combat branches, infantry and artillery. But their doctrine concentrated on decentralized authority, flexibility, speed, and exploitation, a framework that eventually translated into the basis of modern mechanized warfare.

Between 1933 and 1939, the Germans greatly expanded the size of their army and armored forces. Beck backed the establishment of the first three panzer divisions in 1935, and during the same period he ordered the general staff to conduct a war game on the employment of panzer corps. By 1936 the Germans were studying the employment of a panzer army and in 1938 began forming two more panzer divisions. By the start of the war in September 1939, they had fifty-four active divisions, six of which were armored. But for economic reasons as well as the shortage of petroleum available to the Third Reich, the *Wehrmacht* remained a traditional infantry-dominated army. Nevertheless, its leaders had shaped it into a highly mobile and capable force, the perfect tool for Hitler's aggressive policies.

On the basis of their experiences in Poland, the Germans converted four light divisions into panzer divisions, with motorized infantry divisions backing them up. Still, the army that invaded France in May 1940 consisted of less than twenty motorized and mechanized divisions and over one hundred regular infantry divisions. Nevertheless, all these divisions, including the armored, possessed a common doctrinal conception, and all were prepared to fight highly mobile battles.

German preparation went beyond developing a doctrine for mobile warfare and forming panzer units. The Germans expected all officers to be thoroughly familiar with doctrinal and tactical concepts. Whether in exercises or on the battlefield, units had to live up to the spirit of doctrine. When they did not, commanders instituted rigorous training programs to ensure that standards rose. German officers, however, did not learn to apply doctrine blindly; rather they learned to solve tactical and operational problems by using doctrine as a framework or guide, not as a formula. In accordance with their tradition of *Auftragstaktik*, or mission-oriented tactics, commanders were expected to understand the *intent* of their leaders and to take initiative when necessary to accomplish the mission. Thus in an environment that emphasized decentralization and initiative, the Germans prepared their officers and units to function smoothly on a mobile battlefield.

In Britain the educated elite rejected the possibility that their army might ever again fight on the European continent. Nevertheless, Britain produced two of the more original military thinkers during this period: J. F. C. Fuller and B. H. Liddell Hart. Fuller, a tank officer in World War I, wrote extensively on the potential of the tank. Liddell Hart, an infantry officer in the war, extended Fuller's ideas to suggest the possibility of using tanks not only to break through enemy lines but also to drive deep into enemy rear areas as an exploitation force and disrupt its command and control. Under these two men's influence in the 1920s and early 1930s, the British army carried out experiments with armored test forces. Limited defense budgets, however, made it difficult to fund extensive experiments or

Europe, 1919

form armored units. Additionally, the general unwillingness of the British even to consider another war in Europe made the formation of armored units unnecessary and unlikely. It was difficult to see what armored divisions would do for an army that was going to fight only colonial wars. In the end even Liddell Hart abandoned his advocacy of mechanization and argued for an army that would have no continental role.

Nevertheless, the problems confronting the British army resulted from more than a lack of public interest or funds; some were of its own doing. Not until 1932 did the army establish a committee to study the lessons of World War I. When that committee presented its findings, the chief of the imperial general staff prevented the report from circulating in the army. Throughout the interwar period, the officer corps reflected the stratification of British society; social standing contributed more to advancement than did professional competence and tactical proficiency. The army had no common doctrinal framework within which it prepared for war, and the combat branches went their own separate ways.

The British army did conduct a series of remarkable experiments in the late 1920s and early 1930s to examine the potential of armored warfare. Those tests underlined the potential that tanks offered as well as some of the limiting factors. The British failed, however, to incorporate the lessons of these experiments into the development of their armored forces. Ironically, the Germans learned the most from these efforts and began their armored forces in 1933 based on much of what they had learned from observing the British experiments.

The French developed forces and doctrine very different from those of Germany. Facing a potential enemy with nearly twice the population and much greater economic means, they devoted considerable efforts and resources in the interwar period to ensuring their security. Most noteworthy among their accomplishments was the building of the Maginot Line along the northeastern frontier of France. Composed of huge underground fortresses with elaborate electrical, ventilation, and communications systems, the Maginot Line protected key natural resources and large industrial and population centers along the frontier. Though historians have sometimes blamed the disaster of 1940 on a "Maginot Line" mentality, the defensive line accomplished its strategic purpose of shielding vulnerable areas and permitting the concentration of forces along other parts of the frontier.

The French also spent considerable sums on the development of armored forces; by 1940 they had approximately the same number of tanks as Germany. Instead of concentrating their tanks in large armored formations, however, they spread them thinly across the army. They developed large cavalry divisions that resembled German panzer divisions, but they did not form their first armored division until after the Germans overran Poland in September 1939. After devoting years to careful analysis and experimentation, the French prepared to fight methodical battles in which infantry, artillery, and tanks remained under the tight control of higher commanders and moved short distances from phase line to phase line. Thus the French tried to control the battlefield and their troops in a fashion that the battles of

1918 had already proven unrealistic. Their excessive emphasis on firepower robbed subordinate commanders of initiative and flexibility and ruled out the possibility of any grand maneuvers.

The Soviets provide an interesting and tragic contrast. Arising out of the collapse of 1917, the Red Army, largely created by Leon Trotsky, had beaten back both its Russian opponents and invading Poles in 1919–1921. The Soviets then had to create a military organization loyal to the revolutionary regime. Even within the Red Army, serious disagreements existed as to what kind of forces the Soviet Union required for its defense in a hostile world. A substantial group, centered around former tsarist officer Mikhail N. Tukhachevskii, pushed for creation of an elite force on the leading edge of emerging technology and military thinking. Under Tukhachevskii's leadership the Red Army created its first armored divisions in 1931 (four years before the Germans) and organized large-scale paratrooper drops for the 1935 and 1936 maneuvers.

But the idea of a mass conscript army still appealed to many; as a result, the Soviets vacillated and followed both paths. A series of five-year plans, launched by Stalin in 1927, forced the industrialization of Russia and aimed at providing an economic base to support great military forces. But in May 1937, Stalin loosed his secret police on the Soviet military. A devastating purge savaged the army; Tukhachevskii and virtually all of the modernizers died in front of firing squads. The doctrine developed by these "traitors" also had to go; 1939 found the Soviets busily dismantling the Red Army's armored divisions at the moment that the Nazi panzer divisions were winning their first successes.

In many ways the experiences of the U.S. Army in the interwar period reflected those of the British army. In the early 1920s, Congress had passed the National Defense Act which, had it been implemented, would have provided a framework for developing coherent military forces. But it was not implemented. Instead, as "normalcy" tightened its grip on the American public, defense budgets steadily declined in the 1920s; the arrival of the depression in 1929 further decreased funding available to the military. In the 1920s, with a relatively benign international climate, there was some justification in the disinterest that politicians and public displayed toward the military. But the continuing disinterest in the 1930s as war approached is indeed difficult to explain.

The army in the interwar years confronted no opponents. The Indian wars had ended years earlier, and the Filipinos awaited independence. In small, isolated posts scattered around the United States and its possessions, the interwar army possessed neither equipment, nor funding, nor force levels to prepare seriously for war. As one historian of the army has suggested, "The Army during the 1920s and early 1930s may have been less ready to function as a fighting force than at any time in its history."*

*Russell F. Weigley, *History of the United States Army* (New York: Macmillan, 1967), p. 402.

So parsimonious was Congress that the army's annual report for 1934 indicated that it possessed only *fourteen* post–World War I tanks.

Nevertheless, if the army had little chance to experiment with new ways of war, it did develop extraordinary officers who emerged in World War II to lead great citizen armies. Its educational system also provided a framework within which to think about the next war. If its intellectual preparations were weaker than those in Germany on the tactical and operational levels, it is clear that American officers developed an understanding of strategy and logistics that the German officer corps never possessed. Virtually all the important commanders of World War II served lengthy terms in the army's various schools. That intellectual preparation paid enormous dividends when war arrived.

Air War

All of the missions that make up the employment of air power had appeared by 1918. Strategic bombing, interdiction, close air support, reconnaissance, air defense, and air superiority had all played roles in aerial combat during World War I. Yet the full potential of air power, as well as its limitations, remained unclear. Despite the ambiguities that existed within the body of military experience, advocates of air power argued that air forces would be the dominant military force in future wars and that armies and navies would be of little significance. They believed that air power offered a cheap and easy path to victory and an alternative to the costly attrition of the trenches, but only if nations employed air power as a unified force to break the enemy's will. Air forces, in the view of theorists, must not fritter away their strength in supporting ground forces in defending one's own territory, or even in gaining air superiority; instead of "tactical" missions to support the army (or navy), the single proper role for air power must be "strategic" bombing.

Yet within this dogmatic framework, British and American views diverged significantly on the choice of targets. Like Guilio Douhet (the Italian air power theorist), Sir Hugh Trenchard (the first commander of the Royal Air Force after World War I) argued that the most vulnerable target to air attack was the enemy's civilian population. Trenchard believed that the working class could not stand up to the pressures of bombing; under air attack civilians would rebel and demand peace.

In the United States, Brigadier General Billy Mitchell shaped the tone of relations between airmen and the traditional services. That tone was intolerant and uncompromising. Mitchell and fellow enthusiasts denied that the older services would have a role in future conflicts. Unlike other air-power theorists, however, Mitchell recognized that enemy air forces represented a significant hindrance that an air force would have to defeat *before* it could execute successful bombing operations.

In the 1930s, that basic principle disappeared from the American Air Corps Tactical School. The army school was a hotbed of theoretical musings that created an American strategic bombing doctrine. Its approach did not

Father of the Royal Air Force in Britain, Sir Hugh Trenchard believed civilians were a legitimate target of bombers. Destruction of civilian lives and property, according to Trenchard, would destroy civilian morale and alter the entire course of a war.

seek attacks on enemy population centers, but rather on vulnerable sectors of what planners called the enemy's industrial web. Its argument rested on the premise that large formations of bombers, unescorted by defensive fighters, could fly deep into enemy territory and drop their bombs on key industrial targets (such as ball-bearing plants or oil refineries), the destruction of which would cause the collapse of the enemy economy. The problem with this argument lay in the difficulty of carrying out the missions. Could bombers find their targets (particularly in bad weather conditions) and destroy them; could they fight their way through enemy air-defense systems without cover from long-range escort fighters? But the greatest fallacies lay in the arguments that the economies of modern industrialized states were fragile and easily damaged and that the bomber would always get through.

In Germany the new leader of the Luftwaffe was Hitler's ruthless and thoroughly corrupt subordinate, the World War I ace, Hermann Göring, who aimed to make his air force the most formidable in Europe. The idea of strategic bombing appealed both to Göring and to the Luftwaffe's senior leadership. In 1936, however, the Luftwaffe canceled two prototype four-engine bombers because both aircraft designs were already obsolete. Design work continued throughout the 1930s on the four-engine He 177, which the Germans regarded as their future strategic bomber, but a variety of engineering mistakes and technological problems rendered that program a disastrous failure. Thus the Luftwaffe continued to have problems in developing a strategic bombing capability.

Nevertheless, more so than the British and American air forces, the Luftwaffe developed a realistic and balanced air doctrine. Partially as a result of experiences in the Spanish Civil War, the Germans discovered that it was difficult to place bombs accurately on target and that bombing civilians did not necessarily lead to the collapse of morale. In addition, they placed considerable emphasis in their air doctrine on supporting the army. The Luftwaffe preferred the interdiction mission to close air support, but after Spain it also developed the capability to support the army in breakthrough battles. However, through 1940 the Luftwaffe could not support the army's tanks once the exploitation phase had begun.

Naval War

Navies provide an interesting contrast. Their great prophet, the American theorist, Alfred Thayer Mahan, appeared before World War I; by and large navies saw no reason to change their operational approach because of wartime experience. Having developed sonar (called "asdic" by the British—a device that used sound waves to detect submerged submarines out to a range of about 1,500 yards) at the end of World War I, the Royal Navy believed that it had solved the submarine menace and proceeded on that assumption in its planning and preparations for a future war. In 1938, believing convoys would no longer be necessary, it quietly acquiesced to the surrender of western Irish ports essential to convoys in the eastern Atlantic. Ironically, the German navy, having read British pronouncements about ending the submarine menace, believed those reports. Despite their great success with the submarine in World War I, the Germans displayed minimal interest in the U-boat as they rearmed. Also, neither the British nor the German navy paid much attention to air power. British naval air power remained hobbled by the surrender of its assets to the Royal Air Force (RAF) in 1918. Nor did the German navy show much interest in naval air power, and squabbling with Göring's Luftwaffe ensured that the navy received little air support. In both fleets the emphasis remained firmly on the battleship and big gun.

The interesting developments in naval operations came in the Pacific. Both the United States and Japan sensed a great naval clash in the offing. In America, naval airmen, led by Rear Admiral William A. Moffett and helped by Billy Mitchell's wild attacks, convinced more conservative admirals that naval air power represented a significant supplement to fleet capabilities. Much the same thing happened in Japan; by the mid-1930s both navies had developed sophisticated concepts for carrier operations that would soon change the face of naval war.

The Japanese and Americans made significant advances in other areas as well. Both developed amphibious capabilities to seize bases in the wide expanses of the central Pacific. U.S. Marine Corps doctrine provided the departing point for solving the basic problems associated with amphibious war. The willingness to recognize the threat of the submarine was, however, less obvious. The Japanese expended great resources in the 1930s in building up their merchant marine to supply the home islands in case of war; however, they made *no* preparations to defend that merchant marine against

U.S. submarines. The Americans did no better in preparing themselves to meet the threat of U-boats in the Atlantic, even after watching the Germans savage the sea lines of communication to Britain in World War I.

Historians often berate military leaders for preparing for the last war. In fact they would fare better if they prepared for the next war on the basis of what had happened in the last. Unfortunately, they generally do not. Disinterested in the uncomfortable experiences of World War I, military leaders in the 1920s and 1930s preferred for the most part to study what was agreeable and what supported preconceived notions. The results would show all too clearly in the next war.

The Outbreak of World War II

World War I had not solved the German problem, even though defeat in 1918 and the Versailles Treaty hobbled the Germans in the short term. The results of World War I did not limit Germany's long-range potential, for the Reich was still the most powerful nation in Europe. To the east and south, Russia's and Austria-Hungary's collapse had left weak and politically divided states—a region open to German penetration and domination. Only in the west did the Germans have a frontier with a major power, a France weakened by the blood-letting of four years of war.

The Treaty of Versailles did attempt to shackle German potential, but in strategic terms the treaty failed before its signing. Angered by the provisions and burden of the treaty, most Germans refused the obvious explanation for the defeat of 1918 that the Reich had fought the whole world and lost; rather, they believed, erroneously, that their army had remained unbeaten in the field and that defeat had come as a result of traitorous actions by Jews and Communists who had stabbed the front-line soldiers in the back. In the early 1930s the troubles of the newly established Weimar Republic combined with a worldwide depression to destabilize German political life. In the hour of political despair, Adolf Hitler and his evil cohorts grasped the mantle of power.

Hitler brought to office a coherent and consistent ideology. Unlike Marx, Lenin, and Stalin who defined the Left's enemies on the basis of class, Hitler defined evil along racial lines. He believed the Aryan race solely responsible for creating the world's great civilizations and the Jews responsible for subverting and undermining human progress. Moreover, he argued that Germany must acquire a great European empire to provide the living space and resources for the German people; the Reich must acquire land in the east at the expense of the inferior Slavic races, particularly the Russians. In Hitler's vision, the new German empire, free of Jews, would control Europe from the Urals to Gibraltar and from the North Cape to the Alps. This ideologic vision provided the motivation behind the most catastrophic war in human history.

After becoming chancellor in January 1933, Hitler had to consolidate his power and mitigate the depression's economic and social dislocations. Despite the weakness of Germany's position, he embarked on a risky diplomatic course. In 1933, Germany withdrew from the League of Nations; in 1935 it declared conscription and creation of the Luftwaffe; and in 1936 it remilitarized the Rhineland. Hitler also provided the military services with funds to undertake a massive program of rearmament. After all, as he made clear, he was not interested in reestablishing Germany's World War I frontier, but rather in destroying the entire European balance of power.

The rearmament program, however, brought with it considerable economic dislocation. Nazi Germany was a resource-poor nation with few raw materials and limited access to foreign exchange. Consequently the rearmament program ran into trouble almost immediately. In a conference with his military and diplomatic advisors in November 1937, Hitler announced that Germany would have to take greater risks in foreign policy to escape its economic and strategic difficulties; however, he ran into substantial opposition from his ministers of defense and foreign policy and the army's commander-in-chief. Within three months he had dispensed with all three. In the resulting political storm, Hitler doubled the stakes and deliberately manufactured a crisis with Austria. In March 1938, the *Wehrmacht* marched into Austria with no opposition from the French or British. The *Anschluss* (occupation of Austria) brought the Third Reich a number of advantages. Austria possessed foreign exchange, a large untapped labor force, and a geographic stranglehold over Czechoslovakia. Hitler's triumph reduced the political crisis within Germany.

Scarcely had the dust settled on Austria before Hitler turned his attention to Czechoslovakia. Again he courted a crisis, this time to isolate the Czechs, so that the *Wehrmacht* could execute a quick campaign. Hitler's actions alarmed Germany's generals and created strong military opposition to his plans. Throughout spring and summer 1938, the chief of the general staff, Ludwig Beck, wrote a series of memoranda arguing that Germany's strategic situation was desperate; then in late August he resigned in protest. The British prime minister, Neville Chamberlain, resolved to prevent the outbreak of war; he eventually persuaded Hitler to accept the Sudetenland, the German-speaking districts of Czechoslovakia where most Czech fortifications were located. Few in England or France voiced opposition to the Munich settlement at the end of September 1938. Although Winston Churchill strongly criticized the government's policies in the House of Commons, many believed Churchill was a foolish old man for still believing in military power and strategic issues.

The nature of Germany's aims became clear in March 1939, when Hitler ordered his troops to occupy the remainder of Czechoslovakia. Germany's continued economic difficulties lay at the heart of his decision; Czechoslovakia with its foreign exchange holdings and industrial resources offered a tempting target. While the Germans gained much equipment and matériel from their seizure of the remainder of Czechoslovakia (enough to equip eight infantry and three panzer divisions), their actions prodded the

Western Powers into taking action. Hitler's move so outraged the British public that Chamberlain finally embarked on a massive effort to repair Britain's dilapidated defenses and to challenge Germany's expansionary policies. It was too little, too late.

At the end of March 1939, the British precipitously guaranteed Poland's independence. Outraged by this action, Hitler ordered his generals to draw up plans to invade Poland by September 1, 1939. Unlike the year before, the German military fell into line behind Hitler; they raised no objections about the strategic wisdom of invading Poland and unleashing a major war. On his part, Hitler seems not to have taken British and French intervention seriously. As he told his entourage, he had seen his "enemies at Munich and they were worms."

Nevertheless, at the end of August he engineered a pact with Stalin. That deal, the infamous Nazi-Soviet Non-Aggression Pact, divided eastern Europe between the two powers. Germany gained the right to destroy Poland without interference from the Soviet Union; and in return Stalin received eastern Poland, while Finland, Latvia, Estonia, Lithuania and the province of Bessarabia (in Romania) all fell within the Soviet sphere. Stalin also committed his regime to remaining neutral and removed the threat of a two-front war; the Soviet Union would soon send massive quantities of raw materials (grain, oil, manganese, etc.) to prop up a seriously strained German war economy. Stalin clearly hoped that a German-Allied conflict would result in a stalemate, as had occurred in World War I, in which the contending capitalistic powers would fight themselves to exhaustion. The Soviet Union would then be able to step in and dominate what was left of Europe. As for Hitler, the deal promised him peace in the east after he had conquered Poland and enabled him to face the Western Powers with his full strength if they intervened on Poland's behalf.

By August 1939, circumstances had set the stage for another great European war unleashed by German actions, this time motivated by Nazi ideology. Hitler had determined to create a Nazi hegemony from the Urals to Spain. The Germans, along with various lesser Aryan nations, would rule the Reich and exterminate other "subhuman" races such as the Jews and Gypsies. There would be no pity and no quarter; the racial crusade began the moment the Germans crossed the border into Poland.

Poland

On September 1, 1939, the *Wehrmacht* precipitated World War II by attacking Poland. Vigorous German offensive action broke the Polish defenses, while the Luftwaffe struck Polish air bases. Heavy air attacks also occurred against military targets in Warsaw; these attacks were accompanied by considerable collateral damage and casualties among the civilian populace—not surprising given the current technology. On September 3, the governments of Britain and France honored their obligations to the Poles and declared war on Germany. Hitler's gamble that swift military action, the Nazi-Soviet Pact, and the Western Powers' own reluctance to go to war would deter a larger war had failed.

Planning for the attack on Poland had begun in April 1939 in response to Britain's guarantee of Polish independence. Given Germany's great advantages (among others the Reich bounded Poland on three sides), operational planning did not require military genius. The OKH (*Oberkommando des Heeres*, army high command) created two army groups, North and South, to break into central Poland. Army Group North, under Colonel General Fedor von Bock, consisted of the Third and Fourth armies; its assignment was to cut the Polish Corridor—the sliver of Polish territory separating East Prussia from the rest of Germany—and threaten Warsaw from the north. Bock's army group held the 10th Panzer Division in reserve and General Heinz Guderian's XIX Panzer Corps (one panzer and two motorized infantry divisions) for its mobile operations.

The main attack came from Army Group South, commanded by Colonel General Gerd von Rundstedt; it consisted of Eighth, Fourteenth,

and Tenth armies. The first two would protect the flanks of the main drive launched by Tenth Army against Warsaw in the heart of Poland. Of the fifty-five German divisions, Army Group South had twenty-eight, including thirteen in Tenth Army and eleven in Fourteenth Army. The seven panzer divisions were spread among the five German armies.

The Poles were in an impossible strategic situation; their whole country was a flat plain. The only defensible feature was the Bug River, but it lay so far to the east that a defense along it would have forced the Poles to surrender everything of political and economic value before the fighting even began. Unwilling to surrender their territory, Polish leaders chose a forward defense, thereby allowing the Germans to divide the Polish army and defeat it in piecemeal fashion.

Not fully mobilized and spread thinly across a lengthy frontier, the Poles put up a stout resistance. Nevertheless, German armored and motorized units soon broke through. Army Group South achieved the greatest success. By the end of the first day several of its forward units had advanced fifteen miles, and within the first days, its tanks had breached frontier defenses and gained operational freedom. By September 6, its panzer units were halfway to Warsaw and had isolated Polish forces in the Posen sector. Meanwhile, Army Group North sliced across the Polish Corridor. While some elements drove toward Warsaw, Guderian's panzer corps moved across East Prussia and advanced deep behind the Polish capital; this move destroyed the possibility of a sustained resistance behind the Vistula River.

From the air, the Luftwaffe hammered enemy ground forces. In the air-to-air battle, superior numbers quickly told. Along with winning air superiority, the Luftwaffe interdicted the Polish railroad system and severely restricted frantic Polish efforts to complete their mobilization, while close air-support strikes helped the army in its efforts to penetrate Polish defenses. Thereafter, the Luftwaffe found it difficult to provide close air support in the mobile environment, largely because communications between ground and air forces were completely inadequate. Yet air strikes against Polish troops attempting to concentrate west of Warsaw were so effective that the Poles collapsed entirely in that sector.

German breakthroughs and relentless exploitation broke Polish resistance within one week. When the Polish high command moved from Warsaw on September 7, it completely lost control of its military forces. Eager to participate in the victory, the Soviet Union moved into eastern Poland on September 17 to "protect" the local population. By the end of the month Polish resistance had ceased; the Poles had lost 70,000 killed, 133,000 wounded, and 700,000 prisoners. German losses were only 11,000 dead, 30,000 wounded, and 3,400 missing.

The process by which the German army examined its performance after the Polish campaign suggests why it did so well on the battlefields of World War II. By early October, the OKH had gathered "after action" reports from the army groups down to the regimental level; it then established a rigorous training program throughout the entire army to correct the deficiencies and doctrinal weaknesses that after-action reports had highlighted. Over the next six months the OKH ensured that subordinate commands executed that program rigorously. From October 1939 through April 1940 the army trained ruthlessly and endlessly (sixteen hours a day, six to seven days a week), and when the *Wehrmacht* came west in May 1940, few armies in the twentieth century have been as well trained or highly disciplined.

German success did not come from a revolutionary secret developed in the interwar years; rather, it rested on the firm foundation of a coherent, modern doctrine emphasizing speed, exploitation, combined arms, and decentralized command and control. Nonetheless, the Germans had many improvements to make in both their doctrine and their battlefield performance. For example, they emphasized combined arms by including infantry and tank regiments in their panzer divisions, but they did not perfect the combining of those arms until the 1940 campaign in France.

From the beginning, the invaders embarked on Hitler's ideological crusade. Atrocities, unseen by Europeans for centuries, fell on Jews and Poles alike; Hitler demanded the liquidation of Poland's ruling and intellectual elite, an effort that Stalin's NKVD (secret police) pursued with equal enthusiasm in the east. Senior generals had full knowledge of what the Nazis were doing. The chief of the general staff, Franz Halder, noted in his diary after a speech by Hitler: "Poland is to have its own administration. It is not to be turned into a model state by German standards. Polish intelligentsia must be prevented from establishing itself as a new governing class. Low

The Panzerkampfwagen IV had a short-barreled 75-mm gun, weighed about twenty tons, and had a range of about 125 miles. It was the best German tank in the Polish and French campaigns. Throughout the war the Germans considered it a useful tank.

standards of living must be established. Cheap slaves." An even darker fate awaited the Jews.

The Allied Powers did almost nothing as Poland went down to defeat. They never intended to launch a major offensive into Germany this early in the war. Instead, they concentrated on mobilizing and preparing their forces and hoped to halt the Germans when they turned toward the west. A major offensive would occur only after they had halted the German attack in the west. In the meantime, the French sent out patrols that did not even reach the outpost line of the West Wall, despite the fact that one of Germany's key economic districts, the Saar, lay on the other side of the frontier. This lack of action allowed the German war economy to utilize the Saar's industries unhindered for the first nine months of the war. Similarly, Allied politicians and military leaders refused to undertake any action against German imports of Scandinavian iron ore, and they found numerous reasons to allow the Italians to escape into neutrality. Quite rightly the Western media dubbed the period between the defeat of Poland and the following spring as the "phony war." Failure to exert any pressure on the Germans allowed the Nazis to husband their military strength and mitigate their serious economic problems until the great throw of the dice in spring 1940.

The Scandinavian Campaign

While the Germans and the Western Powers faced off inconclusively in central Europe, the Soviets moved against the Baltic states. In fall 1939 they demanded that the Baltic republics allow Red Army garrisons on their territory. Lithuania, Latvia, and Estonia acceded. The Soviets then demanded that Finland cede territory and make similar concessions. The Finns agreed to the cession of territory but refused any terms that compromised their independence. A furious Stalin ordered the invasion of Finland; the time of year (late November) speaks volumes for Stalin's arrogance as well as a misplaced belief that the Finns could hardly wait to join his "workers and peasants' paradise."

Instead of an easy victory, the Red Army suffered humiliating defeat. From December 1939 through March 1940, the Soviets hurled tens of thousands of troops against the Finns. Relying on massive amounts of artillery and human wave attacks, the Soviets finally broke Finnish resistance. The poor performance of the Red Army in the Winter War underlined its weaknesses, particularly in terms of leadership and initiative, direct results of the purges from 1937 to 1939. Soviet troubles in Finland also reflected a hasty mobilization, lack of preparations, and the difficult conditions in the theater. The Red Army's performance in Finland misled the Germans who overlooked the skillfully executed operations of the Soviets against the Japanese at Nomonhan in August 1939.

The Winter War focused attention on Scandinavia. In February 1940, British destroyers sailed into a Norwegian fiord to rescue Allied merchant sailors imprisoned on a German supply ship. The commander-in-chief of the German navy, Admiral Erich Raeder, had been pressing for a campaign to seize Denmark or Norway to outflank Britain and provide U-boat bases to strike deeper into the Atlantic. Hitler now gave his enthusiastic approval for an attack on Scandinavia in early spring.

Denmark represented no significant problem because of its proximity to the Reich; the attack on Norway, however, required an intricately coordinated operation. The Germans had to capture the major harbors and airfields in Norway before the Royal Navy could react. Supply ships and oilers had to move out in advance of attacking forces—transported by warship—and arrive concurrently with naval units. For one of the few times in the war the Germans placed a joint operation under control of the OKW (*Oberkommando der Wehrmacht*—armed forces high command). General Nikolaus von Falkenhorst commanded the landing and ground operations.

All in all, *Weserübung* (code name for the attack) was a risky operation. On D-1 the Norwegians and British possessed clear intelligence that the Germans were launching a major operation in the North Sea. The former, however, failed to mobilize despite the fact that German soldiers had washed ashore on a beach in northern Norway from a supply ship sunk by a Polish submarine. The Royal Navy picked up the German navy's movement into the North Sea but interpreted the intelligence as indicating that the Germans were breaking out into the Atlantic.

Denmark fell with hardly a shot—not so for Norway. Even before the operation began, a British destroyer had rammed and seriously damaged the heavy cruiser, *Hipper*. The naval force running the Oslo fiord met unexpected opposition from the ancient forts guarding the passage and had to retreat and land its remaining troops at the mouth of the fiord after losing the new heavy cruiser, *Blücher*. The Norwegians failed to utilize the respite. Their cabinet ordered a mobilization by mail; and no one thought to block Oslo's airport. By mid-morning German paratroopers had seized the Oslo airfield and the Luftwaffe rushed in troops by Ju 52s (the German transport aircraft); within five or six hours the Germans had bluffed their way into the capital. By that time, the Norwegian government had fled and resistance had begun throughout the country. The Germans achieved greater success elsewhere in Norway. Luftwaffe strikes silenced coastal defenses, paratroopers seized major airports, and the navy grabbed other ports without serious losses.

In the early morning hours of April 10, however, a small force of British destroyers followed the German picket destroyers up the Narvik fiord; in a fierce gun duel they sank four out of ten of the enemy destroyers and all the German tankers. The surviving ships were trapped. Within the week, the battleship *Warspite* sank the remaining German destroyers in Narvik, a force that contained half the destroyers in the German navy.

Despite these losses, the Germans held all the cards, for they controlled the major ports and airfields. The Allies launched two unsuccessful expeditions to drive the Germans from northern Norway. Near Trondheim 240 miles from Oslo, British troops landed but accomplished little. Farther north, an Anglo-French expedition enjoyed more success against German

Scandinavia, April 1940

mountain troops in Narvik, but by the time the Allies took the port (early June) disasters in Western Europe had led to the collapse of the entire effort in Scandinavia.

Meanwhile in early June, despite intimations that an invasion of Britain might be necessary, the German navy launched its two battle cruisers, the *Gneisenau* and *Scharnhorst*, to influence what it regarded as the coming postwar budget debates. They did sink the British aircraft carrier *Glorious*, but both received such extensive damage that they remained in dry dock until December 1940. Whatever its success in Norway, the German navy had suffered irreplaceable losses. At the end of June 1940, it had only one heavy cruiser and four destroyers operationally ready, a force totally inadequate to support a successful landing on the British Isles.

Norway provided few strategic gains for Germany. In the short run the campaign ruled out an amphibious operation against the British Isles; in the long run, it represented a drain on resources that the Germans could have better utilized elsewhere. By 1943, Norway was tying down hundreds of thousands of troops to no useful purpose. After the fall of France, neither the submarine bases nor the secure route for Swedish ore proved to be of crucial strategic importance in the unfolding war.

The French Campaign

Victory over Poland confronted the Reich with serious economic and strategic difficulties. Underlining the Germans' predicament was the fact that the military had done little contingency planning for a campaign in the west. Therefore, Hitler's demand that the *Wehrmacht* launch a fall campaign against the Western Powers caught his senior military advisors with no operational plans and an army unprepared for a major campaign. Consequently, German military leaders argued furiously with their Führer to delay the fall campaign until the following spring; they did not, however, dispute Hitler's strategic or political assumptions. Instead they argued their case entirely on operational and tactical grounds.

Hitler had no clear conception or objective for a campaign in the west; rather, he believed that the Western Powers lacked the political stomach for a great war. Thus he directed the OKH to seize the Low Countries and northern France to the Somme River so that the Luftwaffe and navy could attack the British Isles. Hitler obviously hoped that such a strategy would drive Britain, led by Chamberlain, from the war. Once Britain withdrew from the war, Hitler believed France would not continue the fight alone. In no respect did the initial directive aim to destroy Allied ground power on the Continent; nor was it a replay of the Schlieffen Plan.

When the OKH completed its plan for taking the Low Countries and driving the French back to the Somme, no one concerned, neither Hitler nor the generals, was happy with it. Nevertheless, arguments between Hitler and his generals focused on the readiness of the army for a campaign in the west rather than on German strategy. German military leaders, on the basis of after-action reports from the Polish campaign, remained extremely concerned about the readiness of their forces, particularly the infantry. Despite their objections, Hitler insisted on the launching of an immediate offensive, and on a number of occasions the *Wehrmacht* rolled up on the frontier and prepared to attack with a fundamentally flawed strategy. Only bad weather prevented the Germans from making a serious mistake. Arguments in the high command continued into January, when a courier aircraft, carrying a staff officer and the German plan, went astray and crash-landed in neutral Belgium. The operational details consequently fell into Allied hands. Only at this juncture did the generals persuade Hitler to call off the attack until spring, and a fundamental operational reassessment began.

By January, Hitler had already conceived of launching a major attack through the Ardennes, the heavily forested and rolling countryside between the Maginot Line in northeast France and the flat countryside of western Belgium. His intuition received support from Army Group A's chief of staff, General Erich von Manstein, who independently concluded that a drive through the Ardennes with armored forces could split the Allied front and offer enticing operational prospects. But such a plan possessed considerable risks; if the Allies reinforced the Ardennes quickly, the Germans would not be able to fight their way into the open beyond the Meuse River.

The OKH found Manstein's proposal, supported by his commander, Rundstedt, both self-serving and risky. But after a series of debates with Hitler, a number of war games, and serious reconsiderations within the OKH, the Germans expanded the Ardennes conception to include nearly all the panzer and motorized forces. In the north, Army Group B, under Bock, would seize Holland and advance into western Belgium in order to fix Allied attention on that area. Meanwhile, Army Group A would push its panzers through eastern Belgium and the Ardennes as rapidly as possible; if all went well they would break into the open on the west bank of the Meuse River before the Allies could react. The success of the daring strategy rested on the Germans' moving large armored forces through the Ardennes and over the Meuse before the Allies could concentrate additional forces along the Meuse and trap the Germans in the Ardennes.

While the Germans hammered out their plans, British and French commanders also prepared for the coming battle. They carefully coordinated their strategy and prepared for French forces to hold along the Maginot Line while a combined French and British force rushed forward into Belgium. The Allies, expecting the Germans to launch their attack through central Belgium, much as they had done in 1914, placed few forces along the Ardennes. It was not that the French failed to see that the Germans might attempt a breakthrough in the Ardennes; rather, they believed they could concentrate reinforcements along the Meuse before the Germans could move large forces through the Ardennes and achieve a breakthrough. As the French prepared to fight a methodical battle with a highly centralized command and control system, they failed to recognize the effect that mechanized forces would have on the tempo of operations. Nothing underlines more clearly their misunderstanding of German mobility than General Maurice Gamelin's decision to move his Seventh Army (the only large reserve force available to him and consisting of some of the best mechanized and motorized units in the French army) from its central location near Reims to the far left of the Allied front. Its task now was to move forward to link up with the Dutch. Thus, for strategic reasons of dubious merit, Gamelin dispersed the French operational reserves.

The armies that clashed in 1940 disposed of relatively equal numbers of troops; the Allies, in fact, possessed more tanks, the Germans more

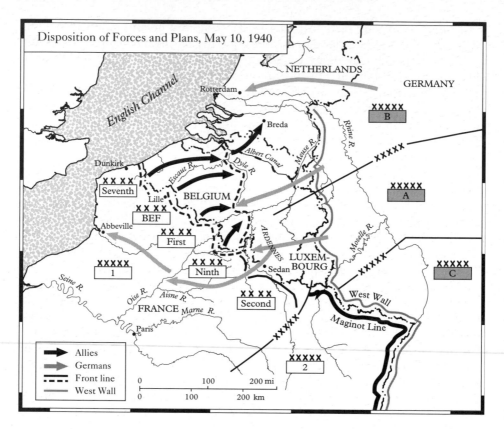

aircraft. But equivalency in forces hid a number of German advantages. On the Allied side, British and French armies had begun to work together only in 1939. The Belgians and Dutch entered the war only after the Germans began their offensive; little or no consultation on either strategic or operational matters had occurred before the Germans struck. Consequently, under the pressure exerted by the German advance the Allied high command never operated effectively or efficiently. On the other hand, the Germans came west with a coherent operational doctrine and conception, executed with ruthless efficiency. The results reflected the thorough intellectual preparations that the German military had made since World War I.

The Opening Moves

The German attack began on May 10, 1940. The Luftwaffe struck across the length and breadth of western Europe. It aimed first to achieve general air superiority; therefore most of its first strikes hit Allied air bases. These raids achieved some successes but met ferocious resistance, resulting in heavy losses. On the first day the Luftwaffe lost more aircraft than on any other day in 1940 (including the Battle of Britain). Some strikes hit the Allied transportation system to delay movement of reserves; significantly, few attacks struck Allied forces moving forward into Belgium and Holland.

Despite heavy losses, the Luftwaffe not only gained air superiority in the first days but also provided strong support to German ground forces. At dawn on May 10, Ju 52s dropped German paratroopers on a series of major targets; the Germans attempted to seize the main airfield near the Hague and capture the government, thus ending Dutch resistance. The sudden descent failed, however, as the Dutch army responded and drove the para- troopers off the airfield. Nevertheless, the strike at the Hague thoroughly distracted the Dutch. Meanwhile other paratroopers seized the major bridges leading into fortress Holland, so that the 9th Panzer Division could sweep through Dutch defenses and into the middle of the country. By May 15, the Dutch position was hopeless. After the Luftwaffe destroyed the cen- ter of Rotterdam, the Dutch, fearing that the Germans would repeat such attacks, surrendered. At the time German propaganda was not slow to draw a connection between terror bombing and the Dutch collapse. But the real credit for the success in Holland rested on the courage and operational imagination with which fewer than 5,000 German paratroopers seized cru- cial communication points in Holland.

To the south of Holland, Army Group B rolled swiftly into Belgium. Airborne forces aided its advance. In one particularly daring and important operation, 180 German troopers landed by glider on top of Eben Emael, the large fortress in the center of the major avenue of approach into central Bel- gium. Within hours, they had blinded the fort and opened the way for Army Group B, which consisted almost entirely of infantry divisions. The swift collapse of the Dutch and of Eben Emael, as well as the hammering advance of Bock's infantry in central Belgium, captivated the attention of the French high command and convinced the Allies that the Germans were attacking as they had expected.

The drive through the Ardennes proceeded flawlessly. Because of Belgian neutrality, the French could do little to hinder a German move through the difficult Ardennes terrain. By the evening of May 12, the three panzer corps had arrived on the Meuse; in the north Hoth's XV Panzer Corps reached the river south of Dinant; Reinhardt's XLI Panzer Corps arrived at the mid-point of the panzer fist; and in the south Guderian's XIX Panzer Corps reached the Meuse near Sedan. The first to cross was Hoth's corps. The 7th Panzer Division, driven by its commander, Erwin Rommel, achieved the first lodgement on the west bank of the Meuse. At great cost to its infantry, 7th Panzer battered the French back and began building a bridge for its tanks to cross. Rommel's success opened the way for Hoth's other division, 5th Panzer, to cross; consequently the northern flank of French forces holding the Ardennes began to dissolve. In the center, tena- cious resistance savaged the infantry of Reinhardt's panzer divisions; they made a small lodgement but could not get their tanks across.

In the south, Guderian crossed late on the afternoon of May 13 as sustained, heavy air attacks punished French defenders. Of the three attack- ing divisions, 10th Panzer Division on the left got less than a company across and lost forty-eight out of fifty of its assault boats. On the right 2nd Panzer ran into equal difficulties; only 1st Panzer Division in the center, led by the 1st Infantry Regiment and the army's *Grossdeutschland* Infantry Regiment,

General Heinz Guderian strongly and enthusiastically supported the Nazis. Though his influence over the development of German armored forces is often exaggerated, he possessed a sophisticated understanding of mobile warfare.

fought its way across and onto the heights overlooking the Meuse and Sedan. This gain allowed German engineers to build pontoon bridges, and in the early morning hours of May 14, 1st Panzer began moving its tanks across the river. The 1st Panzer Division's success opened the way for both the 10th and 2nd Panzer divisions to cross.

The French response to Guderian's crossing was late and uncoordinated. Although some infantry units fought with considerable bravery, others offered only token resistance. French artillery units, whose morale had been eroded by Luftwaffe attacks, panicked and ran; reserves in the area, a few battalions of infantry, dissolved. By the time French commanders launched a halfhearted counterattack, units from the XIX Panzer Corps were across in strength. Several divisions, including the 3rd Armored and 3rd Motorized, were available to the French. The corps commander of these two divisions, General Jean Flavigny, ironically a proponent of tanks in the interwar period, failed to launch a counterattack; instead he parceled his forces out along the disintegrating front, where the growing German tide swamped them. On May 14, Allied air launched a massive effort to knock out the pontoon bridges across the Meuse at Sedan; they met tenacious opposition from German fighters and antiaircraft batteries. The RAF lost forty out of seventy-one obsolete "Battle" bombers attacking the bridges; French losses were as heavy. By now Guderian's forces were rolling west in full flood.

The German leadership suffered several cases of bad nerves. On the evening of May 15–16, Colonel General Ewald von Kleist, commander of Reinhardt and Guderian's panzer corps, intervened to stop the exploitation to the west. Kleist was clearly acting at the behest of the OKW, which feared an attack against the flank of the advancing German forces. Guderian objected strongly and received permission to continue his advance. By evening on the 16th, XIX Panzer Corps had reached Marle, fifty-five miles from Sedan (traveling forty miles on that day alone). That evening Guderian received a peremptory order to halt; infuriated, he reported that he was resigning from command of XIX Corps. At that point, Rundstedt stepped in and worked out a compromise that ordered the corps' headquarters to remain in place while Guderian's panzer divisions continued a "reconnaissance in force"—in effect a license to steal.

The French Collapse

Guderian's breakthrough in the south combined with Hoth's success near Dinant to uncork Reinhardt's panzer corps. Once Reinhardt had crossed near Monthermé, the Germans had achieved a breakthrough of massive proportions, one that ran from Dinant to Sedan, a distance of almost forty miles. A giant fist of seven armored divisions then pushed toward the Channel. Throughout the drive to the Channel, Hitler, OKW, and OKH worried that everything had gone too well. Meanwhile small Allied counterattacks on the flanks of the panzer wedge exacerbated German worries. On May 19, Charles de Gaulle's 4th Armored Division caused some temporary dislocation on the southern flank. On the 21st a more substantial strike by British armor hit 7th Panzer and *SS Totenkoph* divisions, but the intrepid Rommel soon restored the situation. In reality the flanks were solidifying faster than the Allies could respond. Behind the armored advance, German infantry divisions pounded down the roads at over twenty miles per day to relieve the screening forces on the flanks. On May 19, 1st Panzer Division reached Péronne on the old Somme battlefield; the next day 2nd Panzer reached the coast near Abbeville. Ecstatic over reaching Abbeville, neither OKW, OKH, nor Army Group A thought to order Guderian to capture the Channel ports. But the Germans had cut off the whole Allied left wing.

Not until after the Germans crossed the Meuse did the French recognize the location of the main attack. But as Gamelin admitted to Churchill on May 15, they had no reserves. In this desperate hour paralysis gripped French leaders. Unable to deal with the speed of German moves, the French high command collapsed. Thus, there was no effective response as the panzer divisions drove relentlessly toward the Channel. Gamelin's failure to halt the Germans resulted in his removal. His replacement, General Maxime Weygand, arrived from Syria tired and incapable of wresting the initiative from the Germans.

By May 23, Guderian was moving up the Channel coast supported by Reinhardt's panzers to the east. The next day both threatened Dunkirk, the last port through which an Allied evacuation could take place. At that point, the OKW issued one of the most controversial orders of the war—its infamous "stop order," halting German armor. After the war German generals singled Hitler out as responsible for the failure to finish off the Allied left wing. In fact, besides the Führer, a number of senior generals, including Rundstedt and Guderian, shared the blame. The German senior leadership worried that the campaign thus far had proceeded too flawlessly and that their armor had suffered heavy losses; consequently it seemed best to preserve the panzer divisions for the final task of destroying France. At the time there was much that supported the decision: the panzer forces were a strategic weapon of decision, not a siege force, that had suffered heavy losses; much of France had yet to be conquered; and the panzer divisions would have to change their axis of advance substantially for the upcoming campaign.

The halt, however, allowed the British and French to establish a defense line around Dunkirk and provided the commander of the British Expeditionary Force (BEF), Lord Gort, time to save the British army. As early as May 19, Gort had warned London that his forces might have to withdraw from the Continent. Hardly happy with that communication, the War Cabinet instructed the navy's command at Dover to gather vessels for a possible evacuation.

For the next four days Gort maintained the position of a loyal army commander faithfully executing the orders of the French high command. On the evening of May 23–24, however, he broke with that role without fully informing the French and ordered his 5th and 50th divisions (nearly surrounded at Arras) to pull back to the coast. On the next day he used those two divisions to bolster his left flank, where the Belgians were collapsing. Gort's decision ended the prospect of an Allied counterattack from the pocket—an action that French leaders sharply criticized. Despite the con-

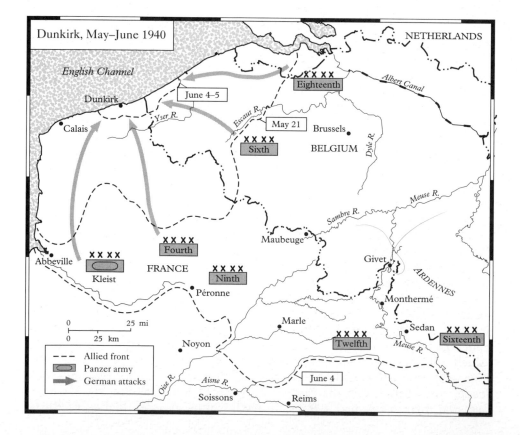

troversy surrounding his decision, Gort managed to cover his northern flank and make the Dunkirk evacuation possible.

As Allied forces streamed into the pocket, the British set in motion a full-scale evacuation, Operation "Dynamo." They had already evacuated 28,000 noncombat troops. Evacuation proceeded at full speed, but the British at first failed to extend a helping hand to the French. The French high command exacerbated the situation by refusing to authorize its commanders to participate in the evacuation; nor did it alert the French navy that such an operation was imminent. By afternoon May 29, the British had evacuated a large number of troops, the French none. At this point Churchill stepped in and ordered that British ships share space on a one-to-one basis with the French; but the damage had already been done.

Fortunately for the Allies, things began to go wrong for the Germans. By May 26, no less than two army groups and four army headquarters were controlling attacks on the Dunkirk perimeter. Not until May 30 did the Germans reorganize their command structure and place Eighteenth Army in control of the Dunkirk perimeter. And it was only on that day that they realized the British were getting away. On May 31, 68,000 Allied troops escaped, raising the total evacuated to 194,000. On June 1 a further 64,000 came out; by now virtually all the BEF had escaped. By the time Operation Dynamo ended on June 3, no less than 340,000 Allied troops had evacuated Dunkirk.

The German failure at Dunkirk was also a Luftwaffe failure. Most of its aircraft were still operating from bases in western Germany; as a result they were farther from Dunkirk than British fighters operating from the British Isles. Spitfire and Hurricane attacks were a nasty surprise to the Luftwaffe, which had had pretty much its own way in the campaign. Altogether the RAF lost 177 aircraft during the air battles over Dunkirk, the Luftwaffe 240. The successful withdrawal should not, however, obscure the extent of the catastrophe. As Churchill commented: "Wars are not won by evacuation." While the evacuation spared the British army and permitted it to fight again, the Germans had completely destroyed the balance of power in Europe.

One should not lose sight of the moral parameters of the Nazi conquest in the west. On May 27 a company of the *SS Totenkoph* Division captured one hundred men of the British Royal Norfolk Regiment. They lined the British soldiers up against a barn wall and machine-gunned them; afterward they bayoneted the wounded. German military authorities brought no charges against the soldiers involved in the incident. Along with the destruction of Rotterdam, this murder of British prisoners suggests the brutality of Nazi conquest.

The End in France

By now a deep malaise had spread throughout the French high command and the government. Premier Paul Reynaud had relieved Gamelin, appointed Weygand as his successor, and brought the aged Marshal Pétain back from Spain. But the change in leadership could not halt the expanding disaster, as the *Wehrmacht* turned to deal with the remainder of France. Its panzer divisions, extricated from Dunkirk, redeployed to jump off positions in north central France. Three army groups (Rundstedt's Army Group A, forty-five divisions; Bock's Army Group B, fifty divisions); and Wilhelm Ritter von Leeb's Army Group C, twenty-four divisions; plus twenty-three divisions in OKH reserve fell on a French army of barely fifty divisions.

Army Group B jumped off on June 5. The French had improved their methods of fighting and, despite overwhelming German superiority, put up tenacious resistance. So tough were the defenses in front of Kleist's panzer group that the OKH pulled the entire group out on June 7 and moved it farther east. Not surprisingly, Rommel's 7th Panzer Division captured two railroad bridges on the lower Somme and in a matter of hours was hustling down French roads toward the Seine River. By the end of the campaign, Rommel's forces had swept to Rouen, sidestepped to the coast to put the French IX Corps (including the British 51st Division) in the bag, and then driven on to Cherbourg. In six weeks 7th Panzer Division captured 97,648 prisoners, 277 guns, 458 armored vehicles, and 400 tanks. Rundstedt's Army Group A attacked on June 9 and rapidly swept the French off the battlefield. Guderian drove to the Swiss frontier, while Paris fell on June 14.

The Anglo-French alliance, barely patched together in the late 1930s, collapsed under the weight of defeat. Late on June 16, Reynaud resigned, and Pétain assumed power. Within two hours he asked for an

The British used more than 850 ships of all shapes and sizes to evacuate Allied troops from Dunkirk. They had hoped to rescue 45,000 men but managed to evacuate 340,000.

armistice. A few days later in the forest of Compiègne, representatives of France signed an armistice in the same railroad car in which the Germans had capitulated in November 1918.

*   *   *   *

In the campaigns of 1939 and 1940, the Germans restored mobility to the battlefield and swiftly defeated Poland, Norway, and France. Their success rested less on a revolutionary idea than on an evolutionary process that had begun in 1917–1918. Through intelligent, careful analysis of the experience of World War I and of the possibilities of improved technology, they developed a doctrine for mobile warfare that rested as much on artillery and infantry as it did on tanks. Placing a greater value on maneuver than on firepower, the Germans shaped their army for mobile operations. Unlike the British and French forces, the armor, artillery, and infantry in the German army spoke the same language—one of speed, exploitation, decentralized authority, and ruthless, aggressive leadership.

Yet, the victory over France did not solve Germany's problems. Despite the doctrinal coherence and effectiveness of the German way of war, the *Wehrmacht* remained a hybrid military organization. Of the divisions that invaded France in May 1940, only eighteen were modern motorized and mechanized units; the remainder, over 80 percent of the force, were World War I–style infantry who marched on foot and depended on horse-drawn transport to bring up their artillery, supplies, and baggage. Additionally, German units possessed diverse equipment, most clearly demonstrated by three panzer divisions' being equipped primarily with Czech tanks. And there was scant prospect that the armament industry would be able to replace horse-drawn wagons with trucks or foreign equipment with German-made matériel. German logistics remained weak at best; the devastating nature of their victory in 1940 hid the sloppiness with which the support structure was able to move supplies forward. Some of Guderian's units, for example, had to depend on French gas stations for their fuel in the drive to the Channel.

Nevertheless, the Germans had achieved an important victory that allowed them to escape the economic constraints under which they had operated thus far. To maintain Germany's newly won position in the world, the Germans would have to recognize how vulnerable they remained in the center of Europe. But they did not; instead Hitler, his generals, and many of the German people drew the conclusion that nothing was impossible for the Third Reich. Instead of using caution, they would now reach out to expand the boundaries of greater Germany to the limits of their dreams.

SUGGESTED READINGS

Bond, Brian. *British Military Policy between the Two World Wars* (Oxford: Clarendon Press, 1980).

Corum, James S. *The Roots of Blitzkrieg: Hans von Seeckt and the German Military Reform* (Lawrence: University Press of Kansas, 1992).

Deist, Wilhelm. *The Wehrmacht and German Rearmament* (Toronto: University of Toronto Press, 1981).

Dennis, Peter. *Decision by Default: Peacetime Conscription and British Defense, 1919–1939* (Durham, N.C.: Duke University Press, 1972).

Doughty, Robert A. *The Seeds of Disaster: The Development of French Army Doctrine, 1919–1939* (Hamden, Conn.: Archon Books, 1985).

————. *The Breaking Point: Sedan and the Fall of France, 1940* (Hamden, Conn.: Archon Books, 1990).

Erickson, John. *The Soviet High Command: A Military-Political History, 1918–1941* (Boulder, Col.: Westview Press, 1984).

Glantz, David M. *Soviet Military Operational Art: In Pursuit of Deep Battle* (London: Frank Cass, 1991).

Hurley, Alfred F. *Billy Mitchell: Crusader for Air Power* (Bloomington: Indiana University Press, 1975).

Knox, MacGregor. *Mussolini Unleashed: Politics and Strategy in Fascist Italy's Last War* (Cambridge: Cambridge University Press, 1982).

Liddell Hart, B. H. *History of the Second World War* (New York: G. P. Putnam's, 1978).

Millett, Allan R., and Williamson Murray, eds. *Military Effectiveness*, Vol. II, *The Inter War Period* (London: Allen and Unwin, 1988).

Murray, Williamson. *The Change in the European Balance of Power, 1938–1939: The Path to Ruin* (Princeton: Princeton University Press, 1984).

————. *Luftwaffe* (Baltimore: Nautical and Aviation Publishing Co., 1985).

Murray, Williamson, and Allan R. Millett. *Calculations: Net Assessment and the Coming of World War II* (New York: The Free Press, 1992).

Taylor, Telford. *The March of Conquest: The German Victories in Western Europe, 1940* (New York: Simon and Schuster, 1958).

Trythall, Anthony J. *"Boney" Fuller: The Intellectual General, 1878–1966* (London: Cassell, 1977).

Winton, Harold R. *To Change an Army: General Sir John Burnett-Stuart and British Armored Doctrine, 1927–1938* (Lawrence: University Press of Kansas, 1988).

2

GERMANY ARRESTED:
THE LIMITS OF EXPANSION

The Battle of Britain

The War in the
Mediterranean, 1940–1942

Libya and Egypt, 1941–1942

Operation "Barbarossa"

$\mathbb{T}$he conquest of France in the stunningly short period of six weeks capped seven years of diplomatic, strategic, and military successes for Adolf Hitler's regime. Though nothing seemed impossible to the victorious Germans, the Third Reich could not strike decisive blows at any of its potential future opponents. Indeed, a careful assessment of Nazi Germany's political and strategic position in summer 1940 would have left cause for sobering doubts; at a minimum it would have concluded that preparations for a long world war, utilizing the entire economic structure of central and western Europe, must begin at once. Instead, the Germans first made a halfhearted stab at solving the British problem by aerial assault, then struck at the Soviet Union, and finally foolishly declared war on the United States. Italian failures also drew the Germans into expensive campaigns in North Africa and the Balkans.

The Germans encountered substantial difficulties in the campaigns against Britain and the Soviet Union. Despite aerial attacks of unparalleled intensity and size, the British proved resilient to air attack and the campaign proved expensive for the Germans in terms of aircrews, aircraft, and industrial resources. In the Mediterranean the British initially met success against the Italians; when more capable German forces and commanders arrived, the opposing forces raced back and forth across the 400-mile North African coastline in seesaw campaigns, but the Afrika Korps failed to drive the British out of Egypt. After the Italians blundered miserably in the Balkans, the Germans intervened and rapidly overran Yugoslavia and Greece, but they failed to extinguish resistance in remote areas. The German airborne attack against Crete also achieved success, but difficulties in the campaign made the Wehrmacht and Hitler leery of such operations in the future. In the east, the invasion of Russia propelled the war to a higher level in terms of numbers of soldiers and equipment involved. Despite initial German successes, the Soviets managed to escape defeat and to bring vast forces to bear against the invaders. As Soviet resistance continued, the Wehrmacht suffered mounting losses and encountered severe logistic problems. By spring 1942 the Germans had won impressive military victories on the ground and in the air, but they had fashioned a noose firmly around their own necks.

The Battle of Britain

Before the House of Commons on June 18, 1940, Winston Churchill warned his fellow countrymen: "What General Weygand called the Battle of France is over. I expect that the Battle of Britain is about to begin." Though most military analysts concluded that it would be a short battle, Churchill did not believe that the war was over. He concluded that crossing the English Channel represented a complex operational problem, which the Germans probably could not solve. Moreover, he recognized that neither the United States nor the Soviet Union could allow a Nazi hegemony over Europe and that Germany's newly won position carried with it inevitable frictions that would result in conflict between the Reich and those two great neutral powers.

Not surprisingly, the British made approaches to both governments. The Soviets, busily engaged in gobbling up the Baltic Republics, in stealing the provinces of Bessarabia and Bukovina from Romania, and in congratulating the Nazis on their successes, exhibited little interest in cooperating with Britain. The United States was another matter. Franklin D. Roosevelt, making an unprecedented bid for a third term with an American people deeply divided over foreign policy, nevertheless made clear over summer 1940 that America was deeply committed to Britain.

By early July, Churchill felt sure enough of Roosevelt to move. With Italy's entrance into the war, the naval balance in the Mediterranean was tipping against the British; not only had the French withdrawn from the alliance, but the British feared that the new regime in France and its fleet might join the Axis Powers. On July 5 the British acted: the Royal Navy seized French ships in British ports; in Alexandria it demobilized and disarmed units of the French navy. Finally, Force H, operating out of Gibraltar and led by battle cruiser *Hood*, appeared off Mers el Kébir in North Africa. The British issued an ultimatum with three options: sink or abandon their ships, join Britain, or be destroyed. The French refused negotiations and were building up steam when the ultimatum expired; Force H opened fire and a deluge of 15-inch shells fell on the French fleet. The attack sank battle cruiser *Dunkerque* and three older battleships and killed 1,250 French sailors. Ironically only two weeks before, French and British troops had been fighting against the Germans.

The attack underlined Churchill's resolve. Not until the end of July, however, did the German high command take the British problem seriously. They then prepared two approaches: first, "Sea Lion," a joint-service, amphibious landing on the British coast; and second, a great air offensive to gain air superiority and wreck Britain's industrial infrastructure. One wonders how seriously Hitler considered the landing in Britain. The Luftwaffe hardly participated in Sea Lion's planning, while the army planned for an invasion the navy could not have supported, even at full strength. The navy, left with only one heavy cruiser and four destroyers after Norway, proposed a landing the breadth of which would not have supported a brigade. Rhine river barges would have transported the landing force. The whole planning process also involved considerable interservice bickering and gross misjudgments. Army planners proceeded as if a Channel crossing were just another river crossing!

None of this bothered the Luftwaffe; Hermann Göring and his commanders planned to win the war against Britain by themselves. At the end of June the Luftwaffe turned to the problem of winning air superiority over the

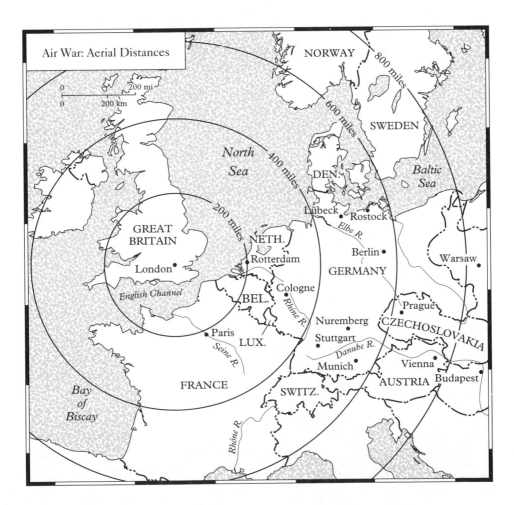

British Isles. On June 30, 1940, Göring issued general instructions. After redeployment, the Luftwaffe would begin a sustained effort to achieve air superiority. Initial targets would be Fighter and Bomber commands, ground-support echelons, and the aircraft industry. Above all, Göring underlined, the Luftwaffe must attack the RAF ceaselessly.

Unfortunately for the Luftwaffe, it entered battle with an intelligence picture that was faulty in every respect. German intelligence calculated that the Spitfire and Hurricane were inferior to German fighters and that British fighter production was between 150 to 300 machines per month. In fact the Spitfire was equal to the Bf 109, and both British fighters were superior to the Bf 110. British fighter production had also reached nearly 500 machines per month by late summer 1940. Moreover, the Germans failed to recognize the importance of British radar and ground control systems.

Building on faulty intelligence, Luftwaffe operational estimates forecast that four days' fighting would break Fighter Command, and that four weeks would destroy the rest of the RAF and the factories on which British air strength rested. Then the Luftwaffe, bombing enemy cities day and night, could protect Sea Lion, if the British still refused to surrender.

Two German *Luftflotte*, Second and Third, deployed in northern France with 2,600 bombers, dive bombers, and fighters; *Luftflotte* Five with 300 bombers and fighters in Norway would strike at northern Britain. One significant weakness affected German strategy from the start: the Bf 109 could barely reach London, while the Bf 110, a long-range escort, could not face RAF fighters in air-to-air combat. Consequently, the Germans could mount daylight strikes only to London; beyond the capital German bombers could fly only under cover of night.

The British victory in the Battle of Britain resulted from years of thought and scientific preparation. Air Marshal Sir Hugh Dowding deserves credit for much of that preparation.

The fact that the Germans confronted a well-prepared opponent was due almost completely to the foresight of Air Marshal Sir Hugh Dowding. As the RAF's head of research and development in the mid-1930s, Dowding supported development of radar; he also put together the specifications and contracts that resulted in procurement of Spitfires and Hurricanes. In 1937 he took over Fighter Command and in that position created a doctrine and force structure to defend Britain from attack. Thus Dowding fought and won the Battle of Britain with a force whose development he had overseen and whose doctrine and organization he had developed—surely one of the most impressive achievements in twentieth-century military history.

Both air forces had suffered heavily in the Battle of France; the Luftwaffe had lost 30 percent of its bomber force, while the RAF had lost nearly 20 percent of its fighter pilots. But the British enjoyed important advantages. They were defending their homeland; since most air battles would occur over Britain, many British pilots who parachuted would return to operations. Moreover, Fighter Command needed only to hold on until fall when bad weather arrived. To succeed the Germans had to win a decisive victory; even then it was doubtful whether Sea Lion could achieve a successful lodgement across the Channel.

To oppose the Luftwaffe, Dowding possessed approximately 900 fighters, between 500 and 600 aircraft serviceable on any given day. Nevertheless, the disparity between Fighter Command and the Luftwaffe was not as great as it might seem; the Luftwaffe possessed a bare equivalency in Bf 109s and the success or failure of air superiority fighters would determine the outcome. Dowding aimed: (1) to keep his command in being; (2) to fight a sustained battle of attrition; and (3) to prevent the Luftwaffe from impairing Britain either economically or militarily. Half of his fighters defended southern England; a substantial number remained north of London. Throughout the battle Dowding could feed in fresh squadrons and pull back the exhausted.

Over July and early August the Germans built up their tempo of operations. They hoped to clear the Channel and achieve a measure of psychological superiority. They succeeded in the former but failed in the latter. Dowding eventually concluded that committing fighters to cover convoys was too costly; in the meantime Fighter Command achieved valuable experience in how German raids built up and how its own system would react.

On July 21, Göring advised his commanders that the objectives of Luftwaffe attacks should be the RAF and its production base. He also underlined that they should strike Fighter Command's morale and urged that the German fighters possess maximum latitude in protecting bombers. Thus bomber raids would bring up enemy fighters, while Bf 109 sweeps sought out and attacked those fighters. Three days later *Fliegerkorps* I mapped out four distinct missions for the campaign. First would be attacks on Fighter Command. But it also singled out Bomber Command and attacks on imports; finally, independent of the first three missions, it urged ruthless "retaliatory" terror raids against British cities.

Officially the Battle of Britain began on August 13, although the RAF noted a sharp increase in operations on the preceding day. On "Eagle

Day" the Germans directly attacked Fighter Command. The most danger-ous attacks struck at radar sites along the coast, but the Germans soon aban-doned this avenue as unproductive. By mid-August the British had lost 148 fighters to 286 aircraft for the Luftwaffe (only 105 Bf 109s). German intelli-gence, however, failed to perceive how British defenses were working. The early air battles should also have alerted the Germans to the weaknesses of their own intelligence; *Luftflotte* Five from Norway received a savage beating from fighters that its intelligence had described as nonexistent.

Adding to Luftwaffe discomfort was a consistent lack of focus and direction. Göring finally recognized the vulnerability of the *Stuka*, a dive-bomber whose lack of speed made it an easy target for British fighters. He made, however, the crucial mistake of tying Bf 109s more closely to the bombers, thus robbing the fighters of their flexibility. Finally, Göring con-centrated Bf 109s under Field Marshal Albert Kesselring's command near Pas de Calais. While this shift enabled the Luftwaffe to pressure RAF bases in front of London, it also relieved the pressure on Fighter Command's structure over the rest of southern England.

As the air campaign developed, Dowding altered his operational conceptions. British fighters no longer pursued enemy aircraft over the Channel but now concentrated exclusively on attacking bombers. In the ten days after Eagle Day, Fighter Command lost 126 fighter pilots killed, wounded, or missing, a 14 percent loss. But enemy fighters and bombers were scarcely in better shape. Throughout the last week of August and into early September, the Germans severely damaged British airbases and sector stations in southern England. Fighter Command struggled desperately to maintain its equilibrium despite mounting losses.

The Germans broke first. Discouraged by British resistance, Hitler and Göring, with Kesselring's wholehearted support, switched from an air superiority strategy to strategic bombing in the hope that it would destroy London and sap British morale. The shift came suddenly. On September 7, Kesselring launched nearly 1,000 aircraft on London (348 bombers and 617 fighters). The raid caught British defenses by surprise; Fighter Command's response was ragged; controllers at sector stations initially concluded the Luftwaffe was striking at southern England. As a result, British fighters failed to attack until enemy bombers were on the way back. In swirling dog-fights, Fighter Command lost twenty-two more fighter pilots, but the Ger-mans lost the same number along with numerous bombers. Damage in London was frightful, and night raids worsened the loss. But the respite allowed Fighter Command to recover.

One week later, Kesselring launched a second blow at London. This time he ran into a well-prepared and rested enemy, eager to attack the raiders. From the moment the Germans crossed the coastline, British fight-ers slashed into Luftwaffe formations. Both sides lost equivalent numbers of fighters; the Germans, however, lost forty-one bombers. What made Sep-tember 15 decisive was the fact that many Luftwaffe bomber crews cut and ran, dropping bomb loads all over Kent. Deceived again by intelligence experts who had erroneously concluded that Fighter Command was beaten, and having suffered heavy losses since May, Luftwaffe crews had had

The British were outraged by the bombing in November 1940 of the cathedral at Coventry and the killing of 554 civilians. Three years later in July 1943, 30,000-40,000 German civilians died under Allied bombs in Hamburg.

enough. Though air attacks would continue, the Battle of Britain was over. The Luftwaffe had not won anything approaching air superiority, and Hitler postponed Sea Lion on September 17. Winston Churchill eloquently expressed the triumph: "Never in the field of human conflict was so much owed by so many to so few."

In retrospect it is hard to see how the Germans might have made a success of Sea Lion, considering the state of their navy and the problems besetting the Luftwaffe. That should not, however, diminish Dowding's accomplishments or the psychological importance of the British victory. Those responsible for Munich and appeasement in the 1930s possessed neither the strategic understanding nor the toughness of spirit needed to make the frightening decisions necessary for the defense of Britain in summer

1940. Only Churchill, called to be the prime minister on May 10, 1940, as German spearheads slashed into western Europe, possessed those qualities. His monumental eloquence and driving leadership imbued the British with the belief that they could win. On the other hand, Dowding's solid, professional leadership ensured that British air defenses made few mistakes. Britain's success made it clear to the world that the Nazis were not omnipotent—a factor of immense importance.

Though the Germans had lost the Battle of Britain, their efforts to cow Britain by terror attacks did not cease; rather, they shifted their emphasis to night bombing. Of all the world's air forces only the Luftwaffe had actually developed the navigational means to bomb in bad weather or at night. Luckily British intelligence provided warning that the Germans possessed such a capability. Through examination of crashed bombers, decryption of German message traffic, and imaginative analysis by a young scientist, R. V. Jones, the British unraveled the German system. Jones convinced his superiors and eventually Churchill of the danger, and as a result British scientists developed effective countermeasures that warped the radio beams on which German navigational systems operated. All this was of enormous importance because British defenses were blind. Air defenses could scramble single-engine fighters in the general direction of incoming bombers, but once airborne the fighters could not intercept their opponents at night. By late 1940 the first experiments with airborne radar were underway, but the sets on which interception depended were unreliable, bulky, and often inaccurate.

The problem confronting German planners in the nighttime offensive was target priority: should the Luftwaffe attack specific segments of British industry such as aircraft factories, or systems of interrelated industries such as imports and distribution, or even popular morale? The nighttime bombing offensive attempted all three strategic aims; not surprisingly it failed. As with daylight attacks, the Luftwaffe lacked either the strength or capability to achieve such wide-ranging objectives, and direct attacks on the British population only spurred the British to pay the Germans back in kind.

The *Blitz* underscored a number of important points. First, the resilience of modern economies and states allowed them to absorb great punishment. Second, the air weapon was a difficult one to wield with precision; achieving accuracy or sustained levels of damage was not easy. Finally, despite claims by airmen that air power would provide an easy solution to the costs of modern war, it was in fact extraordinarily expensive in terms of aircrews, aircraft, and industrial resources.

The War in the Mediterranean, 1940–1942

The focus now shifted to the Mediterranean. For the British the Suez Canal and Gibraltar held the key to their empire in India and the Far East. But

Italy's increasing hostility in the late 1930s forced the British to turn to the route around the Cape of Good Hope. Nevertheless, the greatly increased distances that British shipping had to travel with Italy's entrance into the war gave the British considerable incentive to open the Mediterranean.

The Italians viewed the Mediterranean as *mare nostrum* (our sea) and as the basis for the restoration of the Roman Empire. As such, Benito Mussolini recognized that he would have to expel Britain from Gibraltar and Suez. But fearful of German ambition, he hesitated to request Hitler's aid. Italy would, therefore, begin by fighting its own "parallel war." On the other hand, the Germans, with Hitler's dreams of living space in eastern Europe, had little inclination to look to the Mediterranean for strategic advantage.

Mussolini's Parallel War

On June 10, 1940, Mussolini declared war on the hard-pressed Western Powers. This was a popular move for most Italians, who believed that the British and French had robbed them of the fruits of their victory in 1918. Mussolini's conceptions, as with those of Hitler, were revolutionary. He aimed to use foreign conquest to create a Mediterranean empire and in turn to exploit that "success" to revolutionize Italian society. Mussolini's wars were murderously effective against poorly armed African peoples, but the Italians made only superficial preparations to meet their better armed and prepared opponents. The army focused on defending the Alps rather than preparing for an ambitious and difficult campaign; the air force dreamed of strategic bombing but possessed no ability to intervene in a naval war in the Mediterranean; and the navy felt thoroughly inferior to the Royal Navy.

Because of a lack of strategic and operational planning, the Italians floundered despite opportunities created by the French collapse and British weaknesses. The army's inadequate planning and preparations were symptomatic of all services: Marshal Rodolfo Graziani, army chief of staff, proclaimed in the last prewar conference that "when the cannon sounds everything will fall into place." Such wishful thinking did not make up for inadequate preparation. In the last desperate days of French resistance, the Italians launched a series of ill-prepared attacks on France; lack of success prevented them from taking advantage of the armistice with Vichy France. In early July a force of Italian battleships escorting a convoy to Libya ran into the British eastern Mediterranean fleet escorting a convoy to Malta. Despite advanced warning, greater numbers, and air superiority, the Italians fled in disarray. Arriving late, the Italian air force bombed both fleets indiscriminately but damaged nothing seriously since it possessed no armor-piercing bombs or aerial torpedoes. In September the Italian commander in Libya, Graziani, finally moved on Egypt. A lackadaisical advance got his forces to Sidi el Barrani, fifty miles from his starting point.

Meanwhile, events in the Balkans picked up momentum. Emboldened by the collapse of Europe's equilibrium, the Hungarians determined to regain Transylvania, lost to Romania in 1918. The Germans, given their dependence on Romanian oil, had no desire to see a conflict break out

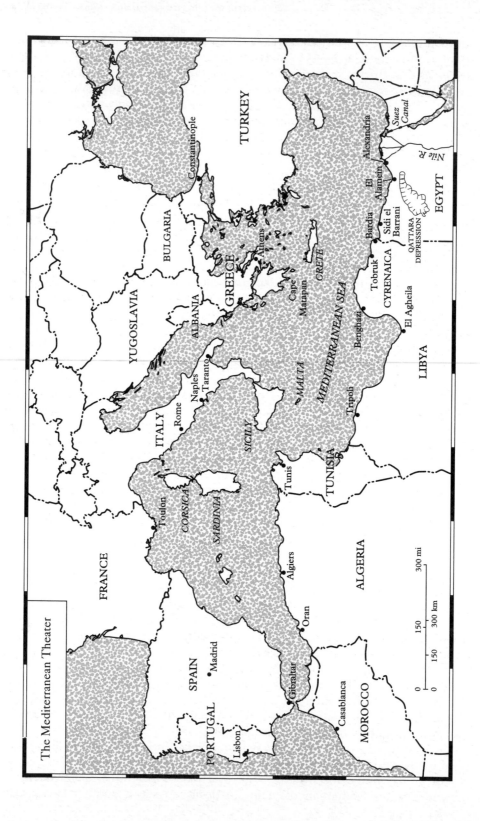

The Mediterranean Theater

between those two states. Therefore, with help from the Italians, they imposed a settlement that returned most of Transylvania to Hungary. Rebellion resulted in Romania; the king abdicated and General Ion Antonescu established a military dictatorship. The Germans, confronting a possible Romanian collapse, stepped in to stabilize the situation. At Romania's request, Hitler sent a military mission—one that by December consisted of no less than a panzer division, a motorized infantry division, two flak regiments, and two fighter squadrons. Ostensibly the German "advisors" were there to help the Romanian military; in fact they were there to guard the oil and warn the Soviets against fishing in troubled waters.

The Italian Collapse

Whatever the positive benefits from the move into Romania, it backfired on the Germans, for Mussolini viewed it as a cavalier disregard of Italian interests. As he told his foreign minister Count Galeazzo Ciano, "Hitler always confronts me with a fait accompli. This time I am going to pay him back in his own coin. He will find out that I have occupied Greece." Mussolini then ordered hurried preparations for an attack despite the lateness of the season.

Launched into northern Greece in early November 1940 from Italian-occupied Albania with little logistical support, in most cases with no winter clothing, and with numerical inferiority, the Italians marched straight into defeat. After initial successes, a combination of bad weather and Greek numerical superiority led to a general collapse. The Italian air force, with neither the inclination nor the preparation to support the army, confined its efforts to terror attacks on Greek cities. A string of incompetent commanders, including General Uboldo Soddu—who whiled away evenings in Albania by writing musical scores for movies—failed to rectify the situation. Not only had Mussolini upset the delicate balance in the Balkans, but he also had made British, and perhaps Soviet, intervention possible. The threat to Romanian oil was obvious; given winter conditions, Germany could do little.

Mussolini's run of troubles, however, had barely begun. On the evening of November 11–12 British torpedo aircraft from the carrier *Illustrious* struck the naval base at Taranto and sank half the Italian battle fleet. With this stroke the balance in the Mediterranean swung permanently in Britain's favor. One month later the British army attacked in North Africa. What the theater commander, General Sir Archibald Wavell, intended as a mere raid resulted in a complete rout of Italian forces. Mutually unsupporting positions around Sidi el Barrani collapsed before the onrush of the British 7th Armored and 4th Indian Divisions driving rapidly westward. Though Italian forces were on the run, Wavell pulled 4th Indian out of the line and transferred it to the strategically useless campaign in Ethiopia. The two-week period during which British forces reorganized was not enough for the Italians to recover; but it did, however, allow the Germans to get across the Mediterranean to Tripoli.

In early January British forces resumed their advance into Libya. Tobruk fell with startling suddenness. As the Italians hustled down the coastal road past Benghazi in a desperate retreat toward Tripoli, the 7th Armored Division sliced across the desert, caught the Italians at Beda Fomm, and destroyed what was left of Mussolini's African army. British forces advanced to El Agheila, where they halted; they had advanced more than 400 miles. There Wavell helped others persuade Churchill that his troops could not reach Tripoli and that the British should aid Greece as quickly as possible. Nevertheless, the British, for a loss of only 2,000 men, had captured 130,000 Italians and stripped the last pretensions of competence from Mussolini's military forces.

The Germans Arrive in the Mediterranean

Italy's disasters in early 1941 threatened to undermine the Axis position in the Balkans and Mediterranean. In response, Hitler's strategy had strictly limited aims: restore a collapsing situation in the Mediterranean; prevent Italy's collapse; and protect the southern flank of German forces gathering for the invasion of the Soviet Union. Since conquering the Soviets represented the heart of Hitler's revolutionary goals, there was no serious consideration among the Germans of alternatives to the eastern campaign.

The commander of the forces deployed to North Africa in early 1941, soon called the Afrika Korps, was a newly promoted lieutenant general, Erwin Rommel. Rommel had had a spectacular career in World War I. In the interwar period he remained in the infantry, but after the Polish Campaign, assumed command of 7th Panzer Division. In the French campaign, Rommel played a crucial role in the breakthrough along the Meuse River. As a reward, he received command of the corps-sized force deploying to aid the Italians. Rommel's orders were defensive; he was to protect Tripoli and support the remnants of the Italian army in North Africa. But Rommel believed that he must strike or be destroyed; he would soon emerge as the war's premier field commander.

Characteristically, Rommel disregarded his instructions and attacked even though only one division had arrived. Coordination between British units new to the theater collapsed in confusion, and Rommel surged east across Libya. By the end of April the Germans had chased Commonwealth forces almost 400 miles and driven them out of Libya except Tobruk. By holding that port, the British complicated the Germans' logistical problems; for the next six months Rommel found himself caught between Egypt's frontier defenses and Tobruk; he was unable to deal with either satisfactorily. Nevertheless, with only one motorized division he had restored the Axis position in North Africa and rocked the British; he had driven his opponents back to where they had begun.

In the Balkans geography constrained Axis actions. Given the limited logistic capacity of Albania, the Italians could not funnel sufficient troops and equipment directly to the front facing the Greeks. To advance against the Greeks, the Germans had to move through Yugoslavia or Bulgaria. The need for action became more critical in March 1941 when British troops arrived at Athens to reinforce the Greeks.

After Erwin Rommel arrived in North Africa in February 1941, he demonstrated a remarkable mastery of mobile operations, but he could not overcome the greater numbers of the Allies and his own shortages of supplies and fuel.

As the Germans built up Field Marshal Sigmund Wilhelm List's Twelfth Army in Bulgaria for its April attack, German diplomats assuaged Turkish fears and intimidated the Yugoslavs into joining the Axis on March 25. But on the evening Yugoslav negotiators returned to Belgrade, Serbian officers overthrew the government. Wildly cheering crowds in Belgrade, bedecked with French and British flags, underlined the mood. Within hours, Hitler ordered the OKW, the armed forces high command, to "smash Yugoslavia." By evening, after conferences with Field Marshal Walther von Brauchitsch (the army's commander-in-chief) and Göring, the Führer signed Directive 25 requiring that Yugoslavia be "beaten down as quickly as possible." Hitler also ordered the Luftwaffe to destroy Belgrade.

German planning rapidly adapted to changing circumstances. Within one week, OKH, the army high command, had altered Twelfth Army objectives to include southern Yugoslavia. Meanwhile, Second Army established itself in Austria and Hungary so it could execute a major attack from the north. As panzer forces from the two armies concentrated their thrusts from the south and north on Belgrade, German infantry would overrun the remainder of Yugoslavia. Along with ground deployments came extensive Luftwaffe redeployments. The code name for the aerial assault on Yugoslavia was "Punishment," an accurate reflection of Hitler's fury. By the time the Luftwaffe had completed attacks on Belgrade, 17,000 people had died.

From the onset the Balkan campaign split into two separate operations: the conquest of Yugoslavia and that of Greece. Fortunately for the Germans, the Yugoslavs failed to mobilize; the ferocious air attacks on Belgrade shattered the government; and the Yugoslavs attempted to defend their

Messerschmitt Bf 110 fighters supporting German operations in Yugoslavia in March 1941.
The Germans had great hopes for the Bf 110 as a multi-role "strategic" fighter, but numerous
design flaws limited its effectiveness except as a night fighter.

entire country. But Nazi forces easily broke through their defenses. Within
five days the Germans had seized Belgrade as the Yugoslav army collapsed in
disarray. Ironically the extent of the success contributed to the undoing of
long-range Nazi interests in Yugoslavia; almost immediately, the OKH began
recalling units for the operations against the Soviet Union. That process left
substantial numbers of armed Yugoslavs in mountains and remote areas.
Though the government had ceased to exist, the German victory did not
extinguish resistance.

The campaign against Greece was a replica of Yugoslavia; XXXX
Panzer Corps outflanked Greek defenses and sent Allied forces pell-mell to
the south. The Greek army collapsed, and the British withdrew by sea in
the face of the Luftwaffe's overwhelming air superiority. Nevertheless, at
the end of April the Royal Navy managed to evacuate nearly 51,000 of the
62,000 British soldiers in Greece.

The Fall of Crete

In retrospect, the strategic prize in the Mediterranean was not Greece but
Crete. Possession of that island would have provided a base for RAF raids
on Romanian oil fields, as well as a base from which to supply partisan
movements throughout the Balkans. The Germans recognized the threat,
and as their forces pushed the British and Greeks southward, German planners under paratroop general Kurt Student were already preparing a strike at
Crete. Student envisioned an airborne attack on Crete's airfields, supported
by coastal landings. But the Italian naval disaster at Cape Matapan at the
end of March, where the British sank three heavy cruisers, indicated that any
attack on Crete must rely almost exclusively on airborne forces. The final
plan was simple: seize the airfields at Maleme, Rhethymnon, and Herakleion
with the Luftwaffe's 7th Airborne Division and then reinforce as rapidly as

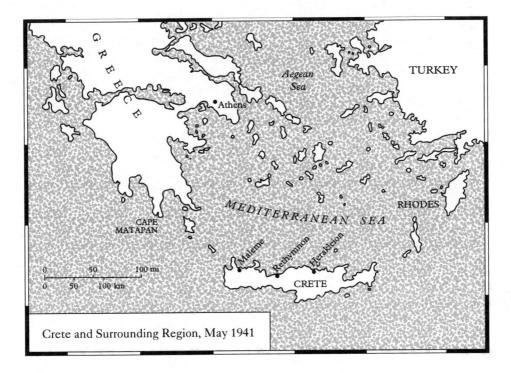

Crete and Surrounding Region, May 1941

possible with the 5th Mountain Division by using Ju 52 transport aircraft. But there were obstacles: the Allies had more troops on Crete than German intelligence reported; the local population proved distinctly hostile; and "Ultra" intelligence informed the British as to the coming attack.

The British had their own problems: many defenders had just been evacuated from Greece; they were short of equipment; and their morale was hardly solid. And despite signals from intelligence indicating that the Germans would launch an airborne assault on the airfields, Major General Bernard Freyberg, commander of Commonwealth forces, emphasized a defense of Crete's shores from the sea rather than from the air. Nevertheless, the attack on Crete, starting on May 20, almost failed. After its towrope parted, the glider carrying the 7th Airborne's commander crashed well before reaching the island. New Zealand troops at Maleme inflicted prohibitive casualties on the paratroops and retained control of the airfield. Without radios, the Germans at Maleme could not notify Student of their desperate situation. Airborne drops at Herakleion and Rhethymnon that afternoon resulted in an even greater disaster. Finally, Italian naval forces, escorting two convoys of reinforcements, ran into the Royal Navy and lost the troop ships they were convoying.

But the British lost the battle for Crete as a result of decisions taken at the end of the first day. The battalion holding the hill overlooking Maleme retreated, despite the fact that it had suffered no more heavily than its opponents. Freyberg's attention remained fixed on the sea, and few reinforcements reached the airfield's defenders—a period during which German paratroopers were particularly vulnerable to counterattack. Once the paratroopers controlled Maleme, however, they could receive reinforcements and heavier weapons; then the balance slowly but inexorably tilted against Commonwealth forces. Despite ferocious Luftwaffe attacks, the Royal Navy eventually evacuated most of Crete's defenders, but the British had lost a crucial geographical position in the Mediterranean. Romanian oil flowed to the Reich throughout spring 1944, hindered by nothing more than a smattering of air raids.

The German victory cost the paratroopers heavily. Nearly 60 percent of the transport aircraft were destroyed or badly damaged in the attack. Attacking airborne forces suffered such heavy losses that Hitler refused to employ them again as airborne forces until 1944. Ironically the allies reaped the lessons of Crete. On the receiving end of the aerial assault, they were far more impressed by the attack than were the Germans. As a result, much of the doctrine and concepts for British and American paratroop forces were derived from German airborne operations against Crete.

Libya and Egypt, 1941–1942

By late spring 1941 the Germans had achieved their short-term strategic goals in the Mediterranean. Rommel had restored the situation in Libya; intervention in the Balkans had repaired the damage done by Mussolini's invasion of Greece; seizure of Crete had driven the Royal Navy out of the Aegean Sea. But there were long-range drawbacks to these successes. While the Nazis had smashed the Greek and Yugoslav governments, they failed to achieve control of the countryside as the withdrawal to support Operation "Barbarossa" began, nor had they disarmed substantial numbers of the troops in remote Balkan areas—precisely the areas most likely to support guerrillas. On the strategic side, the Germans could not exploit their successes in the Mediterranean because they had already decided to invade the Soviet Union.

As Germany turned from the Mediterranean, the Middle East became a strategic backwater. Hitler now aimed to ensure that Italy remained in the war and to prevent the British from achieving a success that might threaten the Reich's southern flank. Rommel was chiefly responsible for meeting these objectives. Despite confronting considerable odds and having to operate at the end of long, tenuous supply lines, he emasculated much of the British military effort and by early summer 1942 even threatened to destroy Britain's position in the eastern Mediterranean.

Rommel on the Defensive

The British enjoyed a number of advantages that make Rommel's success even more remarkable. With the help of Polish cryptanalysts, they broke into the high-grade cipher transmissions of the German armed forces, particu-

larly those of the air force, in 1940. This message traffic contained information about the plans, combat readiness, and intentions of the German high command, Hitler, and senior commanders in the field. The breaking of German codes for much of the war thus provided the British with clear insights into German strengths and weaknesses. "Ultra" (the code name for decrypted messages from the German "Enigma" cipher machine) often provided the British with pinpoint information on the timing and tracking of supply convoys from Italy to Libya, thus allowing the British to intercept and destroy them. The losses kept the Axis forces desperately short of supplies. Sometimes, however, intelligence from Ultra could be misleading because Rommel frequently disobeyed orders from Italian as well as German high commands. The second British advantage lay in air power. Not only did the RAF posses numerical superiority, but its doctrine, developed by open-minded airmen like Sir Arthur Tedder, enabled the RAF to render effective close air support. Unfortunately, that air support could not rectify the weaknesses of British ground forces.

In June 1941, the British held the port of Tobruk in Libya and a front-line position just inside the Egyptian border. British armored forces held a four-to-one superiority in tanks over the Germans, whose armor was split between Tobruk and the Egyptian-Libyan frontier. Rommel, however, had created a number of tank traps, using 88-mm guns, and German defenses were carefully and skillfully sited. On June 15, Wavell launched "Battleaxe," an operation characterized by caution and inflexibility. Hoping to achieve a breakthrough before Rommel could concentrate his forces, the British attacked along the coastal road to drive straight on to Tobruk. Rommel's shrewdly prepared defenses, however, wrecked the attackers' momentum. By nightfall the British had lost half their tanks, while Rommel's armor, still shielded by antitank guns, had not come into play. A sweeping German counterattack around the British flank then drove British armor back in headlong retreat to its starting positions in Egypt. Battleaxe cost the

British ninety-one tanks, while the Germans lost only twelve (most of which they recovered and repaired).

The failure led to Wavell's removal. His replacement as Middle East commander-in-chief was General Sir Claude Auchinleck whose experience had been with the Indian army. From June through November 1941, Auchinleck prepared for another go at the Afrika Korps. For the first time, the British received substantial American aid to supplement their own equipment. Meanwhile Rommel had received barely sufficient supplies to keep his forces going. The German high command gave highest priority for supplies and reinforcements to the battles in Russia, and British air and naval attacks, aided by Ultra intelligence, proved deadly to Axis sea lines of communication. By mid-fall 1941 the British had established a considerable superiority in weapons and divisions in Africa; the RAF had nearly 700 aircraft against 120 for the Luftwaffe and 200 for the Italians; in tank strength the British had 710 against 174 German and 146 Italian vehicles. British weaknesses had more to do, however, with the intangibles of battle, and those came close to causing another defeat.

Operation "Crusader" began on November 11, 1941. One of Eighth Army's two corps, XIII, was to pin the Germans along the frontier, while XXX Corps swept around Rommel's flank to link up with Tobruk. The plan appeared clever, but in reality it split British armor, already weakened by diversion of a brigade of heavy tanks to support XIII Corps' infantry.

The attack got off to a slow start—so slow in fact that Rommel missed what was happening. When he reacted, he moved with usual dispatch; he screened off XXX Corps with antitank guns. Meanwhile, the British committed their armor piecemeal, and the Germans mauled it badly. In one action, Italian forces, showing considerable improvement, imposed a heavy toll on 22nd Armored Brigade, which lost 40 out of its 160 tanks. On November 24, Rommel pulled most of his tanks out of the main battle and dashed for the Egyptian frontier.

The balance on the swirling battlefield, however, slowly tilted to the British. Once Rommel's strike at British rear areas had failed to shake his opponents, he had to withdraw. Moreover, pressure exerted by the British from Malta placed extraordinary strains on the Afrika Korps: air and naval attacks sank nearly 80 percent of Axis supply ships crossing in October and November. Rommel's retreat took his forces back all the way across eastern Libya to El Agheila. Though Crusader appeared to represent a considerable turn in the desert war, the success rested on numerical superiority and German logistical difficulties, not from equality in tactics or battlefield performance.

As German forces retreated through Libya, the balance shifted back in their favor. *Luftflotte* Two (Second Air Force) transferred to the Mediterranean from Russia and launched a massive aerial assault on Malta. Consequently Rommel's forces now received most of the supplies dispatched from Italy. Retreat through Libya also enabled the Germans to fall back on supply dumps and restore their strength while it stretched British supply lines. Finally, Crusader resulted in heavier losses among combat veterans in Eighth Army than in the Afrika Korps.

Rommel Counterattacks

As the British halted near El Agheila in late 1941, having advanced some 400 miles, they repeated their mistake of February 1941: they pulled experienced forces back for rest and refit and pushed brand-new units to the front. Strengthened with new tanks and quick to take advantage, the Afrika Korps came boiling out of its defensive positions in January 1942 and struck the newly arrived 1st Armored Division. That division's three cavalry regiments, newly converted to tanks, knew little about armored operations and less about desert combat; the three British regiments came into play separately and were destroyed separately. The deadly combination of German panzers and 88-mm antitank guns leapfrogging from position to position ruled the battlefield. Rommel's thrust pushed the British back to Gazala, just west of Tobruk, and allowed his troops to reoccupy Benghazi, where both sides, exhausted by two months of combat and movement, settled down to build up for another battle.

In spring 1942, Churchill vociferously pressured his commanders in Libya to attack; Ultra indicated an enormous British superiority in every category of weapon. What intelligence failed to reveal, however, were enemy advantages in leadership, doctrinal coherence, and tactical proficiency. British generals resisted Churchill's urgings and set the date for their offensive in early June; it was too late. On the evening of May 26, Rommel moved, hooking around the British left flank and piling directly into the middle of the Eighth Army.

The British deployment possessed a number of weaknesses. The Gazala Line, approximately forty miles west of Tobruk and held by XXX Corps, reached deep into the desert with its infantry concentrated in strong points, called boxes, protected by minefields and barbed wire. The Bir Hacheim fortress anchored the southern tip of the line. Eighth Army commander, General Neil Ritchie, mistakenly believing that a German attack would come against his center, dispersed his armor to cover both his flank and the expected attack on his center. Auchinleck did suggest a concentration of armor, but Ritchie disregarded the suggestion.

Rommel's move underlines the extraordinary risks he was willing to run; he aimed to encircle the entire Gazala Line and Eighth Army. But things failed to work as he expected. The Germans began on May 26 with a diversionary attack on the center of the Gazala Line where Allied commanders expected an attack; that night the main body of the Afrika Korps moved around the Allies' southern flank. As he moved deep into the Allied rear, Rommel ran into heavy opposition; American M-3 Grant tanks had arrived in quantity and provided a nasty surprise. By the second day, the Germans were in serious trouble. Having moved around the British flank, the Afrika Korps found itself trapped against the Gazala Line with no route through which its supplies could flow; and it was rapidly running out of food, water, and ammunition. Fortunately for the Germans, the British launched a series of piecemeal attacks. Rommel's screen of antitank guns once again devastated British armor, while the panzers remained skillfully camouflaged in hull-down positions. Finally, the Afrika Korps overwhelmed Bir Hacheim

Rommel's operations in the desert relied on the mobility of his tanks, such as the Panzerkampfwagen III. He often massed his armored forces and delivered lightning-like blows against the more numerous but less flexible British forces.

and cleared a passage for supplies. The British had turned a promising situation into a catastrophe after two weeks of fighting.

On June 11, Rommel attacked eastward; on the next day his armor trapped two British armored brigades and destroyed them. A third armored brigade intervened to help its comrades, but again it ran into well-sited German defenses and was also destroyed. Such heavy losses cost the British their advantage in tanks; the Germans now had numerical superiority. Rommel turned north toward the coast and attempted to cut off British infantry withdrawing from the Gazala Line. Though most escaped, their retreat carried them straight to and over the Egyptian frontier in headlong flight.

Chewing its way through the collapsing British, the Afrika Korps headed eastward. On June 19 German forces brushed past Tobruk in pursuit of Ritchie's troops. The port's defenders consisted of 2nd South African Division, the Guards Brigade, and 32nd Tank Brigade with seventy tanks; confident that Rommel was going elsewhere, the defenders settled down. At dawn on June 20 a massive artillery bombardment hit the southeast side of the fortress, followed by the Afrika Korps, which had doubled back overnight. By mid-morning the garrison commander had decided the situation was hopeless and surrendered himself and 35,000 troops.

The Germans confronted the question of what to do next. Luftwaffe air attacks had severely battered Malta, and German paratroopers were preparing to give the coup de grâce. Given Rommel's extraordinary successes, however, did it make sense to stop just as the Afrika Korps rolled up on the frontier with the British in a state of complete demoralization? Rommel argued that he had an opportunity to drive the British from Egypt. Moreover, casualties on Crete, strong British defenses on Malta, and doubts about Italian reliability made an attack on the island a risky affair. Hitler sided with Rommel.

Rommel's pursuit carried him deep into Egypt. Yet his attempt to drive the British out of Egypt ultimately failed. Auchinleck relieved Ritchie and assumed command of Eighth Army. Halting his forces at El Alamein, he established a defensive position between the Mediterranean and the Qattara depression. The new position had no open flank because the Qattara depression, located thirty-five miles south of the coast, was a great salt sea impassable to heavy vehicles. Distances from Libya also complicated the German logistical situation. There at El Alamein in early July 1942 the British held, only sixty miles from Alexandria, and Rommel's slim chances of conquering Egypt faded.

Operation "Barbarossa"

At the end of July 1940, Hitler determined to destroy the Soviet Union. Strategic and ideological reasons lay behind his decision. On the one hand, he recognized that the United States and the Soviet Union represented significant strategic factors that explained British intransigence. But ideology underlay Hitler's decision as well; to him the Soviet Union represented an amalgamation of his greatest enemies, the Jews and Slavs. Not until he had destroyed Stalin's "Jewish-Bolshevik" regime would the biological revolution of Nazi Germany be safe. Finally, according to the Führer's *Weltanschauung*, the Third Reich desperately needed the agricultural and raw material resources of European Russia so that it would no longer have to depend on maritime trade for raw materials and foodstuffs. Without land and space, the German nation, Hitler believed, would never realize its full potential.

Because ideology played a crucial role in "Barbarossa" (the invasion's code name), the Germans came as conquerors, not as liberators; their conquest would bring slavery for Slavs and extermination for Jews. In its wake "special action" task forces of the Waffen SS accompanied each invading army group (three in number) to liquidate Jews, Communists, and other undesirables; these SS units received the wholehearted cooperation of most army commanders. Moreover, the army made its own contribution to the hideousness of war in the east; out of the approximately 3 million Soviet soldiers captured in summer and fall 1941, barely 100,000 survived the war— virtually all were under Wehrmacht, not SS, jurisdiction. The fanatical resistance of the Soviet population in defense of Stalin's malevolent regime largely resulted from the criminal behavior that marked German actions from the onset of Barbarossa.

Planning

By fall 1940 the Germans were deep into planning. The general staff accepted Hitler's assumption that the Wehrmacht could destroy the Soviet Union within one year. Basic to the Nazi approach was a belief that an invasion would catch and destroy the Red Army in the border areas. If that did not occur, several factors would have a negative effect on the course of subsequent operations. The theater itself broadened almost immediately, which would spread out the invaders; moreover, the depths of European Russia would allow the Soviets to trade space for time, while the campaign season itself would be short. Logistic war games gave clear warning that the Wehrmacht would face difficulties in supplying forces beyond a line running from Estonia to Smolensk and into the central Ukraine.

Operational planning by the OKH focused on Moscow as the strategic goal. However, the OKW emphasized that an advance on Moscow would depend on successes on the flanks—clearing the Baltic states to Leningrad and occupying the Ukraine. While differences between OKW and OKH conceptions remained relatively small, Hitler opposed the suggestions of his military advisors. He minimized Moscow's importance and argued that the invasion must achieve success on the flanks: in the north, Leningrad, cradle of the Bolshevik revolution; and in the south, the Ukraine, heartland of Soviet agriculture. To avoid Hitler's ordering a focus on the flanks, Colonel General Franz Halder (chief of the army's general staff) completed the final plan for Barbarossa without addressing this fundamental divergence of views. He obviously hoped that after the first stage of the invasion, the army leadership could persuade Hitler to go for Moscow. Consequently, German conceptions for the invasion contained a significant divergence that the high command refused to resolve until the campaign's mid-point. All of the planning also assumed that the Germans would destroy the Red Army in the border areas.

For the invasion the Germans deployed three army groups. Army Group North, under Field Marshal von Leeb, consisted of Fourth Panzer Group and Sixteenth and Eighteenth armies (three panzer, three motorized infantry, nineteen infantry, and four security divisions). Army Group Center, under Field Marshal Fedor von Bock, contained Second and Third Panzer groups as well as Fourth and Ninth armies (nine panzer, six and one-half motorized infantry, thirty-seven infantry, and one cavalry divisions). Finally, Army Group South, under Field Marshal Gerd von Rundstedt, consisted of First Panzer Group and Sixth, Eleventh, and Seventeenth armies (five panzer, four motorized infantry, twenty-eight infantry, two mountain, four light, and three security divisions). The OKH held two panzer, one motorized infantry, and eleven infantry divisions in reserve.

The objectives for the army groups reflected the planning: Army Group North was to clear the Baltic states; Army Group Center was to advance to Smolensk; and Army Group South was to push toward Kiev and then down the Dnieper bend, while Eleventh Army covered Romania and its oil. Consequently, Leningrad, the Ukraine, and Moscow were all objectives, but there were no clear priorities, no alternatives, and no examination of what the Wehrmacht would do should the Soviet Union not collapse. Even at the operational level, German field commanders were unsure whether the first objective of Army Group Center was encirclement of Soviet forces around Minsk or those farther east at Smolensk.

The German army that invaded the Soviet Union was an extraordinary military instrument. It was thoroughly trained; its doctrine was balanced and realistic; it had honed its battlefield skills by two years of campaigning; and its officer corps was flexible, adaptive, and professional. Nevertheless, its successes hid significant weaknesses. The inadequacies of rearmament in the 1930s forced the army to equip many units with foreign and obsolete weapons. Its panzer and motorized infantry divisions acquired many of their support vehicles by stripping western Europe of civilian trucks—vehicles that were neither designed nor built for the rigors of primitive Soviet roads. Moreover, the Germans were unprepared for the logistic demands of a theater that possessed continental dimensions. Finally, German intelligence did as bad a job in judging Soviet capabilities as it had done in judging the RAF. It underestimated the Red Army and its reserves considerably, miscalculated the recuperative powers of Soviet industry and military organizations, and underestimated the technological sophistication of Soviet weaponry.

The Soviet Union had its own weaknesses. Stalin understood the political vulnerability of his own regime only too well and consequently refused to trade space for time. He moved much of the regular army to the frontier to prevent the Germans from driving into the interior and then refused military commanders permission to make defensive preparations for fear of provoking the Germans. Using estimates more in tune with the tempo of the French army of 1940 than of the Wehrmacht, the Red Army calculated that it could hold the Germans close to the frontier and then counterattack.

Even more disastrously, Stalin's murderous purges of the Red Army had created a legacy of timidity, fear, and incompetence. The Soviet high command was incapable of understanding the German system of warfare or reacting to it. Any Soviet officer who dared to question the great leader's assumptions ran the risk of being accused of defeatism. In June 1941 the Soviet Union and its Red Army awaited the German invasion almost totally unprepared for what was to come.

The First Weeks of Barbarossa

At 0330 hours on June 22, 1941, German artillery from the Baltic Sea to the Black Sea opened fire; large numbers of Luftwaffe aircraft had already crossed the frontier to attack the Red Air Force. The Germans found Soviet aircraft parked wing tip to wing tip. By noon Soviet aircraft losses on the ground and in the air had reached 1,200. Field Marshal Erhard Milch, the Luftwaffe's chief logistics officer, recorded that the Soviets lost 1,000 aircraft on the 22nd, 800 on the 23rd, 557 on the 24th, 351 on the 25th, and 300 on the 26th. German air successes came at the expense of ill-trained and

German Invasion of USSR,
June 22 – December 5, 1941

ill-equipped Soviet aircrews, floundering in impossible tactical formations. Within the first week, the Luftwaffe had gained such a degree of air superiority that for the next five months it could support the army's advance with interdiction and unhindered close air support.

On the ground the Germans were equally successful. Stalin's obdurate refusal to allow his forces to make defensive preparations or to raise their alert status resulted in much of the Red Army's being surprised in indefensible positions. The warning that an invasion was imminent did not go out from Moscow until midnight. Thus few front-line units received any kind of warning. Across the Eastern Front the Red Army, staggered by the ferocity of the blow, struggled to adjust as communications collapsed, rear-area headquarters lost control, and chaos and confusion reigned.

German armor quickly clawed its way into the open; behind it German infantry pounded down the lanes of western Russia sometimes at the rate of thirty miles per day. Manstein's LXVI Panzer Corps, assigned to Army Group North and attacking from East Prussia into Lithuania, broke loose and in four days drove two hundred miles to seize the bridges across

The Germans used self-propelled guns, such as this Sturmgeschütz, to support infantry attacks. They manufactured about 10,500 throughout the war.

the Dvina River at Dvinsk. Manstein then urged commander of Fourth Panzer Group, Colonel General Erich Hoeppner, to push the other panzer corps forward, while LXVI Panzer Corps moved deeper into Latvia. Hoeppner was not sure, however, whether his mission was to sweep the Red Army out of the Baltic states or to guard the flank of the advance on Moscow. Leeb, commander of Army Group North, also remained in the dark as to his next objective but settled on a conservative broad-front advance that allowed Soviet forces to recover their balance and escape from Lithuania and Latvia.

By mid-July, Army Group North had advanced three-quarters of the way to Leningrad, but serious difficulties had emerged. While it had smashed Soviet resistance and driven the Red Army from the Baltic States, the advance of its mechanized units had split into two separate axes: the first to protect the advance on Moscow, the second to push toward Leningrad. Furthermore, spearhead units were at the end of long and tenuous lines of communication, while supporting infantry were far behind and food, fuel, and ammunition were in short supply at the front.

Army Group South ran into serious difficulties from the start. Part of the problem was the fact that many of its formations had fought in the Balkans and had not had time to recuperate. Moreover, the Soviets deployed a high percentage of their forces and best units in the Ukraine, and their commander largely ignored Stalin's order not to undertake preparatory measures. As a result, Soviet troops delayed First Panzer Group's advance.

The Germans did succeed in battering Soviet defenders back to Kiev, but Hitler ordered Rundstedt, the commander of Army Group South, not to attack the city. Not until early August did First Panzer Group break clear and encircle twenty Soviet divisions near Uman. That victory resulted in the capture of 103,054 prisoners and the destruction of three Russian armies, 858 artillery pieces, and 317 tanks.

If advances by Army Group North and Army Group South failed to achieve complete success, Army Group Center's Second and Third Panzer Groups won stunning victories. Here one of the worst sycophants in Stalin's military system, General Dmitrii G. Pavlov, played a major role in the collapse. After service in the Spanish Civil War, Pavlov had persuaded Stalin that mechanized warfare represented a dead end. Consequently, Stalin directed the Red Army to disband its armored formations in late 1939. Despite the fact that German panzer groups had achieved operational freedom at the end of the first day, Pavlov, echoing orders from the *Stavka* (Soviet high command), persisted in shoveling Soviet forces forward to deliver hopeless, pointless counterattacks. Communications between his units died as the Germans rushed forward. The Red Army stood in place, moved forward deeper into the encircling pincers, or simply collapsed. Second and Third Panzer groups swung in and met at Minsk on June 28 to complete the first encirclement. Within the larger Minsk encirclement, Fourth and Ninth armies completed a smaller one around Bialystok. Somewhere around 324,000 prisoners fell into German hands; along with the prisoners went heavy Soviet casualties with 3,300 tanks and 1,800 artillery pieces knocked out or captured.

In early July German successes led Halder to note in his diary:

> On the whole, one can already say that the task of destroying the mass of the Russian army in front of the Dvina and Dnieper has been fulfilled. I believe the assertion of a captured Russian general to be correct that we can calculate on meeting east of the Dvina and Dnieper only disjointed forces which alone do not possess the strength to hinder German operations substantially. It is, therefore, truly not claiming too much when I assert that the campaign against Russia has been won in fourteen days.

In early July Army Group Center's panzer groups renewed their drive. By late July the Germans had completed encirclement of Smolensk despite desperate and often successful Soviet efforts to break out. Waves of Soviet counterattacks from the outside attempted to loosen the German hold on the pocket. Only by August 5 did the Germans complete destruction of the Smolensk cauldron; another 300,000 prisoners fell into their hands, with 3,205 tanks and 3,000 artillery pieces destroyed or captured.

Difficulties

But the German advance came to a halt. At this point the extent of Nazi miscalculations and Halder's overoptimism emerged. Neither the Soviet state nor its military institutions had collapsed, and the logistic realities of

Russian distances exacted a high price on the invaders. Armored spearheads were at the end of over-extended lines of communication. Supplies of ammunition and fuel barely made it to the front, while virtually no rations arrived. Finally a series of savage Soviet counterattacks struck the German spearheads. Though these attacks were uncoordinated and often badly led, they imposed a heavy toll.

Exacerbating German problems was the fact that the Soviets mobilized far more troops than German intelligence had calculated. By July 1, as a result of mobilizing all reservists between the ages of twenty-three and thirty-seven, the Red Army possessed 5,300,000 additional soldiers. The reserve formations these men joined were desperately short of equipment, lacked experienced officers and noncommissioned officers, and were often ill-trained and ill-prepared. They represented, however, a numerically formidable force whose counterattacks fell on the German mechanized spearheads—units already exhausted by the advance, short of ammunition and fuel, and separated by wide distances from supporting infantry units.

The heaviest fighting occurred against Army Group Center. In mid-July, Second Panzer Group had seized the high ground around Yelnya, fifty miles east of Smolensk, as a jumping off point for the attack on Moscow. Eleven Soviet armies attacked across the entire front of Army Group Center, but the nastiest fighting occurred around Yelnya, where no less than six Soviet armies attacked in efforts to break the Smolensk encirclement. Despite considerable doubts as to whether Moscow would be the next objective, the Germans decided to hold the salient. Nevertheless, by early September the Soviets had forced the Germans to abandon Yelnya, inflicted over 40,000 casualties, and wrecked five infantry divisions. The Soviet attacks had an effect beyond the casualties inflicted; heavy, unrelenting attacks forced the Germans to expend virtually all ammunition and fuel that the overextended logistic system brought forward. Consequently the Germans failed to establish the supply dumps necessary for resumption of the advance; nor could they refit the panzer and motorized infantry divisions for the next stage of the campaign.

Despite prodigious marches (in some cases twenty to twenty-five miles per day), German infantry were still far to the rear, and armored and motorized infantry received the brunt of Soviet attacks. Fighting in August increased losses among those units that had borne the brunt of fighting and on whose shoulders further advances depended. Halder's diary entry for August 11 underscores the shifting mood within the German high command:

> The whole situation shows more and more clearly that we have underestimated the colossus of Russia—a Russia that had consciously prepared for the coming war with the whole unrestrained power of which a totalitarian state is capable. This conclusion is shown both on the organization as well as the economic levels, in the transportation, and above all in the infantry divisions. We have already identified 360. The divisions are admittedly not armed and equipped in our sense, and tactically they are badly led. But there

they are; and when we destroy a dozen the Russians simply establish another dozen.

Moreover, Stalin's hand remained firmly on the helm of what had
become a ruthless, desperate effort to survive. In mid-July he reimposed the
commissar system and turned his NKVD—the secret police—loose on
"slackers and defeatists." Nevertheless, the defects that had caused the early
defeats continued to permeate the system. The Soviet military style did not
tolerate failure and rewarded initiative with savage punishment. In the north
tens of thousands of Leningrad civilians dug anti-tank ditches and bunkers
to protect the city, but local authorities refused to stockpile foodstuffs for a
siege or to allow evacuation of the old or even the young. To do so smacked
of defeatism.

Along with a darkening operational situation and supply difficulties,
the Germans magnified their problems by engaging in debate over the campaign's next objectives. Halder and Brauchitsch (commander-in-chief of the
army) argued for a resumption of the advance on Moscow as soon as sufficient supplies arrived. Hitler in turn pressed for an advance on Leningrad
and the Ukraine; nevertheless it was not until the end of August that the
Führer finally forced the military to accept his decision. Only at that point
were German forces in a position to resume their advance. But as the
Wehrmacht entered the final stages of the campaigning season, there were
dangerous signs. By September 1, it had suffered 409,998 casualties out
of an average strength of 3.78 million. Moreover, the eastern army was
short 200,000 replacements; OKH had committed twenty-one out of the
twenty-four divisions in its reserve and virtually nothing remained, while
only 47 percent of the armored force remained "in commission."

In accord with Hitler's decision to advance on the Ukraine, Guderian's Second Panzer Group turned south to slice behind Soviet forces near
Kiev. At the same time Kleist's First Panzer Group, which had advanced
down the Dnieper bend, crossed that river and swung north. As the German
drives gathered steam, Russian commanders desperately appealed to *Stavka*
for permission to abandon Kiev. Stalin still refused to countenance withdrawals. On September 16, German spearheads met at Lokhvitsa in the
eastern Ukraine, one hundred miles east of Kiev; the encirclement encom-
passed four Soviet armies. By month's end after final destruction of the
pocket, the Germans claimed 665,000 prisoners, 824 tanks, 3,018 artillery
pieces, and 418 antitank guns.

While Army Group South completed destruction of the Kiev pocket,
Army Group North advanced to the gates of Leningrad and almost entirely
encircled the city; only a tenuous lifeline remained across Lake Ladoga. The
siege of Leningrad fell on a city that possessed a peacetime population and
minimal supplies of food and fuel; in the first winter over one million of its
citizens would die of starvation.

The Battle of Moscow

With successes in the north and south, Hitler concluded that Stalin's regime
was about to collapse. He therefore authorized an advance on Moscow

before the onset of winter. With Army Group Center launching the main effort, the objectives for Operation "Typhoon" were to destroy the rest of the Red Army and capture Moscow. Hitler and his army commanders expected that Typhoon's success would result in the long-awaited collapse of the communist regime.

Combined with the lateness of the season and the failure to make up for losses suffered over the summer, the supply situation should have caused the Germans great worry. On September 13, commander of Fourteenth Army reported: "at the moment [the supply system meets] current consumption only. The transport situation [has] not thus far allowed establishment of depots sufficiently large to enable the troops to receive what they need in accordance with the tactical situation. The army lives hand to mouth, especially as regards the fuel situation." In effect Wehrmacht units were not in a position to build up crucial supply dumps (including supplies required for winter weather) because the logistical system could barely supply sufficient ammunition and fuel to meet current demands.

In the last half of September, the Germans regrouped for Typhoon, the final push. Second and Third Panzer groups rejoined Army Group Center, along with much of Fourth Panzer Group. To unhinge the Soviets before the other panzer groups moved out, Guderian began Second Panzer Group's offensive two days early and advanced rapidly. Soon after, the other panzer groups also blasted their way into the open. *Stavka* appears to have believed that the lateness of the season precluded further German advances on Moscow. Stalin's demand that the Red Army defend every square inch of Soviet soil spread the defenders out, and there were few reserves to counterattack German breakthroughs. Not until October 5 did Stalin and his advisors recognize that major operations were occurring on the central front. Ironically the Soviets awoke to the danger only through a speech by Hitler in Berlin declaring that a great offensive had begun. Within one week the Germans had ripped open Soviet front lines and encircled two enormous groups of Soviet armies. West of Moscow, near Vyazma, they encircled six armies; near Bryansk, about 150 miles to the south, they encircled three more. When the battle was over, the Germans claimed another 600,000 prisoners. The German advances caused outbreaks of panic and looting in Moscow as the Red Army seemed on the brink of collapse. So great was the booty in material and prisoners that Goebbel's Propaganda Ministry announced that the Wehrmacht had won the war in the east.

At this point the weather broke. Autumn rains arrived to turn roads and countryside into seas of mud. The German advance halted in its tracks, while the *Stavka* desperately hurried forward reinforcements from the interior. The German situation became increasingly desperate. The farther forward the Wehrmacht advanced, the greater the strain on its logistics. The demands of Typhoon and subsequent advances consumed forward stockpiles as well as the ammunition and fuel that arrived through the supply system. That consumption in turn meant that the Germans possessed virtually no stockpiles of fuel, ammunition, or winter clothing.

Despite dropping temperatures, Halder, Brauchitsch, and Bock supported continuing the Moscow drive. German intelligence estimated that

Georgi Zhukov was the Soviet Union's premier expert in mass mechanized warfare. Victor at Moscow, Leningrad, Stalingrad, and Kursk and "liberator" of Berlin, he usually commanded over one million soldiers organized into more than a dozen armies.

the victories at Bryansk and Vyazma had exhausted Soviet reserves. Bock concluded that "the Germans could now afford to take risks." In early November, Halder expressed the pious hope that it would not snow until January so that the advance could continue. Colder weather did in fact allow the advance to begin again, but worsening conditions took a terrible toll on troops, still dressed in summer uniforms. As the weather turned cold, conditions reduced the German soldiers to desperate expedients such as lighting gasoline fires under the crankcases of tanks to warm engines sufficiently to turn over.

The Soviet Counterattack

As the Soviet situation deteriorated, Stalin rushed his most competent commander, Georgi Zhukov, to defend Moscow. Zhukov was as ruthless and effective a practitioner of the operational art as World War II produced; he was one of the few competent Soviet officers to survive the purges. Now in front of Moscow, he waged a delaying defense and for the first time effectively traded space for time. Meanwhile he built up a substantial reserve from reinforcements arriving to defend Moscow (some from as far away as Siberia). Zhukov believed that the Soviets could go over to the offensive once the Germans had exhausted themselves. Not surprisingly, German intelligence picked up little of this threatening situation. By December 4 the Germans had clawed their way to Moscow's outskirts, but they possessed neither the strength nor will to continue. That night temperatures fell to −25° Fahrenheit; one infantry regiment suffered 300 frostbite casualties. On December 6 the Soviets counterattacked.

The Germans had already lost the initiative elsewhere in the east. In the north, savage Soviet attacks kept open their fragile supply line across Lake Ladoga to Leningrad. In the south the Germans had taken Rostov at the end of November; however, Soviet counterattacks threatened to envelop the German spearheads. Rundstedt, the commander of Army Group South, ordered a withdrawal to the Mius River, but Hitler countermanded the retreat, fired the field marshal, and appointed Field Marshal Walther von Reichenau as his replacement. The new commander reaffirmed Rundstedt's retreat order and then suffered a heart attack. Events in the south presaged a crisis throughout the German high command and the collapse of Hitler's confidence in his generals.

As German forces teetered, Hitler made a crucial decision that sealed the Reich's fate. On December 7, 1941, the Japanese struck both British and Americans in the Pacific. Despite his own troubles in the east, Hitler decided to support his ally by declaring war on the United States. In so doing, he enabled Roosevelt to picture the Japanese attack on Pearl Harbor as part of a larger Axis plot; consequently American strategy, developed in consultation with the British in early 1941, identified the Third Reich as the greatest danger. Hitler's decision sprang from several factors: frustration at the desperate situation in the east, anger at Roosevelt's aggressive actions over summer 1941, and a contempt for the United States and its "mongrelized," racially mixed population. Hitler, as with most German leaders, ignored America's economic potential and encountered no objections to his decision. The army, desperately concerned over its situation in Russia, hardly cared about the consequences of America's entry; the navy on the other hand had actively pushed Hitler for a declaration of war on the United States throughout summer 1941 because such a declaration would increase operational possibilities for its U-boats. The Luftwaffe expressed no opinion.

Soviet forces that counterattacked the Germans in front of Moscow on December 6 were well prepared for the harsh conditions of winter. Nevertheless, Zhukov recommended limited objectives for the offensive: namely the destruction of one or two German armies lying in front of Moscow. Stalin, however, ordered a general offensive to destroy German forces across the whole breadth of the Eastern Front. For a period in December and January it appeared that Stalin was right. The headquarters war diary of one German unit recorded the desperate conditions of its troops:

> Discipline is breaking down. More and more soldiers are heading west on foot without weapons, leading a calf on a rope or pulling a sled loaded with potatoes. The road is under constant air attack. Those killed by the bombs are no longer being buried. All the hangers on (cargo troops, Luftwaffe, supply trains) are pouring to the rear in full flight. Without rations, fleeing irrationally, they are

pushing back. Vehicle crews that do not want to wait out the traffic jams in the open are drifting off the roads and into the villages. Ice, inclines, and bridges create horrendous blockages.

The desperate situation resulted in a crisis between Hitler and his generals, with the latter arguing for sweeping withdrawals to more defensible positions. Hitler believed that any retreats could turn into a rout that would repeat the fate of Napoleon's Grand Army in 1812. The Führer, therefore, demanded the army stand firm. Those who ordered retreats found themselves relieved from command or court-martialed. Brauchitsch (commander-in-chief of the army), Bock (commander of Army Group Center), Leeb (commander of Army Group North), Rundstedt (commander of Army Group South), Hoeppner (commander of Fourth Panzer Group), and Guderian (commander of Second Panzer Group) all found themselves summarily relieved. Hitler named himself commander-in-chief of the army. From this point, the German military functioned with the OKH in charge of the east, the OKW in charge of the Mediterranean and west, the Luftwaffe high command in charge of the air war, and the naval high command in charge of the U-boat war. Nowhere except in Hitler's mind did the threads of German strategy come together.

Halder's diary suggests the difficulties that German troops encountered on the Eastern Front:

> 25 December: A very bad day . . . ; 27 December: desperate attempts to check the enemy east of Sukhinichi . . . ; 29 December: *Very bad day!* . . . ; 31 December: *Again an arduous day* . . . ; 3 January: Another dramatic scene with the Führer, who calls in question the generals' courage to make hard decision . . . ; 8 January: *Very grave day.*

By early January Zhukov had driven back both flanks of Army Group Center, but the Germans hung on desperately. In retrospect, Hitler's demand to stand fast saved the Wehrmacht from collapse. The Soviets on their part attempted too much, and their advance flowed into areas possessing little operational or strategic significance. At times their forces cut lines of communication on which the German front depended, but the Germans held the crucial roads and supply centers. Slowly they recovered their equilibrium, while the Red Army, bled white from the fighting of the summer of 1941, found it difficult to maintain momentum. Unlike the German advances over the summer and fall, the Soviet winter offensive failed to gain any significant operational success except to batter the Germans back from Moscow. Yet when the winter was over, the Germans had suffered losses from which their army never recovered. By mid-March the fighting died down as the spring thaw arrived; the two armies began preparations for the summer battles of 1942.

✯   ✯   ✯   ✯

The fall of France in 1940 had not translated into an immediate strategic success for the Germans. The British had possessed an effective and competent air defense system, while the Wehrmacht had possessed neither doctrine, nor training, nor the understanding to make an amphibious assault on the British Isles. Sea Lion was stillborn from its conception. Britain's successful defense raised a number of intractable problems the Germans were incapable of addressing, problems that Italian incompetence only exacerbated. Forced by Italian defeats to move in strength into the Balkans and to support Libya, the Germans repaired the damage for the short run. But since they had little interest in the area, they failed to turn British defeats into a strategic rout.

1941 was the crucial year on which the fate of the world turned. In this year the Germans made a number of crucial mistakes. They failed to mobilize the European continent for the long haul. Then they embarked on an ill-prepared and poorly conceived crusade against the Soviet Union, one in which their operational and tactical excellence could not redress the political and strategic mistakes inherent in their approach to war against the Soviets. Finally, in desperation because of difficulties in the east, they declared war on the United States. Even more quickly than they had in World War I, the Germans had turned the war into a conflict in which everyone was against the Reich.

For Germany's opponents in 1941 the problem was quite different. For them it was a matter of hanging on until their superior resources changed the course of the war. The enormous logistical shortcomings displayed by the Wehrmacht in its invasion of Russia underlined German vulnerabilities. While the Germans could fight battles extraordinarily well, they were less capable of fighting a war of prolonged duration. Unfortunately for them, the outcome of the war ultimately would rest on the capacity to mobilize and project military power over an extended period and over extreme distances. With Nazi expansion halted, the Allies at last possessed the reason, time, and energy to mobilize fully their popular and economic resources. The war that now emerged would increasingly become a clash of economic strength, in which the Allied powers enjoyed significant advantages.

SUGGESTED READINGS

Barnett, Correlli. *The Desert Generals* (Bloomington: Indiana University Press, 1982).

Bartov, Omer. *Hitler's Army: Soldiers, Nazis, and War in the Third Reich* (New York: Oxford University Press, 1991).

Erickson, John. *The Road to Stalingrad* (New York: Harper & Row, 1975).

Fugate, Bryan. *Operation Barbarossa* (Novato, Calif.: Presidio Press, 1984).

Howard, Michael E. *The Mediterranean Strategy in the Second World War* (New York: Praeger, 1968).

Irving, David. *The Trail of the Fox* (New York: E. P. Dutton, 1977).

Knox, MacGregor. *Mussolini Unleashed, 1939–1941: Politics and Strategy in Fascist Italy's Last War* (Cambridge: Cambridge University Press, 1982).

von Manstein, Erich. *Lost Victories*, ed. and trans. by Anthony G. Powell (Chicago: H. Regnery, 1958).

Millett, Allan, and Williamson Murray. *Military Effectiveness*, vol. 3 (London: Allen and Unwin, 1988).

Murray, Williamson. *Luftwaffe* (Baltimore: Nautical and Aviation Press, 1985).

Overy, R. J. *The Air War, 1939–1945* (New York: Stein and Day, 1980).

Pogue, Forrest. *George C. Marshall* (New York: Viking Press, 1963–1987), 4 Vols.

Taylor, Telford. *The Breaking Wave: The Second World War in the Summer of 1940* (New York: Simon and Schuster, 1967).

Ziemke, Earl F., and Magna E. Bauer. *Moscow to Stalingrad: Decision in the East* (Washington: Office of the Chief of Military History, 1987).

3

THE ATLANTIC AND THE PACIFIC: PRODUCING AND PROJECTING MILITARY POWER

The Pacific War, 1941–1942

Mobilizing and Projecting Military Power

The European War at Sea, 1939–1945

The Air War

$\mathbb{W}$ith the entry of the United States and the Soviet Union, the war became a conflict of global dimensions and unprecedented scale. The process of defeating the Axis involved not only translating large populations and economic resources into military means and combining complex technologies into effective production of weapons but also—particularly for the Americans and British—protecting long and vulnerable lines of communication and projecting military power across great oceans. Throughout 1941 and 1942 German U-boats threatened the entire Allied war effort. With forces scattered across the face of the earth, the Allies halted the Japanese, mobilized the resources to fight massive battles, overcame the U-boat threat, and finally began projecting the military power on which victory rested. As the battle of the Atlantic escalated, the British, later joined by the Americans, waged a great air offensive against the Reich. Until the means for a successful assault on Fortress Europe became available, strategic bombing remained the primary means for the United States and Britain to strike Germany.

The naval wars in the Atlantic and Pacific differed greatly. Except for a few unsuccessful raids by surface ships, the battles in the Atlantic revolved around attacks by or attacks on German submarines. In the Pacific numerous large engagements of surface ships, supported by aircraft, occurred. Early in the war, however, it became apparent that the Pacific required a balance of land, air, and sea forces; geography dictated a solution different from that in the Atlantic. Though accepting the Allied strategy of "Germany first," the Americans found themselves shifting more and more resources into the Pacific, and with the attacks on Guadalcanal and New Guinea, they made the first tentative steps in what would become a massive assault across the Pacific. Nonetheless, many dark days remained before the Allies could translate their manpower and industrial advantages into sufficient military power to push the Japanese back in the Pacific and assault Fortress Europe.

The Pacific War, 1941–1942

Origins of the Pacific War

The origins of the Pacific war lay in the deeply rooted expansionist desires of Japan. When Western traders first reached the Home Islands in the mid-sixteenth century, the Japanese proved receptive to European ideas and permitted trade to occur for much of the next century. Beginning in the mid-seventeenth century and continuing for the next two centuries, however, they drove most foreigners out and isolated themselves from the West. But by the mid-nineteenth century they could no longer maintain their isolation and undertook a remarkable transformation to remake Japan. Using the British as models for their navy and the Prussians for their army, they built up effective and efficient military institutions, which defeated the Chinese in 1895 and tsarist Russia in 1905. Those wars gave the Japanese hegemony over Korea, which they annexed in 1910.

A lack of natural resources constrained the Japanese economy as it modernized and expanded, and imports became dependent upon the foreign exchange that exports earned. Until 1929 trade and industry prospered due to the upswing in the world economy. But the burden of industrialization rested on the back of Japanese peasants, and that burden was heavy, especially considering the poverty of the countryside. In 1929, when the world market collapsed and the Great Depression began, all the industrial nations, especially Japan, were hit hard. The reaction of an already xenophobic and nationalistic elite was extreme. The army's officer corps, which drew many officers from the countryside, found the idea that Japan must conquer larger markets most attractive.

Since the Russo-Japanese War, nationalists had considered China an obvious area for Japanese expansion. In 1931, the Japanese army in Korea took matters into its own hands and seized Manchuria, which it then renamed Manchukuo. The League of Nations condemned the action, as did the United States, but no one undertook serious reprisal. For the next six years intermittent military action and political intrigue continued in north China. An army memo explained: "The natural resources of Manchuria are far exceeded by those in North China. There are limitless deposits of iron

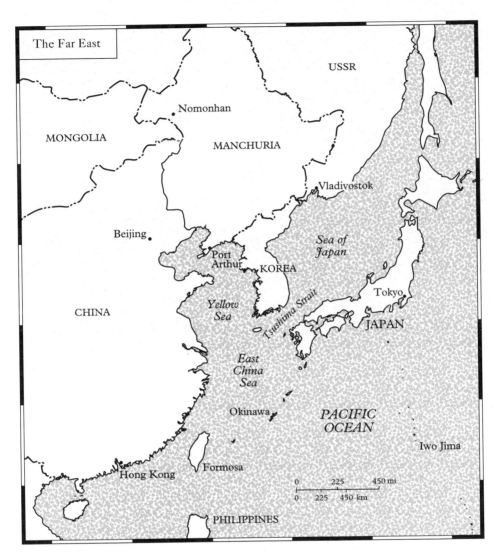

and coal in Shansi province. If we are careless, these resources will end up in English or American hands."*

In summer 1937, the army manufactured an incident at the Marco Polo bridge (near Beijing) between Manchuria and China and initiated major military operations against the Chinese. The home government had no advance warning but approved the operation due to fear of radical nationalists. Thus without addressing the political or strategic ramifications, the Japanese engaged in a full-scale yet undeclared war in northern China. The Chinese factions could not withstand ruthless Japanese assaults, but the

---

*Ienaga Saburo, *The Pacific War, World War II and the Japanese, 1931-1945* (New York: Pantheon Books, 1978), p. 68.

A Japanese infantry squad advances in China. Japanese soldiers distinguished themselves by their stamina, aggressiveness, and obedience. A British field marshal said, "We talk a lot about fighting to the last man and the last round, but only the Japanese soldier actually does it."

Japanese never possessed the strength to occupy all of China. While they occupied major ports and cities along the coast, much of the countryside remained beyond their control. Chinese guerrillas, especially Mao Zedong's Communists, made life miserable for the occupiers.

As if the "China incident"—the Japanese euphemism for their war against China—were not enough, the Japanese army courted several direct confrontations with the Red Army in Manchuria. In summer 1939 the Japanese seized a disputed area in western Manchuria; in late August the Red Army, under the future marshal Zhukov, counterattacked and destroyed a reinforced Japanese division at Nomonhan. Not surprisingly, after that defeat the Japanese army exhibited less interest in fighting the Soviet Union—at least until it had dealt with its China problem.

Americans watched Japanese behavior in China with growing outrage, but even the direct attack by Japanese aircraft on a clearly marked U.S. gunboat in China in December 1937 failed to elicit any American commitment to the Chinese. Moreover, American defense expenditures in Asia remained minimal: the Philippines received little funding, and none of the Pacific islands, on which a naval war depended, received sufficient resources from Congress to defend themselves.

The collapse of the Western Powers in spring 1940 turned Japanese attention toward the colonial empires of Southeast Asia. In June 1940 their foreign minister advocated inclusion of portions of Southeast Asia in a "New

Order in East Asia." The Japanese subsequently pressured the French to permit the stationing of troops in northern Indochina, and in July 1941 they occupied southern Indochina. This move placed them in a position to advance against British and Dutch colonial possessions in Southeast Asia and the Southwest Pacific. Viewing the Japanese move southward as a threat to the Philippines, the Americans finally reacted by embargoing exports to Japan, including oil, and by freezing Japanese assets in the United States. Oil was the essential element in the embargo, for without oil the Japanese economy and military machine would collapse. In October General Tojo Hideki became premier and one month later called for the elimination of British and American influence from the Orient.

Strategy and Plans

American strategy for a war in the Pacific changed dramatically in the inter-war period. Planning initially rested on the "Orange" plan, which the U.S. military developed before World War I as one of the "color" plans (black for Germany, red for Great Britain, green for Mexico, orange for Japan). The "Orange" plan resurfaced after 1918 and called for an "offensive war primarily naval in character" in the Pacific. It emphasized a naval drive through the central Pacific and a great clash of battle fleets. Throughout the 1920s and 1930s, students and faculty at the Naval War College tested and refined aspects of the American plan for the Pacific. In the late 1930s, as international tensions increased, the Americans began modifying these war plans. Designated "Rainbow" to distinguish them from the "color" plans, the new plans faced the possibility of the United States' having to meet the combined threat of Germany, Italy, and Japan. At a meeting of British and American staffs in January 1941, the future allies agreed that the main effort had to be made in the Atlantic, not in the Pacific, and that Germany and Italy had to be defeated first, not Japan. The new plan, "Rainbow 5," provided the main outline of strategy for World War II, but it changed Pacific strategy at the onset of a war from offensive to defensive.

American strategy changed because the combination of German, Japanese, and Italian power confronted the United States with significant threats from both east and west. President Franklin Roosevelt seems to have recognized the danger far earlier than most other Americans including his advisors. The problem then for him was how to push the buildup of U.S. forces to meet the threat without occasioning a political revolt from a population still drunk on isolationism. The fall of France made the danger greater, exacerbating American vulnerabilities in both the Atlantic and Pac-ific. In summer 1940 the president took the extraordinarily courageous dec-ision in an election year to support Britain; but that support could only re-tard the American buildup in the Pacific. Moreover, Roosevelt also 16determined that the United States would pursue a Germany-first strategy, given that nation's potential—a decision he maintained even after war began. But the problem for American planners lay in the fact that at least until 1943, when American industry would finally be producing vast quantities of weapons, equipment, and munitions, they would possess scant military means to deal with immensely complex logistic demands, not to mention opponents far better prepared to fight in the immediate future.

Defense of the Pacific proved difficult. The United States refused to send naval forces to help defend Singapore, which the British viewed as the "Gibraltar" of the Far East. With Japanese-held islands lying across the central Pacific, the Philippines seemed surrounded. Though planners anticipated problems maintaining contact with the Philippines, the United States began pouring units and resources into the islands. After the arrival of additional air and ground units, American strategists hoped to continue fleet operations from Manila and placed great faith in the buildup of heavy bombers in the Philippines both for their deterrent as well as their combat value. Nevertheless, planners did not expect the outbreak of war before spring 1942 and did not anticipate a swing in the balance in the Pacific toward the United States until 1943 when ships authorized in the 1938 building program came into service. Despite heightened tensions and extensive preparations, American commanders refused to believe that the Japanese would actually launch a surprise attack against the United States, particularly against the Pacific fleet at Pearl Harbor in the Hawaiian Islands.

In Japan the army and navy had developed substantially different strategic visions. The army looked toward Asia for expansion; as the dominant service, it had acquired a peculiarly parochial viewpoint, largely ignorant of the outside world. The Imperial navy, however, looked to Southeast Asia; it had acquired a better appreciation for Japan's vulnerability and for the most part urged greater caution in national strategy. Tied down in China, with major commitments in Manchuria on the Soviet frontier, the army could put only a small portion of its forces into the drive that overwhelmed the Western colonial empires in Asia. The navy would have to carry the bulk of the burden.

For decades the Japanese navy had planned for a war in the Pacific against the United States. Even before World War I, the Japanese planned on seizing control of the Philippines and Guam and intercepting and destroying the U.S. fleet when it crossed the Pacific and attempted to protect American possessions. Expectations of a decisive naval battle required highly proficient forces, and the Imperial navy became one of the best peacetime navies in history. It trained long and hard under the most strenuous of conditions; its pilots were outstanding. No other navy was as well-trained to fight at night. As for its technological capabilities, the "long-lance" torpedo was by far the best in the world, while its super battleships, *Yamato* and *Musashi*, were truly awesome representatives of a dying age. Finally, its conception and preparation for carrier warfare fully equalled that of the U.S. Navy, and its aircraft and pilots were initially superior to their American counterparts.

In late 1941 the army and navy established the broad outlines of Japanese war plans. They would attack Malaya and the Philippines simultaneously, seize the Dutch East Indies, and then launch a major offensive into Burma. After capturing Wake and Guam and thereby cutting America's lines of communication across the Pacific, they would establish a defensive perimeter extending west to Burma, east through the Dutch East Indies and

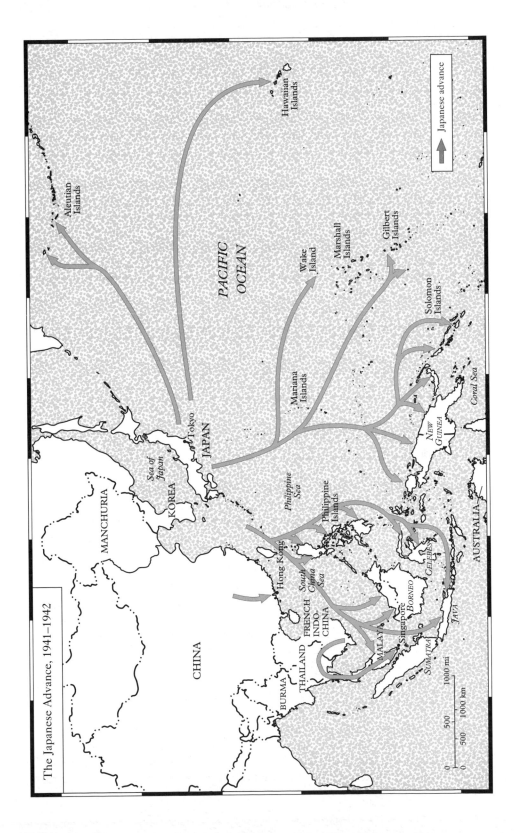

The Japanese Advance, 1941–1942

Japanese advance

PACIFIC OCEAN

Aleutian Islands

Hawaiian Islands

Wake Island

Marshall Islands

Gilbert Islands

Mariana Islands

Solomon Islands

Tokyo
JAPAN

Sea of Japan

KOREA

MANCHURIA

CHINA

BURMA

THAILAND

FRENCH INDO-CHINA

Hong Kong

South China Sea

Philippine Sea

Philippine Islands

NEW GUINEA

Coral Sea

CELEBES

BORNEO

Singapore

MALAYA

SUMATRA

JAVA

AUSTRALIA

0   500   1000 mi
0   500   1000 km

New Guinea to the Gilbert Islands, and north to Wake and the Kurile Islands. The Japanese initially hoped to lure the U.S. fleet into the central Pacific where submarines and aircraft could reduce its strength; their main fleet would administer the coup de grâce in the seas near Japan. But the commander of the Japanese fleet, Admiral Yamamoto Isoroku, unveiled a daring operational plan; his carriers would cross the northern Pacific and attack the American fleet at Pearl Harbor. Yamamoto hoped that the strike at Pearl Harbor would destroy or immobilize the American fleet and allow time for his forces to seize the resources that Japan's war economy needed and to construct an island barrier against an American counterattack. Then, he assumed, the United States would sue for peace, as tsarist Russia had done in 1905. Nevertheless, Yamamoto had had extensive exposure to America, including a year at Harvard University, and recognized the dangers that Japan would run in fighting a long war with the United States.

American intelligence picked up much of the Japanese movement in the weeks before war; historians have pointed to intercepts and other signals that suggested Pearl Harbor as a possible target. As in Europe, decrypts of Japanese signals (in the Pacific called "Magic") would play a crucial role in the eventual Allied victory. But no intercepts or other intelligence could overcome American perceptions of the Japanese as having an inferior military; the subsequent disaster at Pearl Harbor resulted more from this attitude than from poor or mishandled intelligence.

The Japanese Triumphant

In the morning hours of Sunday, December 7, 1941, American peacetime assumptions collapsed. The Japanese carriers had crossed the northern Pacific unobserved. From a point north of the Hawaiian Islands, they launched two waves of aircraft. The attackers reached Pearl Harbor at 0800 hours to discover the American battle fleet at anchor and the defenses at a minimal level of readiness. Japanese torpedoes and bombs found inviting targets, while their fighters destroyed the American aircraft parked wing tip to wing tip on Hickam Field. U.S. opposition was light, and Japanese losses were minimal. By the time it was over, the battleship *Arizona* had blown up; *Oklahoma* had capsized; *West Virginia* and *California* lay buried in mud; and *Nevada* got underway but had to be beached because of extensive damage. Japanese bombs damaged the *Pennsylvania* in dry dock and exploded destroyers *Cassin* and *Downes*. American casualties totaled 2,403 dead and more than 1,000 wounded.

Despite its results, the attack on Pearl Harbor proved to be an operational failure and strategic disaster for the Japanese. On the strategic level, the "sneak" attack united American support to enter the war. On the operational level, the Japanese sank an obsolete battle fleet but failed to destroy either fleet repair facilities or the gigantic fuel reserves, over one million tons. That fuel supply supported U.S. fleet movements for most of 1942; had the Japanese destroyed it, the Americans would have been forced to operate from the West Coast for the next year. Furthermore, American carriers were not in the harbor at the time of attack and thus escaped to fight another day.

Worse disasters soon befell the Allies; Japanese air attacks in the Philippines caught the Far Eastern Air Force deployed in peacetime fashion on Clark airfield. American air strength in the Philippines went up in smoke, even though eight hours had passed since Pearl Harbor. Two days later Japanese aircraft operating from southern Indochina caught and sank the British battleship *Prince of Wales* and battle cruiser *Repulse*. That success, even more than the attack on the American battle fleet, underlined the vulnerability of ships to air attack; the day of the battleship was over. Coupled with losses at Pearl Harbor, the loss of two British capital ships shifted the balance of naval power in the Pacific decidedly in favor of the Japanese.

Another disaster occurred in Malaya where nearly 200,000 British and Commonwealth troops defended the peninsula and Singapore. Despite nearly a two-to-one superiority, the British found the enemy skillful at infiltration and exploitation; the Japanese had little experience in jungle fighting but their tactical skills were outstanding. Under command of General Yamashita Tomoyuki, they outflanked the British from one position to another; by early February they had reached Singapore. On February 15, 1942, barely two months after Japanese landings, Lieutenant General A. E. Percival surrendered the city and its garrison in one of the most humiliating defeats ever suffered by British arms. That defeat reflected the gross overconfidence of British leaders and their failure to prepare their troops to fight in the jungle. It also demonstrated superb leadership and performance by the Japanese.

In the Philippines, American defensive efforts were no more successful, although they lasted longer. When General Douglas MacArthur assumed command of Philippine defenses, he convinced Washington that he could do more than simply defend Manila Bay. With additional reinforcements and supplies, he planned on meeting the invaders on the beaches and driving them into the sea. Shortly after the attack on Pearl Harbor, the Japanese made initial landings on the northern and southern tips of the main island of Luzon; then on December 22 they made their main landings in Lingayen Gulf about 125 miles north of Manila. They easily drove the defenders back, and on December 24, MacArthur ordered his forces to withdraw to the Bataan Peninsula. Abandoning much of their ammunition, equipment, and rations, which had been stockpiled forward near the beaches, the combined American and Philippine force established a twenty-mile defensive line on the northern part of the peninsula, while MacArthur's headquarters and the Philippine government moved to the island of Corregidor in Manila Bay.

By the time MacArthur's forces reached Bataan, they were on half rations; within a few weeks they were receiving less than one thousand calories per day. This inadequate diet largely resulted from MacArthur's faulty prewar strategy that had attempted to defend all of Luzon. By April, Bataan was finished, and in early May, Corregidor surrendered. In the meantime Roosevelt, realizing that he would have a public relations disaster on his

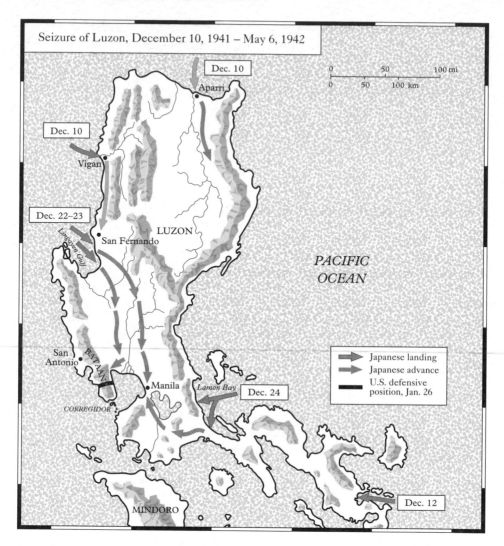

Seizure of Luzon, December 10, 1941 – May 6, 1942

hands if MacArthur fell into Japanese hands, ordered the general to relinquish command to Lieutenant General Jonathan M. Wainwright and move to Australia. There MacArthur assumed command of American and Australian forces in the Southwest Pacific.

Meanwhile, as Japanese forces reduced the Americans in Bataan, they continued their rampage in Southeast Asia and the Southwest Pacific. On January 21 they attacked Borneo with its rich oil resources. At the end of February they destroyed Allied naval forces in the East Indies (present-day Indonesia) in the battle of the Java Sea. On March 1 the Japanese landed successfully on Java, and the collapse of the Dutch colonial empire followed shortly thereafter. The Imperial navy moved at will through the waters in the Southwest Pacific. In late March, Japanese carriers struck into the Indian Ocean; in a one-week operation their forces chased the Royal Navy to Madagascar, while sinking a light carrier and two heavy cruisers.

The Japanese Checked

In spring 1942, the Japanese decided not to halt and erect a defensive perimeter, as their previous strategy suggested, but to use their fleet more aggressively and extend control over the Pacific. To this end they planned two major operations: against Australian forces in New Guinea near Port Moresby and against Midway (1,300 miles northwest of Honolulu) with the hope of destroying the remainder of the American fleet. Both Japanese operations aimed to extend the defense ring of island bases around their conquests and the Home Islands. American fleet intelligence from Magic, however, warned Admiral Chester W. Nimitz, Commander-in-Chief, Pacific (CINCPAC) and allowed him to deploy his weaker American forces against both threats.

To meet the strike against Port Moresby, Nimitz concentrated carriers *Lexington* and *Yorktown* in the Coral Sea off the eastern tip of New Guinea against an enemy force of two fleet carriers and one light carrier. The subsequent battle of the Coral Sea on May 4–8, 1942, was a new type of sea battle, waged by exchanges of air strikes, without the opposing surface ships ever making direct contact. American air attacks sank light carrier *Shoho* and damaged the larger *Shokaku*; even more significantly the air battles severely weakened the air components of both Japanese carriers so that neither would be available for operations in the immediate future. Japanese air attacks lightly damaged the American carriers; both, however, continued launching and recovering aircraft. But, a series of massive internal explosions wracked the *Lexington*. The ship's position was soon hopeless, and it had to be sunk by escorts. With the *Yorktown* also damaged, American losses in the Coral Sea were heavier, but the Japanese called off the amphibious attack on Port Moresby.

Approximately three weeks earlier, the Americans had launched an audacious raid against the Japanese Home Islands by flying B-25 bombers off the carrier *Hornet*. The operation was the brainchild of navy and army planners; it soon received the support of General Henry H. "Hap" Arnold, chief of army air forces. A relatively junior air reserve officer, Lieutenant Colonel James H. Doolittle, who had a reputation as one of the great flyers in the interwar period, put the force together. The navy provided the *Hornet*, and by the end of April 1942 the force was at sea ready to launch its aircraft. The plan was to launch the bombers close enough to the Home Islands so that the B-25s could reach China and reinforce the Chinese air force. However, the task force ran into a Japanese picket line of fishing vessels. Fearing compromise, the attackers launched early. Although they surprised the Japanese, they did not have the range to reach friendly airfields, and most crashed in China. The damage caused by Doolittle's bombers was minimal; however, an outraged and humiliated Japanese high command advanced the date for the Midway operation and set in motion the crucial confrontation in the Pacific war.

The Japanese designed an excessively complex plan to lure the American fleet to its destruction and to seize Midway by amphibious assault. No less than six different divisions of the Imperial fleet had separate responsibilities. In a diversionary operation, a strike force of two light carriers would attack American bases in Alaska and occupy two islands in the Aleutian chain, Attu and Kiska. Four battleships would provide a screening force to cover that raid. On the next day, the main carriers under Admiral Nagumo Chuichi would pound Midway, while behind them Admiral Yamamoto with superbattleships *Musashi* and *Yamato* would move up to destroy the American fleet, if it intervened. Finally another fleet moving from the southwest with two battleships, six heavy cruisers, and a small aircraft carrier would protect amphibious forces on their way to Midway.

The Japanese plan, even given its excessive complexity, might have worked. Intelligence from Magic, however, gave the game away even before the enemy left port. As a result, the feint at Alaska failed to fool Nimitz; the Midway garrison received extensive reinforcements of air and ground forces; and the American fleet, including the carriers *Yorktown*, *Hornet*, and *Enterprise*, was at sea ready to intercept the Japanese carrier force. The American battleships remained in San Francisco because they were not fast enough to keep up with the carriers—an indication of how rapidly the battleship had declined in American naval eyes. The *Yorktown*'s presence underlines the importance of Magic; the carrier returned to Pearl at full speed from the Coral Sea. Initial estimates were that it would take ninety days to repair damage it had suffered in battle; however, given the emergency, the *Yorktown* steamed out of Pearl Harbor forty-eight hours later after desperate emergency repairs.

The Japanese suspected nothing about these preparations. For the first time in the Pacific, luck turned against them. On June 4, their carriers and supporting vessels arrived north of Midway; all of the scouting aircraft took off on time except for the aircraft scheduled to search the sector where the American fleet lay waiting. Nagumo launched half of his aircraft for an attack on Midway, while the other half, armed with torpedoes and armor piercing bombs, remained on the carrier decks. Two hours later with no hostile reports from search aircraft, he ordered these weapons changed to high-explosive bombs to execute a second strike on Midway. As rearming proceeded, the search aircraft suddenly reported American fleet units. Additional moments passed until the aircraft reported one American carrier; with this warning, Nagumo decided to rearm the aircraft on the decks with the weapons needed to strike the American fleet. Meanwhile, heavy air attacks from Midway-based aircraft exacerbated Japanese problems. The attacks did no damage, but they made the task of rearming more difficult, as Japanese ships maneuvered at full speed.

Here again luck intervened. The first American carrier aircraft to find the Japanese were torpedo bombers, first from the *Hornet*, then from the *Enterprise* and *Yorktown*. Japanese fighters and antiaircraft guns slaughtered the American aircraft, which failed to achieve any hits; but low-flying torpedo bombers pulled Japanese fighters down to sea level. Shortly after the last torpedo bomber had gone in and just as the Japanese carriers turned into the wind to launch aircraft, the dive bombers from *Yorktown* and *Enterprise* arrived overhead. With no interference, they attacked the Japanese carriers, whose decks remained full of armed and fueled aircraft, high-explosive bombs, and ammunition for land targets (the munition handlers had not yet returned the downloaded weapons to the magazines). In a remarkably brief period they wrecked three carriers (*Akagi*, *Kaga*, and *Soryu*). Shielded by a rain squall, the last carrier, *Hiryu*, escaped damage for the moment and then launched aircraft against *Yorktown*, achieving a measure of revenge; three bombs and two torpedoes from the *Hiryu*'s aircraft severely damaged the American carrier and eventually contributed to its loss. Later that afternoon, pilots from the three U.S. carriers (those from the *Yorktown* were flying off other carriers) found the *Hiryu* and left it sinking as well. In early evening, the U.S. fleet pulled off to the east to avoid a night surface engagement.

Midway was a major success for the U.S. Navy; American aircraft had destroyed four Japanese carriers. Even more important the Japanese lost most of their flight crews—the best trained in the world—in the flaming wreckage. The threat to Midway was gone, and initiative in the Pacific now swung tentatively to the Americans.

The Counteroffensive

By this point, command relations in the Pacific had solidified. The size of the theater—the entire expanse of the Pacific and Indian oceans—made some division inevitable. But interservice as well as political realities resulted in the creation of two distinct American efforts. There was some irony in this state of affairs, because in Europe the Americans were preaching to their British allies about the need for a single, united command against the Germans. In the Pacific, however, they waged anything but a unified effort.

The division of responsibility resulted as much from personalities as from strategic necessity. MacArthur's escape from Bataan presented

After World War II Douglas MacArthur complained in a somewhat self-serving fashion, "[F]ailure to unify the command in the Pacific . . . resulted in divided effort, the waste, diffusion, and duplication of force, and the consequent extension of the war with added casualties and cost."

Roosevelt with a difficult decision. To bring him back to America would have caused considerable pressure to place him in a high military position; if left in a united Pacific command, his date of rank made him superior to any American officer, a state of affairs unacceptable to the navy, particularly since the Pacific was an ocean and MacArthur was a soldier. As a compromise, the Joint Chiefs of Staff (JCS) divided the Pacific in half and gave MacArthur command of the Southwest Pacific and Admiral Nimitz the Central Pacific. The two separate commands would cooperate as necessary.

Immediately after Midway, MacArthur proposed to attack the main Japanese base at Rabaul on New Britain; to achieve that goal, he argued that he needed two carriers and an amphibious division (marines). This self-seeking proposal met a self-seeking response. Admiral Ernest King, the chief of naval operations, proposed that Nimitz take command of all MacArthur's ships and aircraft; the army would merely provide forces to garrison islands that the navy and marines captured. After a week of acrimonious debate, the JCS hammered out a compromise that it published in a directive on July 2, 1942. The decision represented a less risky approach and reflected the real balance of American and Japanese forces in the Pacific. An advance on Rabaul would take place, but in three stages. The first included a landing in the southern Solomons on the islands of Guadalcanal and Tulagi (a tiny island twenty miles off the northern coast of Guadalcanal). Seizing them would protect communications to Australia. Stage two would involve an advance along the northeast coast of New Guinea and culminate in the third stage, a direct assault on Rabaul.

The Tulagi-Guadalcanal operation in August 1942 opened the American counteroffensive. When marines landed at Red Beach on Guadalcanal on August 7, they encountered little resistance because Japanese construction crews had no protecting troops. Outside of the initial landings and seizure of the airfield, nothing else went right. The lack of beach personnel and suitable landing craft resulted in supplies being unloaded on the beach haphazardly; congestion also prevented some landing craft from discharging their cargo. Then the commander of the naval task force, Vice Admiral Frank J. Fletcher, pulled his carriers out of the area almost immediately after the landing.

Disaster followed. An Allied force of heavy cruisers and destroyers under command of Rear Admiral V. A. Crutchley of the Royal Navy guarded the landings. As Fletcher's carriers exited the area, an Australian patrol aircraft spotted Japanese warships heading south from Rabaul into "The Slot" which was formed by the parallel lines of islands making up the Solomons. However, the pilot failed to report his sighting immediately. Moreover, he described the enemy force as three cruisers, three destroyers, and two sea plane tenders. In fact it consisted of five heavy cruisers, two light cruisers, and a destroyer, all of which were heading at full speed towards Guadalcanal. The report did not get to Allied fleet commanders until 1700 hours, even though the initial sighting had occurred at 1030.

Five Allied heavy cruisers and five destroyers protected the anchorage near Guadalcanal where the merchant ships were still unloading sup-

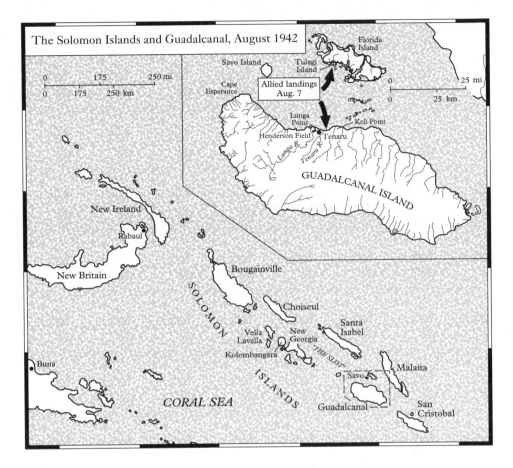

The Solomon Islands and Guadalcanal, August 1942

plies. Around 0130 hours, the attackers struck. None of the Allied vessels spotted the Japanese until it was too late. Though one lucky American shot caused minor damage on an enemy cruiser, the Japanese sank four cruisers and damaged two destroyers and one heavy cruiser. Fearing Allied aerial attacks at dawn, the Japanese admiral broke off the action and retreated; by so doing he permitted the invasion to continue.

The battle of Savo Island was a disaster for the U.S. Navy. It was even more humiliating than Pearl Harbor, for at least in December 1941 the United States had been at peace. The next morning after dumping some supplies on the beach, the support vessels weighed anchor and abandoned the marines who consequently had no barbed wire, no construction equipment, and only minimal supplies of ammunition and food. They were at the end of long and tenuous lines of supply, but they enjoyed one priceless asset: Japanese engineers had almost completed construction of Guadalcanal's airfield. On August 15, four U.S. destroyers slipped into Guadalcanal with aviation fuel, ammunition, and ground crews. Five days later, twelve dive bombers and nineteen fighters arrived at the newly named Henderson Airfield. Possession of the airbase gave marines a crucial advantage in coming weeks.

The Pacific war had exploded on the United States and the colonial empires of Southeast Asia. Now with Hitler's declaration of war, the Americans were in a two-front war. Given the reaction of the American people to Pearl Harbor, the Pacific theater represented a strong and continuing area of interest to American military planners. Yet in the long run, Germany was the greater danger. For Roosevelt and the JCS, strategy became a delicate balancing act between the requirements of a "Germany first" strategy and the political realities of public demands that U.S. forces avenge Pearl Harbor. In early 1942, the Japanese sweep through Southeast Asia and the Southwest Pacific had threatened the entire theater; only the Coral Sea and Midway provided a breathing spell. Now with the commitment to Guadalcanal and New Guinea the Americans had made the first tentative steps forward. But shortages of resources and heavy demands of a two-front war represented strategic and logistical problems that the Americans could not fully solve until 1944.

Mobilizing and Projecting Military Power

The United States

The Japanese attack on Pearl Harbor caught the United States in the first stages of a massive mobilization of its industrial and manpower resources. In no sense was the nation or its military prepared for war. In the 1920s and 1930s the United States had spent less than 2 percent of its gross national product on defense; even with the start of World War II, U.S. defense expenditures were less than five billion dollars. In 1940 those expenditures ballooned to nearly twenty billion, while the peacetime proposals of both army (which included the air force) and navy for expansion reached over one hundred billion dollars. In summer 1940, the fall of France led Congress to pass the first peacetime draft in American history. But the draft and buildup of American military power met strong opposition from many. In summer 1941 with Britain still isolated in western Europe, with the Japanese pursuing an evermore threatening policy in the Pacific, and with Nazi armies slicing through the Soviet Union, the Congress of the United States renewed the peacetime draft by *one* vote. Those drafted were hardly much happier; a movement among draftees called themselves the "Ohio" gang—"over the hill in October."

Anger over Pearl Harbor dissolved opposition to American involvement in the war; Americans rallied behind the president and the military in support of the war effort in a fashion that has never been seen, before or after, in U.S. history. The problem was how to translate economic strength and popular enthusiasm into military power. American leaders, political as well as military, had the experience of U.S. mobilization in World War I to use as a model and therefore avoided some of the mistakes that had beset mobilization in that conflict. Economic mobilization began in August 1939 when Roosevelt created several boards to plan for conversion of industry to war production, to control consumer prices, and to coordinate use of scarce materials. Prewar efforts functioned poorly, but by early 1943 the nation's economy had converted to a wartime footing and functioned relatively smoothly. Though the United States relied on numerous controls and boards, the many voluntary measures of its mobilization contrasted sharply to the mandatory approach of the Soviet Union, Britain, Germany, and Japan.

In May 1943, the Office of War Mobilization under James F. Byrnes, a former Supreme Court justice, received complete control over establishing priorities and prices. Strict regulation of rents, food prices, and wages went into effect, as did rationing of items such as meat, shoes, sugar, and gasoline. The combined effects of conscription and expanded industrial production produced a labor shortage and increased bargaining power for workers. The National War Labor Board, created after Pearl Harbor, served to arbitrate disputes and hold wage rates down. As a result, prices and wages soared during 1942, but they leveled off in 1943 and remained steady until the end of the war.

The labor shortage also encouraged large numbers of American women to join the work force. In addition to those serving in the military, many women found jobs in hospitals, factories, transportation, offices, and farms. Though most withdrew from the labor market after 1945, their participation during the war contributed to significant changes in the economic status of women in American society. African-Americans also benefited from the labor shortage; many found previously closed jobs open to them. They also found more opportunities in the military; one (Benjamin O. Davis) became an army general for the first time and more than 600 became pilots. Though treated somewhat better than they had been in World War I, they continued to suffer from prejudice and mistreatment, and the practice of segregating blacks from whites continued.

When the Japanese struck Pearl Harbor, American mobilization had been underway for about a year and a half. As U.S. industry strained to meet the needs of its allies and its own rapidly expanding forces, severe shortages appeared. By 1943, however, the dividends of the economic mobilization and the strengths of American industry became apparent. The results of that effort were truly awesome. In 1944 alone the U.S. aircraft industry produced 73,876 combat aircraft. In *all* of World War II the Germans produced only 86,311. In 1941, two years *after* Nazi Germany had started World War II, its factories produced 3,256 tanks for the entire year, including 698 made in Czechoslovakia. In 1943, two years after it entered the war, Soviet industry was producing over 1,300 tanks per month; American production that same year was over 2,400 per month. Similarly, the naval buildup in the Pacific reached extraordinary levels; by 1944 a new *Essex* class fleet carrier or an *Independence* light carrier was arriving in Pearl Harbor every month, and in some months one of each. By the battle of Leyte Gulf in October 1944, the attacking U.S. fleet possessed no less than seventeen fleet carriers. One also needs to recognize that in addition to

M-3 Grant tanks being produced in Chrysler Corporation's Tank Arsenal in Detroit, Michigan. During the war, the Detroit Tank Arsenal produced 22,234 tanks, or about 25 percent of all tanks produced in the United States.

projecting power around the world and supplying huge quantities of weapons to Allies, Americans also grew, processed, and transported large amounts of food and foodstuffs that prevented their allies from starving. Finally, the United States bore the immense financial and economic costs involved in the Manhattan project, which resulted in production of the atomic bomb. No other nation or economic system could have financed such a development during the war.

But there were difficulties in the early years of American mobilization. The shipment of military equipment to Britain and then the Soviet Union in 1940 and 1941 provided a shield for American preparations. Such shipments, however, also deprived U.S. military forces of equipment that was vital to preparations for war. Even in 1943, lend-lease shipments were a significant drain on equipment stocks. Other difficulties included priorities. In 1942 German successes in the battle of the Atlantic threatened to cut the sea lines of communication between Britain and the United States by sinking many merchant vessels. That same year, the American shipbuilding industry produced three million tons of merchant vessels; in response to Britain's desperate plight as well as the demands of military forces deployed around the world, industry increased production to nine million tons in 1943. Nevertheless there was a cost: production of such large numbers of merchant vessels adversely affected the production of landing craft essential for Allied amphibious attacks on Fortress Europe *and* the Japanese island empire in the Pacific.

The production of weapons represented only part of the problem; turning millions of young men into efficient and effective combat units was another. Critics of the tactical and operational competence of American forces in World War II often use as their model of comparison the performance of German soldiers. Such a comparison is fundamentally false. German rearmament began in 1933; it represented an effort that government as well as the officer corps knew would lead to a major conflict. The Germans had six years of peace and one and a half more of relatively light combat to prepare their ground forces. Moreover, they usually were on the defensive when they faced the Americans.

But the Americans, beginning the mobilization of their economy and their military in September 1939, found themselves in heavy combat on land, sea, and in the air within two years of the initiation of their effort. On the day that Germany invaded Poland, the U.S. Army possessed 14,486 officers and 175,353 enlisted men. Six years later at the end of World War II, the army possessed 891,663 officers and 7,376,295 enlisted personnel. Over those six years, the performance of American ground forces steadily improved as commanders and units gained combat experience. And there is no doubt that American naval and air forces were distinctly superior in qualitative as well as quantitative terms to their enemies by 1943. Though the ground forces may have lagged qualitatively behind their naval and air contemporaries, particularly in the early part of war, there were exceptions. The 88th Infantry Division in the Italian campaign consistently proved itself superior to its German opponents, as did the American airborne divisions. Nevertheless, there is considerable evidence that many American combat units did not match their German opponents on the ground.

A number of reasons explain this state of affairs. On the negative side, U.S. forces initially relied on the M-3 Grant but then in 1942–1943 replaced it with the M-4 Sherman tank, which was more mobile and mechanically reliable than German tanks, but which could not match German Panthers or Tigers in killing power. Recognizing the need for a heavier tank, the Americans built the M-26 Pershing but manufactured only 700 before Germany surrendered. Consequently, American armored-fighting vehicles remained qualitatively inferior to those of their opponents. Additionally, the system of manpower allocation to the armed forces sifted out too many of those who scored highly on intelligence tests into the army air forces, the navy, and innumerable technical positions and left too few among those who had to do the fighting on the ground. To make matters worse, the army all too often regarded soldiers as interchangeable parts that it could shift from one unit to another with little regard for unit cohesion.

Manpower demands on the U.S. population limited the options of military leaders. The war required that millions of Americans be involved in the manufacture of military matériel. Then the services needed millions more; at the war's end the army possessed 5.9 million men and women, the army air forces 2.3 million, the navy 3.4 million and the marine corps nearly half a million. All these military forces required enormous support to get overseas and then to fight a massive *two-front* war over distances that no other combatant had to consider. Originally army planners had foreseen the need for ground forces in excess of two hundred divisions. The realities of fighting the war in the Pacific and the air assault on the Reich forced the Army's chief of staff, General George C. Marshall, to scale back the program to ninety divisions.

That decision resulted in serious but unavoidable consequences. By the end of the war eighty-nine out of those ninety divisions had been committed to combat—scarcely much margin of security. In Europe the fighting forced American commanders to commit infantry and armored divisions to sustained combat, often beginning with Normandy and continuing through Nazi Germany's collapse. Consequently, there was little opportunity (with the exception of airborne divisions) to pull divisions out of the line to rest, refit, and retrain and to give combat units a chance to absorb replacements outside the front lines. In the Battle of the Bulge, this situation had the serious consequence of leaving General Dwight D. Eisenhower, the Allied supreme commander, with a reserve pool of two airborne divisions for the *entire* front—from Holland to Switzerland—on which American troops were fighting. Nevertheless, the main concern for American planners was balancing between the requirements for manpower in the work force and the military in order to sustain the economy as well as operations in the field. Whatever the drawbacks of having only ninety army divisions, it reflected serious choices with which American leaders for the most part grappled more effectively than did their German counterparts.

Great Britain

No country mobilized more extensively than did the British. The nature of the German threat, which lay across the straits of Dover, barely twenty miles away, underlined the desperate situation confronting Britain in June 1940. In 1939 the British had devoted 2.8 percent of their labor force to military service; by 1944 that number had grown to 24.1 percent. Similarly in 1939, 6.4 percent of the labor force worked in defense-related industries; by 1944 the number had grown to 17.7 percent. The hardship and pressures that this unprecedented mobilization placed on the British is captured by a 1944 report.

> The British civilian has had five years of blackout and four years of intermittent blitz. The privacy of his home has been periodically invaded by soldiers and evacuees. In five years of drastic labor mobilization, nearly every man and every woman under fifty without young children has been subject to direction to work, often far from home. The hours of work average fifty-three for men and fifty overall; when work is done, every citizen who is not excused for reasons of family circumstances, work, etc., has had to do forty-eight hours a month duty in the Home Guard or Civil Defense.

Supplies of all kinds have been progressively limited by shipping and manpower shortage; the queue is part of normal life. Taxation is probably the severest in the world, and is coupled with continuous pressure to save. The scarce supplies, both of goods and services, must be shared with hundreds of thousands of United States, Dominion, and Allied Troops; in the preparation of Britain first as a base and then as a bridgehead, the civilian has inevitably suffered hardships spread over almost every aspect of his daily life.

The war effort raised enormous problems. Britain's industrial plant and processes were antiquated and out of date. Yet on a relatively weak economic base the British produced almost as many aircraft as did Nazi Germany, which had all of western and central Europe upon which to draw. In armored fighting vehicles the British produced 27,896 to 46,837 for the Reich. When one considers that the Americans produced 88,410 armored fighting vehicles, and the Soviets 105,251, one gets a sense of how extraordinarily outnumbered the Germans were. But no matter how extensive Britain's mobilization, there were factors they could not overcome. Weaknesses in the industrial base placed limitations on what they could do; the antiquated nature of British industries, particularly the motor industry, had serious consequences. The inadequacy of British tanks throughout the war was one glaring example; the failure of much of the truck fleet on which General Sir Bernard Montgomery's advance in 1944 depended was another.

Germany

Of all the national economic performances, however, it was that of Nazi Germany that left the most to be desired. Hitler's Reich had launched World War II on a most inadequate economic base, one that had contributed to Hitler's belief that the Third Reich must expand to gain the economic resources required for its long-term security. Through the fall of France in spring 1940, Germany lived a precarious economic existence; only the incorporation of Austria in March 1938 and the seizure of Czechoslovakia in September 1938 and March 1939 prevented economic collapse and allowed rearmament programs to proceed. By 1938 the Reich was devoting 18 percent of Germany's gross national product to military spending.

The conquests of Poland, Scandinavia, the Low Countries, and France placed their economic and industrial resources at the disposal of the Reich and brought the Balkans and neutrals like Switzerland, Sweden, and Spain within the Nazi economic orbit. Germany possessed economic resources and industrial capacity the likes of which the Reich had never had before. But Hitler and his senior leadership drew the inaccurate conclusion that the existing production levels in Germany were sufficient to win the war. Moreover, fearful of Nazi Germany's political stability, they hesitated to bring into effect the kind of complete mobilization that Churchill instituted in Britain from 1940 until 1943. Consequently the Germans refused to introduce measures that would have mobilized their population and manpower for total war. At the precise moment that their actual (Britain) and potential (the United States and the Soviet Union) opponents were setting in motion massive mobilization and rearmament programs, the Germans continued business as usual with eight-hour shifts and six-day work weeks. Neither aircraft nor tank production, nor any other crucial indicators showed significant upward movement. Even more important was the fact that the Germans made few efforts to draw on the European economy to expand future production; instead they busily stripped factories in western Europe of machine tools and shipped them back to industrial plants in the Reich that were still working only single shifts.

This short-sighted approach continued through December 1941. However, defeat in front of Moscow, accompanied by loss of much of the army's equipment, and collapse of the Luftwaffe's logistic system (exacerbated by the brutal Russian winter) finally awoke German leaders to the fact that they needed to undertake desperate measures to fight a world war. The death of the armaments minister, Fritz Todt, in February 1942, led Hitler to make one of his more inspired decisions: the appointment of his personal architect, Albert Speer, as Todt's replacement. The thirty-six-year-old Speer possessed extraordinary managerial and leadership skills, as well as keen commonsense. He set about to allow Germany's industrial magnates and firms maximum latitude to expand production. Nevertheless, severe constraints limited options in the economic sphere. Despite the seriousness of the situation, Hitler refused to allow total mobilization of Germany's resources. For ideological reasons, he forbade mobilization of German women to support the war effort; consequently a substantial labor source remained untapped throughout the war in stark contrast to what was occurring elsewhere in the world.

Hitler's decision limiting economic mobilization also reflected his misreading of the lessons of World War I. He believed that the severe pressure in 1918 for armaments production had resulted in the collapse of morale and revolution in Germany. Nevertheless, the Nazi regime undertook extraordinary measures to stoke the war economy; it mobilized slave labor from across Europe; and Nazi authorities soon dragooned millions of French, Russians, Italians, Poles, and other nationalities into German factories.

From spring 1942 a steady and impressive upswing of weapons and munitions production occurred. That growth proceeded through summer 1944 despite Allied strategic bombing attacks. Nonetheless, increases in German production from 1942 to 1944 remained substantially behind those occurring in the United States, the Soviet Union, and Britain. The lost years of 1940 and 1941 were years that the Germans could not make up.

Equally important was the fact that Allied strategic bombing severely retarded German production. Across the Atlantic the Americans increased aircraft production by use of mass-production techniques; the Willow Run aircraft plant of Ford in Michigan possessed a factory floor over two miles long. B-24s began at one end as a tail assembly and rolled out the other as completed aircraft. In Germany the exact opposite occurred as air attacks forced the Germans to decentralize aircraft production into small, inefficient manufacturing operations. Moreover, the quality of the work significantly declined over the course of the war as more slave workers occupied crucial production positions. These unwilling slaves, undernourished and subjected to horrendous treatment, were hardly eager to turn out first-class products for their rulers. The result was a significant decline in quality of weapons produced by German industry.

Defeat at Stalingrad in February 1943, followed shortly thereafter by collapse in North Africa, finally persuaded Hitler to allow Joseph Goebbels and Speer latitude to extend war and mobilization measures throughout German society. But the Führer still held back on some measures, particularly regarding the wider employment of women in German industry. Meanwhile, strategic bombing attacks destroyed German cities and disrupted industries. By 1944 the impact of enemy bombing caused serious consequences in oil, aircraft, and transportation. Desperate efforts to squeeze the last products out of the German economy prolonged, but could not alter, the final result: catastrophic national defeat.

The European War at Sea, 1939–1945

While the opening campaigns of the war were unfolding on land, the crucial campaign of World War II had already begun in the North Atlantic. From the outbreak of war, German U-boats waged a tenacious struggle to sever lifelines between the British Isles and the rest of the world. Had they succeeded, there would have been no second front, no air campaign against the Third Reich, and few supplies for the hard-pressed Soviets; and Britain itself, confronted with starvation, might well have sued for peace. As Churchill commented: "The only thing that ever really frightened me during the war was the U-boat peril."

First Battles

Neither the British nor the Germans had prepared for the battle of the Atlantic. Having developed sonar (called asdic by the British) at the end of World War I, the Royal Navy comfortably assumed that it had solved the submarine menace. During the interwar period it did little serious preparation for protecting convoys; and it constructed few antisubmarine vessels. With the outbreak of war, it could protect only the most important shipping routes.

The Germans for their part displayed no more foresight. Before the war, the commander-in-chief of the navy, Admiral Erich Raeder, emphasized creation of a great battle fleet that would eventually be capable of challenging Britain on the seas. When the war began, the Germans had two battleships and two near completion, three pocket battleships, three heavy cruisers, and five light cruisers. They also had fifty-seven submarines, about half of which were capable of sustained operations at sea. With the outbreak of war in September 1939, Raeder recognized that since war had come early, the navy could not challenge Britain on the surface; it had to use its ships as raiders, while its submarines executed attacks on British commerce.

In fall 1939 German submarines achieved some notable successes; they sank the aircraft carrier *Courageous* and battleship *Royal Oak*. But their number was so small that after an initial wave of attacks, they inflicted minimal damage. The picture was not much rosier for the surface navy. The Scandinavian campaign cost it virtually all its strength, either sunk or damaged. Nevertheless, German successes in spring 1940 altered the Reich's strategic position. The commander of the U-boats, Admiral Karl Dönitz, moved submarine bases to the west coast of France and then launched an energetic anticommerce campaign.

By fall 1940 the U-boat force, while not significantly larger, had achieved a high level of effectiveness. Dönitz spread the submarines in patrol lines across the most likely lanes approaching the British Isles. When one made contact, it reported by radio the location, size, and direction of movement to Dönitz, who then concentrated his submarines in wolf packs against the enemy. Eventually, overcontrol by radio would cost the Germans dearly, but now it worked.

On October 5, 1940, Convoy SC-7 departed Canada with thirty-four slow merchant vessels. Its escort for much of the journey was a single sloop; its opponents were some of the great U-boat aces of the war. In mid-ocean another sloop and a corvette joined up. Eventually two more corvettes arrived. None of the escorts possessed radar; they had not trained together; and the sonar on some of the corvettes was obsolete. The result was a slaughter; SC-7 lost twenty ships with two others damaged. At the same time that U-boats were savaging SC-7, the fast convoy HX-79 departed Halifax for Britain. This convoy had a larger escort, including two armed merchant cruisers, two destroyers, four corvettes, a minesweeper, and three trawlers. But the escort fleet was no better trained. Attacking U-boats sank nearly 25 percent of HX-79's merchant vessels.

The arrival of winter provided a covering blanket over convoys. But in spring 1941 shipping losses in the Atlantic began an ominous upswing. In March losses were 243,020 tons; in April 249,375 tons; in May 325,492 tons; and in June 310,143 tons.

While British losses mounted in the U-boat war, the Germans moved to change the surface equation. Raeder hoped to make a great raid against British shipping by uniting the new battleship *Bismarck* and heavy cruiser *Prinz Eugen* (in the Baltic) with battle cruisers *Scharnhorst* and *Gneisenau* (in Brest). But *Scharnhorst* needed repairs, and an RAF Coastal Command aircraft torpedoed *Gneisenau*. Nevertheless, the Germans launched *Bismarck* and *Prinz Eugen*, as well as a number of supply ships and weather ships, on the raid. As the heavy German ships approached the Denmark Straits, British cruisers picked them up and began shadowing. On May 24 battle cruiser *Hood* and the new battleship *Prince of Wales* attacked, but the Germans destroyed *Hood*, while mechanical problems forced *Prince of Wales* to break off action. *Prinz Eugen* escaped to the south and eventually entered Brest. Crippled by a rudder jammed by British attacks, the *Bismarck* did not get away and on May 27 was finally sunk by the British battle fleet. This ended German attempts to challenge British dominance of the ocean.

Intelligence Intervenes

As a consequence of the *Bismarck* breakout, the intelligence equation in the Atlantic underwent a drastic change. On May 8, 1941, escorts of convoy OB-318 damaged a U-boat and forced it to the surface. After capturing the crew, British sailors boarded the badly damaged submarine and extracted the Enigma enciphering machine and its settings for the next seven weeks. Seizure of a weather trawler at the end of May (sent out to support the *Bismarck*) provided further access to Enigma settings, allowing teams at Bletchley Park (headquarters of British code-breaking efforts) to break into the German naval codes for the first time in the war. The first information from decrypted German transmissions allowed the Royal Navy to sweep up German supply and weather ships; the British destroyed six German tankers and three supply ships after determining their positions. Recognizing that such a clean sweep could hardly have been the result of luck alone, the Germans executed a major enquiry into the security of the message traffic but concluded that destruction of the tankers and supply ships resulted from the efforts of the British secret service.

The Germans had recognized that the British might capture Enigma settings and read transmissions for short periods of time, but they never believed that the British could do this on a sustained basis. They were wrong. Bletchley Park soon began reading U-boat message traffic on a regular basis. The opportunity came from Dönitz's close control of the U-boat war and the numerous transmissions to and from boats at sea, which provided the British with the cribs needed to break into the codes. The intelligence from these decrypts then allowed the British to maneuver convoys around U-boat patrol lines. Sinkings due to submarines dropped dramatically: in July 1941 down to 94,209 tons; in August to 80,310 tons; in September 202,554 tons; in October 156,554 tons; in November 62,196 tons; and in December 124,070 tons. The rise of losses in September reflected the fact that Luftwaffe long-range aircraft picked up the movement of Gibraltar convoys. This British success in the last half of 1941 is the only time in the war where intelligence was decisive by itself. In December 1941 the Germans introduced an additional rotor into the Enigma machine, and the British could not read U-boat message traffic for most of 1942.

The German High Point

The situation in the Atlantic took a drastic turn when Hitler declared war on the United States on December 11, 1941. Dönitz immediately sent a few long-range boats to the east coast of the United States. By mid-January five boats were off the coast from New York to Cape Hatteras, and the slaughter began. The Americans were totally unprepared. No convoy system existed. American destroyers plied up and down coastal waterways like clockwork, so that U-boat commanders always knew where they were. Some American cities along the coast refused to darken their lights. The five U-boats achieved stunning success; between the onset of Operation *"Paukenschlag"* on January 12 and the end of the month, the Germans sank forty ships, all sailing independently. Totals rose rapidly as the Germans reinforced and extended operations to the Caribbean and then to the north coast of South America. In February, U-boats sank 65 ships in American waters, in March 86, in April 69, in May 111, and June 121.

Despite the losses, the Americans stubbornly refused to establish convoys. The commander of defensive operations off the eastern seacoast believed "that a convoy without adequate protection is worse than none." Consequently he concentrated defensive forces in hunting down submarines by patrolling. Such efforts were uniformly unsuccessful; not until April did the Americans sink their first U-boat. The Americans also did not possess a system to integrate intelligence into operations. The British Operational Intelligence Center provided a guide for what was needed, but the U.S. Navy refused to heed British advice until late spring. Equally harmful was the lack of training and doctrine among the naval forces deployed against the U-boats. Initially in 1942 the Americans blamed their failures on a lack of resources, but as a veteran of the effort later admitted, the key factor was human error.

At the beginning of May, the U.S. Navy adopted convoys off the East Coast. That change led Dönitz to shift his emphasis to the Caribbean. Again the U-boats enjoyed a rich harvest of ships sailing independently. In May 1942 U-boats sank forty-one vessels of nearly 250,000 tons in the Gulf of Mexico; thirty-eight more of 200,000 tons went to the bottom in the Caribbean. The Germans had extended the range of U-boats into this area by use of submarine tankers, known as "milk cows." In May and June twenty U-boats operating in the West Indies and Caribbean sank nearly three quarters of a million tons of shipping, virtually all of it sailing independently. This catastrophe forced the Americans to begin convoys throughout the Caribbean; losses again dropped dramatically. The Germans now had to turn back to attacking convoys crossing the North Atlantic; the easy war was over.

The use of U-boats for purposes other than attacking sea lines of communication hampered the campaign in the Atlantic. In winter 1942, Hitler ordered a number of submarines to move into the Mediterranean to help Rommel. Similarly in spring and summer 1942, Hitler held back some U-boats to cover Norway. Then in November 1942, in response to Allied landings in North Africa, he ordered U-boats to attack the landing force. This redeployment cut down on the boats available in the Atlantic precisely at the moment when Allied convoys had lost many escorts to protect the North African landings.

But German difficulties in the North Atlantic were not entirely due to the diversion of submarines. Dönitz's method of controlling his boats created a situation advantageous to Allied intelligence, both in fixing enemy

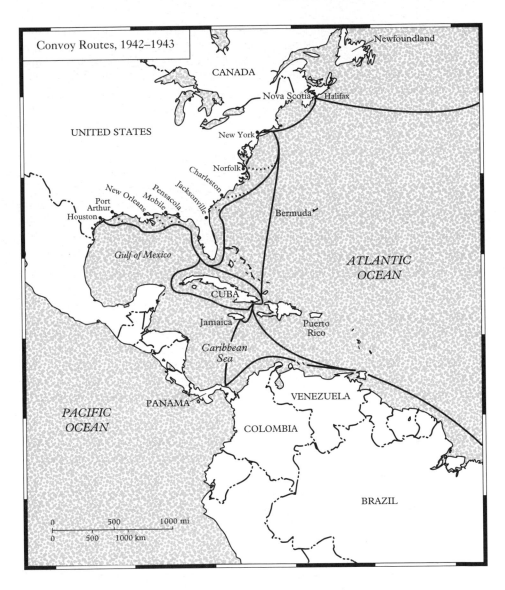

boats by direction finding and in breaking German naval codes. Furthermore, Dönitz attempted to win the war in the Atlantic with a minuscule
staff. For the first several years of the war that approach sufficed, but with
no organic research unit, with a narrowly focused intelligence effort, and
with its small number of officers immersed in day-to-day operations, the
German submarine command fell behind the smoothly running organization
that the Allies eventually put together. As one opponent remarked, Dönitz's
system was "an eighteenth-century way of war in a twentieth-century age
of technology."

During 1942, nevertheless, the Germans sank no less than 8 million
tons of shipping and suffered few losses. Dönitz possessed approximately
150 U-boats in commission or being constructed in September 1941, and

the operational fleet reached 212 boats by September 1942, with an additional 181 preparing for sea duty. By mid-1942 approximately thirty new boats joined the fleet each month. In November total sinkings reached 729,000 tons despite the diversion of many U-boats to North Africa. The climactic moment was now approaching in the Atlantic.

Allied Victory

Despite the large numbers of German submarines, several factors favored the defenders. In December 1942, Bletchley Park again broke into German naval codes, but that intelligence became available sporadically. On some days code breakers could break in quickly, on other days only after long delays. Nevertheless the British and Americans could build up a more complete picture of German operations in the Atlantic, and they now cooperated daily in exchanging intelligence about U-boat operations. The presence of so many U-boats in the Atlantic, however, made it difficult for the Allies to slip a convoy through without its being sighted.

But in 1943 other factors also affected the balance. The number of escorts increased dramatically; nearly all now possessed radar. An improvement to radar—the shifting of microwave frequencies to higher levels—rendered the German detection and jamming equipment useless. Sonar capabilities had considerably improved; depth charges were also better, and some escorts possessed "Hedgehog" rockets that allowed them to attack submarines without losing sonar contact. Allied antisubmarine doctrine and training had also noticeably improved, so that escort groups worked as effective and efficient teams. Finally, escort carriers provided air cover throughout the mid-Atlantic gap where land-based air power had not reached, while long-range aircraft equipped with radar proved a deadly danger to U-boats caught on the surface.

In January 1943 evasive routing of convoys, based on Ultra intelligence, combined with bad weather to lower shipping losses to 200,000 tons. In February losses rose to 360,000 tons, and in March they reached 627,000 tons. In March a series of convoy battles favored the Germans. In a period during which no Ultra intelligence was available to Allied naval commanders, forty German U-boats concentrated on convoys SC-122 and HX-229. In a four-day battle they sank twenty-one merchant ships for the loss of only one boat.

April saw more great battles, but this time the Germans were the losers. In the last week of April, two wolf packs totaling forty-one boats attacked convoy ONS-5. The attackers sank twelve merchant vessels, but the reinforced escort group sank seven U-boats, while severely damaging another five. In April the Germans lost the same number of boats as in March, fifteen. Then in May the battle went completely in favor of the defenders. A combination of escort and air attacks imposed an unacceptable level of losses on U-boats. Allied antisubmarine forces sank forty-one boats during the month. Dönitz concluded that his submarines could no longer meet the Allies on an equal footing; he withdrew them from the North Atlantic.

The battle of the Atlantic was by no means over. Unable to attack Allied convoys in mid-Atlantic, U-boats sought targets in distant waters. Here again, intelligence played a crucial role in leading Allied escort groups to German supply submarines on which long-distant voyages depended. But raids by U-boats off the coast of South Africa and into the Indian Ocean represented only pinpricks that did little overall harm to the Allies. Dönitz had to wait for technological changes to alter the balance. By mid-1945 the Germans were on the point of launching submarines that could move at fifteen knots underwater for short periods of time. Had these boats been available in 1944, the Germans might have negated Allied advantages and resumed a full-scale offensive against Allied commerce.

Allied success in the North Atlantic in May 1943 came at a point at which the American shipyards had begun turning out 10,000-ton *Liberty* ships in enormous numbers. The opening of the Mediterranean, which destruction of Axis forces in Tunisia had made possible, freed up millions more tons of shipping. Through the sea lanes of the world, America could now project its immense military and industrial power in both European and Pacific theaters. With their failure in the Atlantic, the Germans lost their only hope of blocking American troops and industrial products from the coasts of Europe. Significantly, the German navy had played a major role in persuading Hitler to declare war on the United States to prevent such movement. Just as in World War I, the German submarine campaign had failed to live up to the navy's expectations.

The Air War

The Opening Moves

The air war began later than prewar theorists had expected and took much time to work into high gear. Through May 1940, RAF Bomber Command found itself hamstrung by rules of engagement forbidding attacks even on warships tied up at dock. With the German onslaught in May 1940, these restrictions disappeared. For the next ten months, Bomber Command attacked precision targets in Germany, especially oil plants and transportation. But Bomber Command, because its past experiences in the war indicated clearly that daylight bombing attacks would suffer prohibitive casualties, decided to make its attacks at night for most of the rest of the war. The hope was "that the accuracy of night bombing [would] differ little from daylight bombing." Not until summer 1941 did the British discover how unrealistic such hopes were. Then an analysis of mission photographs indicated that only one in three bombers was hitting within five miles of the target; in other words, Bomber Command had a difficult time even in hitting cities.

Such inaccuracy pushed the British toward what they euphemistically described as "area bombing" to "dehouse" the German population. The British decided to undertake a bomber offensive because they wanted to escape the terrible casualties of the last war and because the collapse

Air Marshal Sir Arthur T. Harris fervently believed that only a strategic air offensive could win the war for the Allies in a reasonable amount of time and at an acceptable cost. He also believed, "One cannot win wars by defending oneself."

of France made strategic bombing the only avenue for striking Germany directly. The meager results obtained in 1941 led to pressure for utilization of bomber aircraft in other areas, such as the battle of the Atlantic. Moreover, by the end of 1941 loss rates for bombers had risen significantly as German night defenses improved.

In January 1942 disenchantment with bombing results led to appointment of Air Marshal Arthur T. Harris to head Bomber Command. Harris possessed an unshakable belief in strategic bombing. Fortified by a strong personality and intolerant of differing views, he was an ideal candidate to shake the command's lethargy. Harris understood the need for operational successes both to bolster the morale of his crews and to counter those who argued for diversion of bombers to other tasks. The development of the first significant navigational aid, Gee, allowed the British to bomb with greater accuracy for short distances onto the Continent. In March 1942, the first demonstration of Gee's effectiveness came when Bomber Command took out the Renault factory near Paris. One month later, Bomber Command destroyed Lübeck; postraid reconnaissance indicated that the attack had destroyed 40 to 50 percent of the city. At the end of April, British bombers blasted Rostock and a nearby Heinkel factory.

But Harris's greatest triumph of the year came in May. By scraping together training units and every bomber in his command, he put 1,000 aircraft over Cologne and swamped the night defenses. The British achieved an unheard-of concentration in bombing; with a low loss rate (3.8 percent), Bomber Command devastated the city but killed only 384 civilians, small casualties compared to what was to come. Photo reconnaissance indicated the attack destroyed 600 acres of Cologne. Bomber Command, nevertheless, did not achieve a similar success for the remainder of the year, and the cost remained high. From May to September the British lost 970 bombers; in May 1942 the Command's average number of aircraft had been only 417. The loss rate for the period was 233 percent.

Selected Aerial Targets in Germany

As the bomber offensive expanded, the Luftwaffe responded. In September 1939, Germany did not possess an air-defense system similar to that of Fighter Command. To defend the Reich, the Germans deployed a large number of searchlights and antiaircraft guns. The Luftwaffe also possessed single-engine fighters but committed few of them to home defense because it saw the mission of its fighters as winning air superiority over enemy airspace. In July 1940 the Luftwaffe established the 1st Night Fighter Division under General Joseph Kammhuber. Its mission was to protect Germany from RAF incursions. Kammhuber received a disparate group of aircraft, none of which carried radar. He introduced intruder missions into British airspace to attack RAF bombers taking off; this line of attack showed promise until Hitler ordered it discontinued in summer 1941. Thereafter the Germans never resumed intruder attacks in British airspace.

Throughout 1941, Kammhuber introduced an increasingly effective air-defense system that soon posed a formidable threat to British night operations. Using a belt of radar stations from Denmark to northern France, the system provided early warning as well as ground-control intercept to night fighters equipped with radar. It possessed one considerable weakness: each ground-control site controlled only one fighter and thus one intercept at a time. If the British concentrated their bombers in time and space, they could swamp defenses; but through the end of 1941, that occurred rarely.

In 1942 Bomber Command became a formidable weapon. Despite the heavy damage to Lübeck and Rostock, the OKW did not become alarmed. The devastating attack on Cologne was another matter. Believing these raids signaled a British attempt to start a second front, the Führer decided to reply to the attacks with retaliatory raids and "revenge" weapons such as the wasteful V-2 rocket. Regardless of the vulnerability of the Allied bombers, the Germans remained faithful to Douhet's theories about the futility of countering offensive air power and refused to devote significant resources to their night-fighter defenses.

The Bombing Campaign in Full Gear: Bomber Command

1943 saw an upswing in Allied air attacks on the Germans. Beginning in March 1943 Harris's force battered the Ruhr for three months. These raids marked the beginning of a series of Bomber Command successes. In May 1943 a highly select bomber group took out several dams in the Ruhr River valley, but German air defenses imposed a loss rate on attacking bombers that was close to unbearable. Then in July 1943 the British introduced "Window" (strips of aluminum that reflected to German radar the same signature as a bomber). By dropping out bales of these strips the British blinded the air-defense system. Combined with the arrival of new four-engine bombers, the Halifax and Lancaster, the British dealt out sledgehammer blows.

On the evening of July 27–28, Bomber Command delivered a devastating attack against Hamburg. Conditions were perfect. Hamburg was easy to find; the weather was warm and dry; Window blinded German defenses; and the city's firefighters were on the west side of the city putting out persistent, smoldering coal and coke fires. The marker flares went down perfectly in the center of the city, probably on the great lumberyard where Baltic timber arrived for distribution to Germany. Most of the following bombers dropped their loads of incendiaries and high explosives into the glowing cauldron. The fire then pumped superheated air straight up into the stratosphere, at the same time sucking in fresh air from outside the city. Winds approached 300–400 miles per hour, while temperatures reached close to 1,000 degrees. The raid burned a four-mile hole in the city's center; between 30,000–40,000 perished. After the war Speer claimed that if Bomber Command had repeated its Hamburg success four or five times in succeeding weeks, Germany would have collapsed. But Bomber Command could not repeat its success. In August it took out the bomb research and experimental station at Peenemünde on the Baltic coast. Since German night defenses were recovering from Window, the attacking force of

Destruction in Hamburg. Sir Arthur Harris believed such destruction pointed the "certain, the obvious, the quickest, and the easiest way to overwhelming victory."

597 lost forty bombers (6.7 percent). In October Harris's forces created another firestorm at Kassel.

At this point Harris determined to destroy Berlin. Though his offensive did not win the war, it came close to destroying his command. Berlin lay deep in Germany and Luftwaffe defenses could pick up and follow the great bomber stream throughout its course over the Reich. Rather than guide individual fighters to bombers, the Germans now guided night fighters into the bomber stream and then allowed the fighters to identify and attack individual aircraft. Also, a new German radar, SN2, allowed night fighters to tear away Window's veil. The weather in winter 1943–1944 was appallingly bad, so that virtually all bombing took place through clouds. Although Harris's attackers damaged Berlin extensively, their target was enormous, and the British did not attain the concentration achieved over Hamburg.

British losses rapidly rose. In December 1943 the British lost 170 bombers; in January 1944, 314; in February, 199; and in March, 283. Considering that the Command had a front-line bomber strength of 1,224 in January 1944, such losses were staggering. On the evening of March 30, 1944, Bomber Command struck Nuremberg; many of the attackers hit Schweinfurt instead; the Germans shot down 108. Such disastrous losses forced Harris to call off nighttime area bombing attacks on central Germany. While Bomber Command had dealt out devastating blows, it had not broken enemy morale, and by March 1944 its rate of attrition had reached unsupportable levels.

The Bombing Campaign in Full Gear: The American Effort

In summer 1942 the first bomber units of the U.S. Army Air Forces (USAAF) arrived in England to begin daylight operations on the Continent. The Americans brought with them a belief that during daylight hours they could fight their way through German defenses with great formations of heavily armed B-17s. These bombers would then attack the vital centers of Germany's industry and, by destroying certain crucial targets, cause the collapse of the enemy's economic system. While American air commanders recognized that the Luftwaffe was a formidable force, they believed that their numbers and disciplined flying could overwhelm the German air defenses without the support of long-range escort fighters. Initially, however, they had too few bombers to launch B-17s into German airspace; American raids thus initially struck at Nazi-occupied France within supporting range of friendly fighters. Nevertheless, this rather limited experience led Brigadier General Ira C. Eaker, Eighth Air Force commander, to write his superiors that "bombardment in force—a minimum of 300 bombers—can effectively attack any German target and return without excessive or uneconomical losses." Eaker's strength, however, did not reach that level until late spring 1943 because of the diversion of bombers to support "Torch" and operations in the Mediterranean.

The question of what to attack became a divisive issue. The German aircraft industry had to be a primary target because the Luftwaffe was a far more ferocious opponent than expected. Attacks on other industries offered the possibility of weakening the German economy, but most industries, such as oil, contained a larger number of targets than Eighth Air Force's force structure could attack. Consequently, through a selection process largely determined by the number of targets, the Americans settled on the ball-bearing industry as the weak link in the German economic structure.

At Casablanca in early winter 1943 British and American political and military leaders agreed that Allied air forces should wage a "combined bomber offensive" by day and night to put relentless pressure on the Reich's population and industry. Unfortunately the agreement in principle proved difficult to implement, at least as far as finding a common focus for the offensive. Harris stood firm in his belief in "area bombing" and in his contempt for attacks on specific targets, which he derisively described as "panacea targets." The Americans, on the other hand, persisted in their belief that by making precision attacks on industrial targets they could cause the collapse of the German economy. There was thus little room for a common approach until 1944.

American raids began reaching into Germany in early summer 1943. Heavy blows fell on the Ruhr in July; on August 17, Eaker dispatched a massive force to take out the Messerschmitt factory at Regensburg and the ball-bearing works at Schweinfurt. The latter complex produced half of Germany's ball bearings. But the attacks ran into a slew of German fighters. Of 146 bombers in the Regensburg force, the Germans shot down twenty-four

(16.4 percent). Because the bombers continued on to North Africa, thereby disconcerting the defenses, they avoided higher losses, but sixty of the bombers that reached Africa had to remain to be repaired or salvaged. The forces attacking Schweinfurt (230 bombers) lost thirty-six more aircraft (15.7 percent). Twenty-seven more bombers had to be written off after returning to England because of extensive damage.

From August through October 1943, Eaker threw great unescorted formations of B-17s into German territory without support from long-range escort fighters. Surprisingly the provision of such fighters remained low on his list of priorities. American aircraft continued to attack Luftwaffe production facilities and ball-bearing factories. Losses, however, were horrendous. In maintaining its aerial offensive, Eighth Air Force suffered a nearly 30 percent crew loss each month—a rate ensuring that few bomber crews ever completed the twenty-five missions required to return home. On October 14, "Black Thursday," Eighth again attacked Schweinfurt; the long flight across Germany took a terrible toll. Luftwaffe fighters and antiaircraft shot down sixty bombers, seventeen more were written off, while 121 were damaged but repairable. So heavy were the losses that Eighth had to call off deep-penetration raids. The Luftwaffe had won one of the last, but temporary, victories achieved by Germany in the war.

The Schweinfurt raids of 1943 against the ball-bearing industry represented a terrible threat to the German war economy. After the war, Speer admitted that continued attacks on the industry would have brought the economy to a halt. But Eighth Air Force could not endure such losses from continued attacks. Moreover, the Germans discovered that their industrial concerns possessed large backlogs of ball bearings, that the Swedes and Swiss were willing to sell them to the Reich, and that in some weapons they could substitute roller bearings (easier to manufacture) for ball bearings.

Yet for all its failings in 1943, the air offensive provided substantial benefits to the Allied cause. Attacks on the aircraft industry caused German production of new fighters to fall by an average of 200 fighters per month from its peak in July 1943. In November 1943 new fighter production was 300 under the total for July (576 versus 873). While attacking American forces suffered high losses, they inflicted heavy casualties on the enemy. Admittedly, they could not maintain that effort in the face of such losses, but the attacks seriously affected the Germans.

The British raids also had a serious, though indirect, impact. Well into 1944 the Germans emphasized production of bombers to strike back at the Allies. Moreover, by 1943 they embarked on an enormously costly program to build V-1 and V-2 rockets to pay the British back for area bombing. In the end the V-1 and V-2 program used up resources equivalent to the production of 24,000 fighter aircraft.

But the largest diversion of German military strength came in the area of antiaircraft defenses. In 1940 the air-defense system consisted of 791 heavy batteries, equipped with high velocity 88-mm, 105-mm, and 128-mm guns; by 1943 the number of batteries had risen to 2,132 with over 10,000 antiaircraft guns. That total represented a considerable investment in manpower and material that the Germans desperately needed elsewhere. This was especially so since, from a German point of view, Flak was not cost effective against high-flying aircraft. The 88-mm Flak weapon, for example, required 16,000 shells to hit an aircraft at high altitude. Every night these weapons fired large amounts of ammunition into the skies over the Reich to reassure the population that the Luftwaffe was defending the country against enemy bombers.

The Luftwaffe

From the beginning of the war, the Luftwaffe suffered from a poor support structure. Göring was incapable of providing long-term guidance; General Hans Jeschonnek, the chief of staff, focused entirely on operational concerns; and intelligence was a disaster. Most seriously, the production and maintenance structure was in complete shambles. One of Göring's closest confidants, General Ernst Udet, controlled this crucial sphere of Luftwaffe activity. Udet had been a great ace in World War I, a barnstormer in the 1920s and 1930s, and then a rising star in the resurrected Luftwaffe, but he possessed few managerial skills. Göring selected him nevertheless in 1938 to run the Luftwaffe's production and design establishment. Udet soon had more than forty different offices reporting directly to him. By summer 1941 production programs were way off target; technological development had stalled; and confusion reigned. In the summer of 1941, Göring finally reinstated Field Marshal Milch in the process; soon afterward, Udet committed suicide.

Milch possessed great managerial skills, and since the air war rested on industrial management, Milch's appointment was crucial to getting the Luftwaffe back on track. But the Germans had lost one full year and were already behind the British and Americans. In a hurried trip to the Eastern Front in September 1941, Milch discovered hundreds of broken aircraft littering forward airfields because of shortages in spare parts; the supply system had almost entirely broken down in the vastness of Russia. By December operationally ready rates for German bombers had fallen to 32 percent, for fighters to 52 percent, and for the whole Luftwaffe to 45 percent. These figures underline the difficulties that the Luftwaffe, conceived in terms of central European requirements, now confronted in fighting a conflict possessing continental distances.

For the Luftwaffe the war now became one of three fronts: the Eastern Front against an increasingly effective Red Air Force, equipped not only with its own production but with American and British aircraft as well; the Mediterranean against a growing tide of Anglo-American air power; and the great night and day attacks of the Combined Bomber Offensive. Against this massive threat, Milch struggled to increase aircraft production. Since Germany controlled the industrial capacity of central Europe, he achieved considerable increases in aircraft production. But British and American bombing did retard those efforts in 1943. More important, Germany's enemies had already geared up their economies for massive production increases.

In 1942 the Germans felt the first pressure from Allied production superiority. In Russia the quality of German aircrews made up for the Red Air Force's superiority in numbers. In the Mediterranean, however, the RAF exercised increasing influence over the conduct of operations. Air Marshal Sir Arthur Tedder, perhaps the greatest airman of the war, developed a force that could gain and maintain air superiority over the battlefield, while the desert air force's interdiction and close air-support strikes rendered crucial support to the army. Moreover, its antishipping attacks, supported by Ultra, undermined Rommel's logistical support.

At the end of 1942 the roof fell in on the Luftwaffe. Hitler and the senior military leaders made two serious mistakes. In response to Operation Torch, the invasion of North Africa by the British and Americans, the OKW moved large forces across to Tunisia. To support the commitment, the Luftwaffe had to use much of its Ju 52 transport fleet; that commitment shut down the training program for bomber pilots. The air battle to protect the tenuous logistic lines to Tunisia put the Luftwaffe at a severe disadvantage, especially since Ultra intelligence kept the Allies fully informed of Axis supply movements. Undersupplied and vulnerable on North African airfields, the Luftwaffe confronted increasingly effective Allied air attacks on its supplies and base structure. By March 1943 the Germans and Italians had to stop ship movements to Tunisia; movement of supplies by transport aircraft proved equally as costly. The air battle in the Mediterranean continued through the summer, when the Germans finally conceded defeat in the Mediterranean.

Events on the Eastern Front followed a similar pattern. Almost concurrently with Torch, the Soviets launched a counteroffensive against German Sixth Army at Stalingrad. Hitler, bolstered by Göring's promise that the Luftwaffe could keep Sixth Army supplied, refused any thought of abandoning Stalin's city. The transport fleet, already stretched by Tunisia, had to rush into the breach. Despite heroic efforts, the Russian winter made airlift operations impossible. Operationally ready rates plummeted, losses mounted. The Luftwaffe never came close to providing the 600 tons per day that Sixth Army required. Throughout the winter, fighting swirled around Stalingrad and forced the Luftwaffe to provide constant support for hard-pressed ground troops. In March 1943, the spring thaw brought a short pause to ground operations in the east. The air battles, however, continued, and the Luftwaffe took particularly heavy losses over the Caucasus.

Meanwhile, Army Group Center prepared for the climactic battle of the Eastern Front, the clash of armor at the Kursk salient. The Luftwaffe concentrated nearly 2,000 aircraft over Kursk. *Luftflotte* Six supported Army Group Center's drive with 750 aircraft, while *Luftflotte* Four supported Army Group South's attack with 1,100 aircraft. In 1943 a substantial proportion of Luftwaffe frontline strength still remained committed on the Eastern Front: 84.5 percent of all dive bombers, 27 percent of all fighters, and 33 percent of bombers. On the first day of Kursk, German pilots flew 3,000 sorties and fought a great air battle over the salient. But the Germans never established air superiority, and the Red Air Force interfered significantly with German air and ground operations. After the failure of the German offensive at Kursk, the Soviets launched counteroffensives against Army Group Center and Army Group South. The Luftwaffe desperately attempted to stave off defeat on the ground but suffered heavy losses that severely affected its capabilities. At the same time, its best fighter squadrons moved from the Eastern Front to meet the American bombing offensive.

In July and August of 1943 the Luftwaffe fought three great air battles. In the Mediterranean the Anglo-American attack on Sicily and air raids into Italy cost the Luftwaffe 711 combat aircraft in July and 321 in August (1,032 for the two months); in defending the skies over western Europe, it lost 526 in July and 625 for August (1,151 for the two months); and in the east the Luftwaffe lost 558 in July and 472 in August (1,030 for the two months). The loss of 3,213 combat aircraft in two months out of a force structure of approximately 5,000 combat aircraft was simply no longer supportable. Given the threat to Germany's cities and industries, the Luftwaffe had to come home to defend its base. After September 1943, German soldiers on the Italian and Eastern fronts would seldom see their air force. The skies over the battlefield belonged to the Allies.

★   ★   ★   ★

The entry of the United States into World War II resulted from substantial miscalculations on the part of two Axis partners, Nazi Germany and Imperial Japan. In the end success in the war rested on the great industrial mobilization of the Allies' economies on which military might depended. For the Americans as well as the British the second piece of the puzzle was the ability to project military power over the world's oceans, and that required mastery over the substantial U-boat threat. Until their naval forces had mastered that threat, the economic and military potential of the Western Powers remained open to question.

For the Americans and the British, the defeat of France in May 1940 meant that their ground forces could not engage the enemy on the European Continent until 1943 or 1944. That in turn forced the Anglo-Saxon powers to rely on air power to strike at the sources of Nazi military power. From the retrospective view of fifty years, the Combined Bombing Offensive failed to achieve its stated operational objectives in 1942 and 1943. But it did at least strike the Germans hard, and it moved from being a considerable nuisance to posing a real threat to the stability of the Reich's war economy.

What was indeed remarkable was the unprecedented scale of the Allied effort in harnessing men, women, machines, and raw materials to the war effort. The successes of German and Japanese armies and navies in the first war years provided the incentive and popular support in Allied countries. The political skill and ruthlessness of the American, British, and Soviet leaders then provided the framework and means to translate large populations and economic power into military might.

SUGGESTED READINGS

Beesley, Patrick. *Very Special Intelligence*: *The Story of the Admiralty's Operational Intelligence Center* (London: Hamish Hamilton, 1977).

Buell, Thomas B. *Master of Sea Power*: *A Biography of Fleet Admiral Ernest J. King* (Boston: Little Brown, 1980).

Fuchida Mitsuo. *Midway, the Battle That Doomed Japan* (Annapolis: Naval Institute, 1955).

Hastings, Max. *Bomber Command* (New York: Dial Press, 1979).

Hayashi Saburo. *Kogun: The Japanese Army in the Pacific War* (Westport, Conn.: Greenwood Press, 1978).

James, D. Clayton. *The Years of MacArthur*. 2 vols. (Boston: Houghton Mifflin, 1970).

Millett, Allen, and Williamson Murray. *Military Effectiveness*, vol. III, *World War II* (London: Allen and Unwin, 1988).

Milward, Alan. *The German Economy at War* (London: Athlone Press, 1965).

Morison, Samuel Eliot. *The Two-Ocean War*: *A Short History of the United States Navy in the Second World War* (Boston: Little Brown, 1963).

Murray, Williamson. *Luftwaffe* (Baltimore: Nautical and Aviation Publishing Co., 1985).

Prange, Gordon W., with Donald M. Goldstein and Katherine V. Dillon. *At Dawn We Slept*: *The Untold Story of Pearl Harbor* (New York: McGraw-Hill, 1981).

———. *Miracle at Midway* (New York: McGraw-Hill, 1982).

Ienaga Saburo. *The Pacific War*: *World War II and the Japanese, 1931–1945* (New York: Pantheon Books, 1978).

Spector, Ronald H. *Eagle Against the Sun*: *The War with Japan* (New York: The Free Press, 1985).

Townsend, Peter. *Duel of Eagles* (New York: Simon and Schuster, 1970).

U.S. Army Air Forces. *Ultra and the History of the United States Strategic Air Force in Europe vs. the German Air Force* (Frederick, Md.: University Publications of America, 1980).

Webster, Sir Charles, and Noble Frankland. *The Strategic Air Offensive Against Germany, 1939–1945* (London: Her Majesty's Stationery Office, 1962).

Winton, John. *Ultra at Sea: How Breaking the Nazi Code Affected Allied Naval Strategy During World War II* (New York: William Morrow and Co., 1988).

4

THE EASTERN AND MEDITERRANEAN FRONTS: WINNING BATTLES OF MEN AND MACHINES

To Stalingrad

Defeat in the East, November 1942–October 1943

The Mediterranean, 1942–1943

The East, 1944

By early 1942 the Nazi surge toward the frontiers of Europe had exhausted itself. The Wehrmacht, nevertheless, possessed the capability to launch major offensives and represented a determined opponent, capable of defending its position with tenacity even though at the far reaches of its logistic capabilities. But the productive and mobilized strength of the Allies exercised a growing and eventually overwhelming impact on operations. Moreover, Allied superiority in personnel and logistics allowed them to fight massive battles that played to their strengths, while minimizing those of their opponents. Along with these advantages went Allied superiority in intelligence and deception. Virtually every action that the German military undertook was now open to the prying eyes and ears of Allied intelligence. Moreover, the Allies could screen their intentions and plans almost entirely. Only Hitler's "intuition" at times caught glimpses of what was coming, but the Führer possessed neither the discipline nor consistency to act coherently on such visions.

In the Mediterranean, the British defeated Rommel at El Alamein and drove Axis forces from Egypt and Libya. As the British pushed the enemy back, the Allies used their advantages in sea and air power to land on the coast of North Africa. For the first time, the Americans entered the land battle against the Germans and after some initial difficulties played a major role in the Axis defeat in North Africa and then in the landings in Sicily and Italy. On the Eastern Front, the Soviets, through the skillful use of deception, magnified their growing superiority in weapons and their improving operational performance. In their offensives, they drove the Germans back hundreds of miles. In the end the Allies battered the Wehrmacht back to the Reich and ended whatever chance the Germans had of escaping their fate.

To Stalingrad

As spring 1942 approached, the Germans surmounted the desperate situation on the Eastern Front; they had prevented the terrible conditions of the winter campaign from degenerating into a collapse. Nevertheless, they confronted difficult challenges for the upcoming spring offensive. Halder, still chief of the general staff, and senior ground commanders argued that the army should remain on the defensive, rebuild the forces shattered by the winter, and await increases in production. Hitler, however, believed that Germany must destroy Soviet military potential before American industry came into play. By this point Hitler's word almost always carried the day.

In early April the OKH issued Directive 41 for a summer campaign. In the north, German forces were to link up with the Finns and finish the destruction of Leningrad. Army Group Center would stand on the defensive, while the major effort occurred in the south. There mobile units would clear the Soviets from west of the Don River and then strike into the Caucasus. Initially Hitler accorded Stalingrad little importance. The main objective was Soviet oil with the proviso that Stalingrad's capture might block movement of petroleum up the Volga River.

Several factors underlined how much Nazi capabilities had declined since 1941. Operation Barbarossa had called for a German offensive along the entire front, but by 1942 the Wehrmacht could launch a major offensive only in the south. Moreover, as German armies advanced into the Caucasus, their left flank would become increasingly exposed to Soviet counterblows from the north, and the Germans lacked sufficient troops to cover that flank. As a result, only by persuading their Romanian, Italian, and Hungarian allies to provide armies could Hitler launch the summer 1942 offensive. More ominously, the OKH had to strip other armies in the east of equipment and troops to prepare Army Group South for its role.

Before that offensive began, however, two major battles occurred. The Soviets picked up German preparations and at Stalin's direction launched a spoiling attack at Kharkov, Army Group South's main logistics base. The *Stavka* argued against the attack, for it believed that the Red Army should hold onto its reserves until German intentions became clear. On Stalin's orders, however, the offensive began on May 12; it soon broke through the German front. For a short period it appeared that the Russians

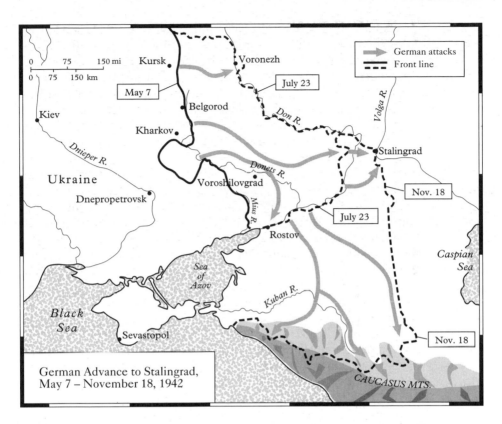

German Advance to Stalingrad,
May 7 – November 18, 1942

might reach Kharkov and its crucial supply dumps. But strong German forces contained the breakthrough and then launched a counterstrike at the salient's thin neck. Soviet commanders pleaded to retreat, but Stalin demanded that the attack continue. In effect, Soviet forces had advanced into a sack, and the German counterattack cut them off. Not only did the Germans capture 240,000 Soviet troops, but they also destroyed most of the Soviet armored reserves (1,200 tanks).

A second disaster for the Soviets followed on the heels of the first. In June 1942, Manstein, now commander of Eleventh Army, conducted a skillful attack on Sevastopol, the main Soviet naval base on the Crimean Peninsula. In ferocious fighting, German troops broke through the port's fortifications and crushed the Soviet garrison. As a reward for the successful siege, Hitler promoted Manstein to field marshal. The Führer, however, vetoed the new field marshal's suggestion that Eleventh Army form a reserve behind Army Group South's drive into the Caucasus. Instead most of the army's infantry and artillery (and Manstein) moved north to conduct siege operations against Leningrad. The few units remaining found themselves parceled out among the attacking armies of Army Group South.

On June 28 the summer offensive began. The Germans planned on launching a multiphased operation that would include sequential attacks from the left to right of Army Group South, followed by an advance into the Caucasus. On the left, in the first phase of the campaign, three panzer, three motorized, and nine infantry divisions struck due east toward Voronezh. By July 2 the Germans were on the city's outskirts, and by July 6 they had taken the city. Their success froze the *Stavka* because the German attack suggested an opening move against Moscow. However, the Germans turned south down the Don, while Hungarian divisions moved to cover the widening northern flank. On June 30, Sixth Army jumped off from the center of Army Group South and attempted to encircle Soviet units along the Don; but the *Stavka* finally persuaded Stalin to order a timely retreat and the German pincers closed on thin air.

As the Nazi advance accelerated, OKH divided Army Group South into Army Groups A and B, and on July 13 Hitler fired Field Marshal Bock for a second time. In effect, the Führer became commander of Army Group South and directed the offensive from his East Prussian headquarters. In the south Army Group A battered its way into Rostov, crossed the Don, and turned south. The gateway to the Caucasus was open. As Bock commented shortly before his relief, however, the battle had been "sliced in two." While Army Group B moved east toward Stalingrad and the Volga River, Army Group A moved south into the Caucasus. For the present, Hitler focused on the southern advance and shifted forces to Army Group A; this delayed the eastward move toward Stalingrad. Other delays came from both army groups having already encountered serious logistic difficulties, particularly the lack of fuel. The capture of Soviet oil fields in the Caucasus failed to alleviate these problems, since the Soviets did a thorough job of sabotaging wells and refining equipment.

In August, Hitler's erratic attention swung from the Caucasus to Stalingrad. On August 23, Sixth Army reached the Volga River north of the

Though the Germans occupied the center of Stalingrad, the Soviets refused to stop fighting. The Germans described the subsequent combat as a *Rattenkrieg*, a war among rats.

city; on the 24th it launched its first attacks on the suburbs and began fighting its way into the city. As fighting intensified, Hitler pulled forces out of the Caucasus and funneled them into the cauldron of Stalingrad's built-up area. The Soviet defenders prepared to hold out to the last. In the wreckage caused by constant air attacks and artillery bombardments, they established strong defenses and scattered numerous snipers. Street by street, building by building, German infantry dug the Soviets out of their defensive positions. Particularly savage fighting took place in Stalingrad's tractor works and in the city's great grain elevator. The close combat and hand-to-hand fighting, in some areas from floor to floor, maximized Soviet strengths of dogged stoicism and determination while minimizing German tactical flexibility and mobility.

Driven by Hitler's fanatical determination, the bitter battle had considerable strategic effects. The fighting ended whatever chance the Germans had to cut the Soviets off from oil supplies of the Caucasus. Moreover it reduced German reserves across the Eastern Front, while exhausting the Wehrmacht in a pointless battle of prestige. By early November Sixth Army had fought its way across the lunar landscape of Stalingrad. Although the Soviets held only a tenuous position on the banks of the Volga, they had pulled Sixth Army into a vulnerable position. Ill-equipped and poorly trained Romanian, Italian, and Hungarian formations protected its flanks; German forces in the Caucasus were exhausted; virtually no reserves were available; and winter was again closing in on a supply system stretched to the breaking point. Hitler, however, believed that the summer offensive had fought the Soviets to exhaustion. The generals were not so sure, but by this point in the war, they had learned to keep their opinions to themselves. German intelligence picked up some Soviet troop movements north of Stalingrad but reported that "only local attacks are expected."

Defeat in the East, November 1942–October 1943

Disaster at Stalingrad

In September 1942 the Soviets began preparations for a massive counteroffensive. Over the next two months, *Stavka* deployed nearly one million men, 900 tanks, and a vast array of artillery forces, including one-third of their rocket launchers, on Sixth Army's flanks. Their plan had limited aims—to break through the defenses north and south of Stalingrad and then to encircle German forces in the city. In the offensive the Soviets displayed significant improvements over the tactical and operational performance of earlier efforts.

On November 19, in the midst of a swirling snowstorm, units from five Soviet armies, including a tank army—a sign of growing Soviet operational skills—smashed into the Romanians north of Stalingrad. By early afternoon they had destroyed Romanian defenses and were in the open; their advance gained an average of fourteen miles on the first day. The XXXXVIII Panzer Corps attempted to plug the breach, but its obsolete collection of tanks had little chance against Soviet armor, equipped with T-34s. On the 20th two Soviet armies broke the Romanians south of Stalingrad. The Soviets split Fourth Panzer Army and drove some of its units into the pocket with Sixth Army. On November 23, Soviet spearheads advancing from north and south met late in the afternoon forty miles west of Stalingrad and isolated Sixth Army.

Decision making within the German high command now broke down, a sure indication of Hitler's destructive influence. On November 19 the Führer was in Berchtesgaden attempting to repair a deteriorating situation in the Mediterranean. As reports of trouble in the east arrived, he hurried north in his command train to OKH headquarters in East Prussia to deal with the Soviet emergency. During much of that trip, however, he was out of touch with the various command sections. Hitler provided no instructions to the commander of Sixth Army, General Friedrich Paulus, and by this point in the war no one remained in the high command willing to make independent decisions. On November 21, Hitler ordered Paulus to stand fast in Stalingrad "regardless of the danger of a temporary encirclement." When one of Paulus's corps commanders, General Walter von Seydlitz-Kurzbach, ordered his troops to retreat in preparation for a breakout, Hitler reacted angrily.

To deal with the deteriorating situation, Hitler created Army Group Don, consisting of four armies, and appointed Manstein to its command, but it took the field marshal nearly one week to assume control. During that period, Manstein advised Hitler that while a withdrawal from Stalingrad might be necessary, it would be best to wait until reinforcements arrived, since Sixth Army was tying down huge Soviet forces. The OKH, supported by many ground and air commanders on the scene, argued for an immediate breakout. Hitler, committed to holding on the Volga, temporized.

Göring, with the aid of some army commanders, provided the final ingredients for disaster. As early as November 21 Sixth Army had examined the possibility of an aerial bridge. The Luftwaffe's General Wolfram von Richthofen immediately warned Sixth Army that the Luftwaffe did not possess sufficient strength. Göring, however, assured Hitler that the Luftwaffe could supply Sixth Army, just as it had supported a corps and a half of German soldiers in the Demyansk pocket over the previous winter; the Luftwaffe chief of staff, despite a massive commitment of transport aircraft to Tunisia, offered no opposition to Göring's promise.

For the time being the Soviets strengthened their hold on Stalingrad. The Germans desperately attempted to patch together a relief force—not surprisingly, few of the reinforcements promised by Hitler arrived. The besieged required an airlift of 600 tons per day; under the best conditions the Luftwaffe could supply 350 tons. Airlift forces consisted of a hodgepodge of Ju 52s, Ju 86s, and He 111s. To cobble together even these aircraft the Luftwaffe stripped its bomber transition schools of their inexperienced crews; maintenance conditions were appalling, and operational rates fell to 10–20 percent during periods of bad weather. On only three days in December did transports reach a 300-ton level; on most days less than 100 tons arrived in Stalingrad.

In mid-December, Manstein launched his offensive to break through to Stalingrad; LVII Panzer Corps drove to within thirty-five miles of the city on December 19, but no farther. Manstein appears to have urged Hitler to order a breakout, but the Führer refused because neither Manstein nor Paulus would assure him that one would succeed. One observer of the Führer during this period concluded that he "seemed no longer capable of making a decision." On December 26, Paulus reported his army incapable of a breakout unless German troops outside the city first opened up a supply corridor.

In fact, it was too late. On December 16 the Soviets attacked the Italian Army along the Don northwest of Stalingrad. The Soviets ripped a one-hundred-mile gap in Army Group Don's flank, and Manstein had to shift forces to contain the breakthrough and abandon all ideas of relieving Sixth Army. The collapse along the upper Don placed an even greater burden on air supply, while Soviet capture of the airfields at Tatsinskaya and Morozovsk in early January forced the Luftwaffe to move its bases almost 200 miles from the pocket. This relocation ended any significant air bridge to Stalingrad.

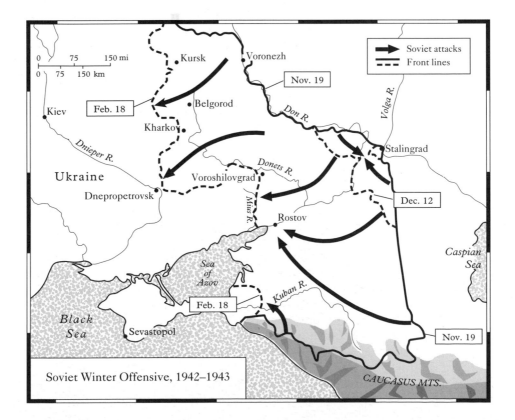

Soviet Winter Offensive, 1942–1943

Throughout January, Soviet forces drove toward Rostov and the Donets Basin. The question now was whether the Red Army would reach Rostov and cut off Seventeenth and First Panzer Armies in the Caucasus. The defenders at Stalingrad would have to hold to the end, in hopes of tying up Soviet forces, while Army Group Don desperately attempted to stabilize a collapsing situation. After Paulus rejected the final surrender ultimatum, the Soviets began their last attack on January 10. By February 2, the Germans had surrendered. Out of 250,000 soldiers trapped in the Stalingrad pocket, approximately 90,000 became prisoners; barely 5,000 survived the war.

The Germans Recover

As Stalingrad capitulated, the Germans strove to stabilize the situation along the southern front. Hitler did allow Army Group A to withdraw from the Caucasus, but part of it became shut up on the Kuban peninsula opposite the Crimea. During the third week in January, a new series of Soviet attacks ripped into Army Group B and virtually destroyed the Hungarian Second Army. The Soviets had achieved operational freedom from Voronezh to Voroshilovgrad, a distance of over two hundred miles. By mid-January, they had captured Belgorod and almost reached Dnepropetrovsk. The Germans had to abandon Kharkov on February 15.

Despite Soviet gains, the Germans managed a recovery; they were falling back on their supply dumps, while the Soviets were outrunning their supply lines. A lack of focus also worked against the Soviets; their spearheads were neither mutually supporting nor strong enough to achieve independent success. Significant German reinforcements also arrived. Hitler permitted the transfer to Manstein's Army Group of about 100,000 soldiers from Army Group A in the Crimea and seven fresh divisions from western Europe. In addition, Luftwaffe forces, reorganized under Richthofen's driving leadership, provided enhanced air support. From February 20 to March 15, Luftwaffe squadrons provided 1,000 combat sorties per day versus an average of only 350 in January. By this point the Soviet advance had left the bases of the Red air force far behind, thereby making air support incapable of intervening in the battle.

Despite Hitler's anger at the loss of Kharkov, Manstein persuaded him that Army Group South (now reformed from Army Group Don and parts of Army Group B) could reestablish control of its northern flank only by temporarily relinquishing control of that city. Supported by Richthofen's aircraft, a German counteroffensive began on February 19. The sudden eruption of the German forces caused a collapse of the overextended Soviet forces. By mid-March, Army Group South had recaptured Kharkov and driven the Soviets back to the Donets River, a gain of almost one hundred miles. The spring thaw finally arrived, and both sides, exhausted after fighting that had lasted continuously from July 1942, collapsed.

The Battle of Kursk, July 1943

Even as SS troops battered their way into Kharkov, Hitler issued a directive for the coming summer. Since the Wehrmacht no longer possessed the offensive power to win a decisive victory in a short campaign, the Führer's directive suggested instead a series of limited offensives, first at Kursk then at Leningrad, to reduce Soviet reserves and to improve defensive positions. After discarding several options, Hitler settled in mid-April 1943 on a major offensive, "Citadel," against the Kursk salient north of Kharkov.

The original conception was that Citadel would begin as soon as spring conditions provided solid ground for maneuver. But there were risks; the sectors north and south of Kursk were vulnerable to a Soviet counter-strike. The overall situation led Manstein to suggest that the Wehrmacht remain on the defensive and counterattack any Soviet summer offensive. Such an approach, however, would have entailed considerable risks and perhaps even the surrender of territory, the last thing Hitler was willing to

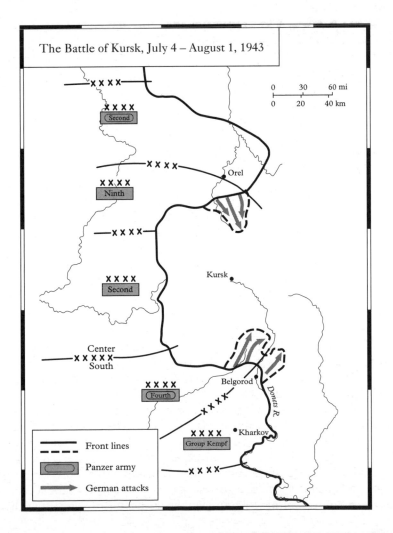

countenance. In the end the plan called for the major effort to occur on the southern shoulder of the Kursk salient. Army Group South would break through Soviet positions and then drive deep behind Kursk to link up with another drive launched on the northern shoulder by Army Group Center's Ninth Army. The hoped-for result would pinch off the Kursk salient and Soviet forces defending it.

Above all, Hitler hoped to achieve a major psychological victory over the Red Army. He argued, "The victory at Kursk must have the effect of a beacon seen around the world." In May he postponed Citadel until June or July despite opposition from some generals, including the OKH chief of staff, Colonel General Kurt Zeitzler. Hitler believed the postponement would allow a buildup of the armored forces with Tiger tanks and the new Panthers. Manstein and Günther von Kluge, commanders of the army groups involved in the operation, disagreed, believing that any delay would result in Soviet countermeasures. Nevertheless, Hitler postponed Citadel to early July. An uneasy calm settled on the Eastern Front as both sides prepared for the coming battle.

The Soviets had improved considerably in operational skill and in their use of intelligence. In April they picked up German intentions to launch a major strike at Kursk and in May began preparations on both shoulders of the salient. German intelligence never divined the massive scale of Soviet defensive and offensive measures to meet the attack. By this point in the war, Stalin was displaying greater trust in his generals. Zhukov and others advised him to remain on the defensive, and he accepted their advice.

The extent of Soviet preparations underlines the trap into which the Germans were walking. Soviet first-line defenses on both sides of the salient were two to three miles deep and contained three to four trench lines with numerous bunkers and strong points. Behind this line the Soviets constructed a second defensive zone at depths varying between six and eighteen miles. Twenty-five miles farther back they laid out three more lines on a similar scale. The fortification zone extended more than one hundred miles and included more than half a million mines. On the northern shoulder the Soviets achieved a density of forty-eight antitank guns per mile of front. Four armies, including a tank army, defended the northern shoulder of the Kursk salient; six armies held the southern side, while five armies of the Steppe Front stood immediately in reserve. Three more armies stood north of Kursk and two south; these forces could reinforce the salient should things turn bad. If the front held, the Soviets intended to use these reserves in major counterattacks. German intelligence gave no indication about the extent of enemy preparations.

On the German side, the growing strength of ground forces reflected the success that Speer had had in mobilizing the European economy. The Luftwaffe possessed nearly 2,500 combat aircraft, more than half of which would support Citadel. In the north, Field Marshal Walter Model's Ninth Army contained three panzer corps with twenty-one divisions, including one panzer grenadier and six panzer divisions, as well as 900 tanks; Manstein's Army Group South contained four panzer corps with twenty-two divisions,

Konstantin K. Rokossovskii wore a set of stainless steel false teeth as a result of his imprisonment and torture by the secret police before World War II for "anti-Soviet" activities. After regaining Stalin's favor he displayed a great flair for mobile warfare and played a key role in the battles of Moscow, Stalingrad, and Kursk, as well as Operation Bagration.

including six panzer and five panzer grenadier divisions, as well as 1,000 tanks. The entire battle would involve some 4,000 Soviet and 3,000 German tanks and assault guns.

On July 5, Citadel began. On the northern shoulder, Ninth Army attacked on a thirty-five-mile front and initially enjoyed limited success. Its attack broke through Soviet front-line defenses and had reached the second line by day's end. By July 6, Marshal Konstantin K. Rokossovskii, commander of Soviet forces in the north, had put in two tank corps and an infantry corps from his reserves, while *Stavka* moved additional units forward. By the next day Ninth Army's assault had stalled along a heavily fortified ridge thirteen miles beyond its start line and still well short of Rokossovskii's third defensive line; attempts to break through on July 10 and 11 failed entirely and Model could characterize the battle only as "a rolling battle of attrition"—exactly the kind of battle that played to Soviet strengths and minimized German mobility.

In the south, Manstein's offensive hardly got off to an auspicious start. As German troops moved into jump-off positions in the predawn hours of July 5, General Nikolai F. Vatutin, commander of Soviet forces in the south, unleashed a massive preemptive artillery bombardment. The surprise bombardment inflicted heavy casualties on German troops and demonstrated that the Soviets were fully informed about the coming attack. Nevertheless, the first hours went well. Fourth Panzer Army, consisting of XXXXVIII Panzer Corps and II SS Panzer Corps, attacked along a thirty-mile front. Within two hours they had penetrated front-line positions and had seemingly broken through. But by early afternoon the Germans began to recognize the weaknesses in their intelligence picture. They were, in fact, in the midst of a defensive position, the depths of which they scarcely could imagine. Moreover, in early afternoon a drenching thunderstorm flooded the battlefield and halted XXXXVIII Panzer Corps. Finally, while Fourth

Panzer Army made relatively good progress, Detachment Kempf (a temporary combination of two corps under General Werner Kempf) on its right flank had hardly advanced. In the air the Luftwaffe provided 3,000 sorties a day over the salient; however, even this level of effort was insufficient to eliminate Soviet aircraft that were defending their ground forces and attacking advancing Germans.

On July 6 and 7, Manstein made some progress in the south. The II SS Panzer Corps led the movement forward. Detachment Kempf continued to have difficulties, and Fourth Panzer Army had to detach a division to secure its flank. The ferocious fighting and extensive mine fields throughout the enemy's deep defensive positions imposed terrible losses on German tank forces. By July 9, the army's *Grossdeutschland* Division had already lost 220 out of 300 tanks.

Manstein's attacks from the south finally began to show results. By July 11, II SS Panzer Corps had advanced about twenty-five miles, and the Soviets were forced to use reserves from the Steppe Front. On the same day Kempf's III Panzer Corps had finally broken into the open. Despite desperate Soviet resistance, Kempf linked up with II SS Panzer Corps and trapped a substantial number of Soviet troops. On July 12 nearly 1,800 German and Russian armored vehicles clashed on a small battlefield near Prokhorovka in the largest tank battle of the war. When it was over, the Germans had lost over 300 tanks, and the Russians 400; but the Russians had held. Manstein still had two fresh divisions and believed that his forces could reach Kursk. He was undoubtedly wrong because the Soviets still held four armies in reserve.

Beginning on July 10, however, events elsewhere intervened: Anglo-American armies landed in Sicily, and Mussolini's regime teetered on the brink of collapse. Amidst concerns about Soviet forces north and south of Kursk, Hitler terminated Citadel to reinforce the Mediterranean. Only Manstein urged continuation of the Kursk battle, but his reasoning largely rested on a belief that no other alternatives existed. In retrospect, Kursk was a disastrous failure, for it had consumed most of the German army's replenished reserves and armored forces. It was the last important German offensive in Russia.

The Soviets Counterattack

After halting Citadel, the Soviets seized the initiative and launched a series of attacks across the breadth of the Eastern Front. They relied on methods quite different from those of the Germans; instead of boldly relying on deep penetrations and double envelopments, the Red Army utilized several thrusts that aimed to push back the enemy on a broad front. If the Germans halted one thrust, the Russians shifted to another. With a 2.5:1 advantage in the air, the Soviets used their air forces for close ground support and air defense, and with an even greater advantage in artillery, they used preparatory fires on the same scale as those used in World War I.

The first Soviet move came against the Orel salient lying directly north of Kursk. Three Soviet armies attacked the northern side of the salient on July 12, 1943. By using forces previously committed to the Kursk battle, Model prevented a Soviet breakthrough. In this rare case Hitler sanctioned retreat from the salient, for he desperately needed troops to shore up a collapsing Fascist Italy (Mussolini fell from power on July 25).

Manstein confronted more daunting problems in the south. Soviet attacks stung his forces at their northern and southern extremities. Hitler refused to make the hard decisions demanded by the desperate plight of German forces; Manstein warned that the Führer must either provide his army group with twenty divisions or abandon the Donets Basin. The best solution might have been a phased retreat of about 150 miles to the Dnieper and reinforcement of that line. Hitler dithered, however, and the northern flank of Army Group South dissolved. Soviet forces took Belgorod on August 5, drove west, and forced the Germans to evacuate Kharkov for the last time on August 21. A desperate counterattack by two divisions finally halted the Soviet advance and permitted Eighth Army and Fourth Panzer Army to reestablish contact and new defensive lines, but the Soviets had advanced nearly eighty miles.

Soviet Offensives, July 7, 1943 – April 30, 1944

Soviet attacks
Front lines

Along the Mius and Donets rivers, Soviet offensives rocked First Panzer Army and a reconstituted Sixth Army. First Panzer Army held; on August 18, however, the Soviets broke through Sixth Army by concentrating massive artillery on a narrow front. Germans attempts to pinch off the breakthrough with attacks on its shoulders almost succeeded, but fierce Soviet attacks blocked the counterattack. Manstein urged Hitler to abandon the Donets Basin. The Führer remained obdurate; not until August 31 did he approve withdrawal of First Panzer and Sixth armies forty miles to a new defensive line. As the two armies pulled back, their desperate plight finally forced Hitler to abandon the Donets Basin and permit a withdrawal of about 140 miles. Sixth Army had to hold in front of the Dnieper because its retreat would isolate the Crimea; Hitler was desperately afraid that the Russians would use that peninsula to launch air attacks against Romanian oil fields.

Despite his permitting abandonment of the Donets Basin, Hitler refused to allow Fourth Panzer and Eighth armies on Army Group South's northern flank to fall back on the Dnieper, but that flank unraveled so fast that by late September, the Red Army and the Wehrmacht were in a desperate race for the Dnieper. Many retreating Germans escaped to the far side, but the Soviets made several hasty river crossings and established bridgeheads from which they could resume their advance.

The bridgeheads made the German position desperate. North of Kiev the Soviet advance severed connections between army groups South and Center; on the lower Dnieper, the Soviets crossed the river and seized a bridgehead north of Dnepropetrovsk thirty miles wide and ten miles deep. By this time they had already won a great victory against Army Group South. Their forces had advanced an average of 150 miles on a front of 650 miles and had regained the Ukraine's most valuable agricultural and industrial areas. Despite Hitler's demands for scorched earth, the hastiness and lack of planning characterizing Army Group South's retreat minimized the damage that the Germans could inflict.

Unrelenting Soviet pressure eventually cut off German forces in the Crimean peninsula. Against thirteen German and two Romanian divisions, the Soviets on October 9 launched forty-five infantry divisions, three tank corps, and two mechanized corps, supported by 400 batteries of artillery. As the Soviet drive gathered momentum and approached the Black Sea west of the Crimea, Kleist and the Romanian dictator, Marshal Antonescu, begged Hitler to abandon the peninsula and allow Seventeenth Army to retreat. Hitler, however, refused, and by November the Soviets had isolated Seventeenth Army in the Crimea. The entire position along the lower Dnieper had now unraveled. One hundred miles to the north, Soviet forces expanded the size of their bridgehead across the Dnieper. Another two hundred miles to the north, Soviet forces seized Kiev; nowhere on the southern front could the Germans stabilize the situation. Only the arrival of autumn rains eventually brought relief to the hard-pressed Wehrmacht.

The fighting over summer and fall 1943 represented the first stage in the collapse of the Nazi position in the east. The constant battles wore German infantry down and forced the panzer divisions to act as fire brigades.

The 2.5 million German soldiers on the Eastern Front had been insufficient to alter the growing imbalance. The OKW considered conscripting women but dropped the idea because of Hitler's violent opposition. As for the Soviets, they had had about 6 million soldiers and had learned their lessons well over the past two years. Their massive attacks and multiple thrusts effectively combined armor, infantry, and artillery and overwhelmed German defenders. On the intelligence side, they enjoyed an enormous superiority, and they skillfully used deception to blind their German enemy almost entirely.

The Soviets also used partisan operations to advantage. Hitler's racial policies and brutal treatment pushed many Russians into guerrilla warfare. By early 1943 approximately 250,000 Soviets operated as partisans behind German lines. Usually organized into brigades of 1,000 men and women, the partisans extended Soviet power into Nazi-occupied territory, conducted raids, demolished roads and railroads, cut telephone lines, and provided intelligence. Those near the front lines usually took orders from the staffs of the closest Soviet armies and launched operations in coordination with major offensives. Their superiors passed commands by radio and air; supplies came from low-flying aircraft. In the two years of most intense partisan warfare, German forces suffered approximately 300,000 casualties, including thirty general officers and more than one thousand officers. Although partisan operations did not change the course of the war in the east, they compelled the Germans to diffuse their already overextended forces.

While extraordinary battles in Russia continued with savage fury, Hitler drove his police and military—willing participants—to complete the racial cleansing of eastern Europe. This extermination of the Jews and the further enslavement of the Slavic masses continued until the final collapse of the Nazis. By 1942–1943 the great killing camps such as Auschwitz and Treblinka were spewing their ashen clouds of slaughtered Jews and other unfortunates over the landscape of eastern Europe; long trains of cattle and freight cars transported the victims—a diversion of scarce transport that even affected the Wehrmacht's logistics. Meanwhile, Ukrainians, Russians, Poles, and others in slightly higher racial categories—as defined by Hitler—were dragooned by the millions to serve as slave laborers in the great industrial undertakings of the SS and German industry. If not murdered, they were brutalized, starved, and mistreated. If Germany could not win the war, then at least the Reich could live up to the Führer's promise given before the war that he would free Europe of all its Jews however the war might turn out.

Although Hitler's racial policies and refusals to abandon territory contributed to the catastrophe, the problem lay deeper. The extent of German miscalculations in planning and executing Barbarossa were now apparent. Above all, the Germans were not fighting "subhuman" barbarians, but an enormously gifted people, whose military efforts early in the war had been seriously impaired by the mistakes and prejudices of Stalin. The Soviets had now emerged as a skillful and resourceful foe.

The Mediterranean, 1942–1943

While Soviet armies had begun the arduous task of retaking territory, the Western Powers finally were able to overcome German tactical and operational performance by improved battle effectiveness of their own, as well as increasing numerical superiority in manpower and equipment. Still unprepared for a direct assault on Fortress Europe, British and American commanders undertook to push the Axis from North Africa, open the Mediterranean to Allied shipping, and drive Italy out of the war. In this they were to be successful, but only after heavy fighting. The battles of North Africa would prove particularly important to correct the significant deficiencies that had appeared with the first commitment of American troops to battle.

El Alamein

The disastrous defeat on the Gazala Line and at Tobruk in June 1942 threatened to undermine the British position in the Middle East. At this point, the British theater commander, General Sir Claude Auchinleck assumed control of Eighth Army. As its beaten remnants streamed eastward, he determined to stand at El Alamein, sixty miles west of Alexandria. Unlike other defensive positions in the desert, El Alamein had the advantage that it could not be flanked; to the south lay the Qattara Depression, a great dry salt sea that could not support heavy vehicles.

Furious at the May and June defeats, Churchill sacked Auchinleck and appointed General Harold Alexander in his place as the theater commander. On August 13, Lieutenant General Bernard Law Montgomery assumed command of Eighth Army. Montgomery was an inspired choice. Admittedly he was a careful, prudent general who rarely took risks, but his approach reflected the caliber of his forces. In his memoirs, Montgomery explained that he built up the Eighth Army by concentrating "on three essentials: leadership, equipment, and training. All three were deficient."* Other problems identified by Montgomery included discipline, confidence, and morale. As he acted to restore Eighth Army, he made the ground and air forces work closely together and ended the practice of fighting in brigade-sized units. In the future divisions would fight as divisions. As additional supplies and new weapons poured into Egypt, Montgomery overcame deficiencies in equipment and established huge supply dumps. Over a period of three months, he fought the battles of Alam Halfa and El Alamein with a flawed instrument, but his success reflected a realistic appreciation of British weaknesses.

At the end of August, Rommel began the battle of Alam Halfa with an attack similar to the one he had used along the Gazala Line in May 1942.

---

*Bernard L. Montgomery, *Memoirs* (London: Collins, 1958), p. 103.

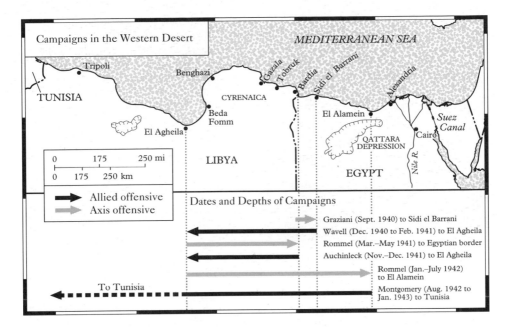

Campaigns in the Western Desert

MEDITERRANEAN SEA

Tripoli

Benghazi

Gazala
Tobruk
Bardia
Sidi el Barrani
Alexandria

TUNISIA

CYRENAICA

El Alamein

Suez Canal

Beda Fomm

QATTARA DEPRESSION

Cairo

El Agheila

0   175   250 mi

0   175   250 km

LIBYA

Nile R.

EGYPT

Allied offensive

Axis offensive

Dates and Depths of Campaigns

Graziani (Sept. 1940) to Sidi el Barrani
Wavell (Dec. 1940 to Feb. 1941) to El Agheila
Rommel (Mar.–May 1941) to Egyptian border
Auchinleck (Nov.–Dec. 1941) to El Agheila
Rommel (Jan.–July 1942) to El Alamein
Montgomery (Aug. 1942 to Jan. 1943) to Tunisia

To Tunisia

That is, he launched a diversionary attack along the coast and on the British center and then sent his main attack against their southern flank. As the Germans drove into the British rear, RAF fighter bombers hammered their columns. Extensive minefields hampered the Afrika Korps' effort to cut off British forces, while British armor fought a solid defensive battle. On September 2, Rommel pulled back after suffering heavy losses and established defensive positions between the coast and the Qattara Depression.

Montgomery now began preparing Eighth Army for what would be his most famous battle, El Alamein. His initial concept involved an attack on each flank of the German position, but reservations about the readiness of his armor to fight a mobile battle resulted in a more straightforward plan. The main attack would occur against Rommel's northern flank, while diversionary attacks pinned German units in the south. Artillery would batter enemy defenses, engineers would clear lanes through enemy mine fields, infantry would then drive through those defenses, and finally the armor would break out. It was a simple plan that relied on firepower and numerical superiority.

The operation, however, failed to go according to plan. With Montgomery having some 230,000 troops and Rommel only 80,000, the set-piece attack began on October 23 with a powerful artillery bombardment, followed by infantry assaults. But gaps cleared by the engineers were too narrow, and the infantry failed to secure the far ends of the lanes. As a result, British armor became entrapped in mine fields. Fortunately for the British, Rommel was home on sick leave, and German commanders responded slowly. They launched a series of piecemeal attacks and suffered heavy casualties; by the end of the first day 15th Panzer Division had lost three-quarters of its

General Bernard L. Montgomery usually wore a black beret, a pullover sweater, and khaki pants. Though he seemed a cranky eccentric, he improved the performance of his units, generated greater confidence among his troops, and soon drove Rommel out of Egypt and Libya.

tanks. But the Germans continued fighting, while British armor remained stuck in mine fields.

To weaken German infantry and tanks, Montgomery began what he called a "dog fight." On November 2, after one week's hard fighting, he launched a powerful thrust against the German center. With the British possessing 600 tanks and the Germans only 30, Rommel, who had rushed back to Africa, started pulling his infantry back on November 3. But Hitler stopped him. Amidst the confusion, Montgomery launched another attack and broke through German defenses. Subsequent efforts to cut off the Afrika Korps, however, failed because British forces moved too slowly. Rommel began a rapid retreat across Egypt into Libya, eventually reaching Tunisia. Montgomery's pursuit was slow and methodical as he established airfields along his route of advance and opened ports for logistical support. But he had achieved what none of his predecessors had managed; he had defeated Rommel.

Operation "Torch"

Meanwhile on the western coast of North Africa major events were in motion. During the Arcadia Conference in December 1941, Churchill had proposed a landing on the shores of French North Africa. The Americans, however, displayed scant interest; from the first, they felt that a "Germany-first" strategy demanded immediate action in Europe. In May 1942, Roosevelt even promised Vyacheslav Molotov, the Soviet foreign minister, that the Western Powers would open a second front in 1942. Planning did begin for a descent on the French coast, should the Soviet Union appear on the brink of collapse, but such a venture represented only a desperate effort to distract the Germans.

The strategy preferred by the American military leaders, particularly General Marshall, the U.S. Army's chief of staff, was to build up military capabilities for a direct assault on western Europe sometime in 1943. However, the U.S. Navy, feeding on prewar preparations and popular attitudes,

In North Africa, General Dwight D. Eisenhower gained experience and developed the skills in high-level command and coalition warfare that were essential for his future success as Supreme Allied Commander.

pushed for a Pacific strategy; and the British doubted whether a landing in western Europe could be successful in 1943. For a while, Marshall moved toward the navy's urgings that the United States turn to the Pacific. Roosevelt, however, refused to countenance such a recasting of American strategy. Instead he demanded a major initiative in Europe in 1942—if not against German-occupied France, then in the Mediterranean—because he recognized the political necessity of a commitment of American troops in Europe to keep his nation focused on defeating Germany. American military leaders eventually agreed to Torch, landings to occupy Algeria and Morocco and co-opt the Vichy French.

The commander of Torch was an obscure American general, Dwight David Eisenhower. Ike had not seen combat in World War I, but he possessed gifts of diplomacy and tact as well as operational competence. His political skills were essential to getting Anglo-American forces to work together on the operational level. Initially, he had some weaknesses as a commander, but he displayed great capacity to learn. If not Rommel's equal on the battlefield, he far surpassed most German generals in his political and diplomatic skills and in his understanding the wider aspects of war.

Considerable wrangling took place between American and British leaders about the location of the landings; the final plan focused on Algeria and Morocco. Following landings at Casablanca, Oran, and Algiers, Allied forces would advance east by land and sea against Tunisia. The initial landings in North Africa on November 8 went well, especially considering the Allied troops' lack of combat experience. The French resisted the invasion tenaciously at first; Hitler's lack of trust in the Vichy regime, however, resulted in those forces possessing obsolete matériel and inadequate ammunition stocks. Coincidentally, Vichy's number-two man, Admiral François Darlan, was present in North Africa and eventually agreed to an armistice.

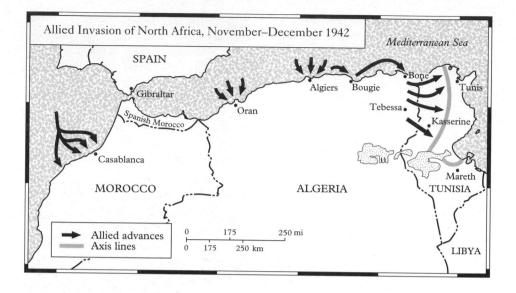

Allied Invasion of North Africa, November–December 1942

Hitler's response was, as usual, swift and ruthless. While Nazi troops occupied Vichy France, paratrooper and Luftwaffe units, flying from Sicily, won "the race of Tunisia" before the Allied forces could get there. By seizing Tunisia, the Germans kept the Mediterranean closed to Allied shipping for another six months and thereby exacerbated worldwide shipping shortages plaguing Allied logisticians. But the price was too high. The decision to fight in Tunisia resulted from Hitler's desire to support Mussolini's decrepit regime; it was perhaps the worst decision that Hitler made in 1942. It committed the remainder of Fascist Italy's military power and substantial numbers of German troops to defend a hopeless position, and it forced Axis naval and air power to fight at a severe disadvantage. The result was a defeat almost as great as Stalingrad, one entirely resulting from German miscalculations.

Though the opening moves in Tunisia had favored the Allies, German paratroopers and armor halted and then pushed the Americans and British back to Tunisia's western frontier. By January, Rommel had escaped from Libya and arrived in southern Tunisia where all the Axis forces in North Africa concentrated. However, Rommel commanded only a portion of Axis forces, while units in northern Tunisia fell under command of Colonel General Jürgen von Arnim. Immediately after his arrival in Tunisia, Rommel sensed an opportunity; Montgomery's hesitant pursuit gave the Germans a relatively free hand, while Anglo-American forces in Algeria were strung out along the Tunisian frontier. The Allied First Army included the American II Corps, commanded by Major General Lloyd R. Fredendall, who refused advice, deployed his troops badly, and located his headquarters deep underground and far behind the front lines. Rommel suggested an armored drive sweeping up from southern Tunisia to destroy Allied supply dumps in eastern Algeria and perhaps even to trap First Army against the coast. In addition, he hoped to give the Americans a severe mauling that would affect their confidence for the rest of the war. Fortunately for the

Allies, the Desert Fox received little support for the proposed attack, and much of the German armor remained under Arnim.

The battle began on February 14 when Rommel's 10th and 21st Panzer divisions punched through thinly held passes in central Tunisia. After pushing back Combat Command A of the U.S. 1st Armored Division and surrounding the 168th Regimental Combat Team, the Germans advanced west toward Kasserine. A counterattack by Combat Command C of the 1st Armored Division failed disastrously, and veteran German forces fought their way through Kasserine Pass. After Arnim had convinced Italian headquarters in Rome to deny Rommel's proposal for a deep encirclement, and after Arnim had refused to release one of his panzer divisions, Rommel advanced north in two columns. One column turned north ten miles east of Kasserine, while the other turned north at Kasserine. Both columns encountered spirited resistance from British units in prepared defensive positions and were halted; on February 22 German forces began withdrawing. Allied ground strength, Arnim's refusal to support Rommel, and German weaknesses had enabled Rommel to achieve only a tactical success.

Immediately after Kasserine, Rommel turned south against the British who had finally arrived from Egypt. Though he attempted to knock them off balance, intelligence from Ultra alerted his opponents, and Montgomery dealt the Afrika Korps a stunning defeat. German forces lost more than one-third of their tanks. Seriously ill, Rommel left Africa a few days later.

With Rommel's defeat, the Axis position in North Africa steadily deteriorated. Ultra allowed Anglo-American air power to interdict the Axis supply lines from Italy. By March the Germans had abandoned the sealift; thereafter, the Luftwaffe's hard-pressed air transports had to provide logistic support: ammunition, fuel, food, and personnel. Again Ultra provided ample intelligence, and Allied fighters destroyed protective screens of Axis fighters as well as the transports themselves. The end came in early May, as the Allies mopped up the remnants in Tunisia. The Germans had lost heavily in the air; the Wehrmacht's ground losses represented the OKH's Mediterranean reserves, while the destruction of Italian ground forces, the last to surrender, left Mussolini with little to defend the homeland. After Tunisia, the Duce's regime enjoyed neither respect nor authority among a disillusioned population.

The victory in North Africa was particularly important for American ground and air forces. Their opening exposure to combat had not been auspicious; some U.S. units in Kasserine Pass had collapsed under the pressure of what was a large-scale raid by German forces. But American commanders set about with determination to repair their deficiencies and learn from experience. As Rommel suggested shortly before his death, American ground forces had been inferior to those of the British when the Germans first encountered them, but the Americans had shown a great capacity to learn. The story of the U.S. Army was thus one of steady, consistent improvement in battlefield performance. Typical of this American improvement was that of air-ground cooperation in Tunisia. The system in place as the campaign began proved generally unworkable; but the Americans had the very effective model of the RAF-British army system to copy. Not only did they dispense with the old, but they improved the British system and subsequently used it with enormous effectiveness in Normandy.

Attack on Sicily and Italy

After the Axis surrender in Tunisia in May 1943, the Allies began preparing for the next phase in the European war. At the Casablanca Conference in January 1943, General Marshall had made a last appeal for a cross-channel invasion in 1943, but Churchill's eloquence convinced Roosevelt that the Allies should maintain their momentum in the Mediterranean and direct their efforts toward Italy. Though American military leaders still preferred an early cross-channel invasion, the advantages of defeating the Italians, opening the Mediterranean to Allied shipping, and enlarging the air offensive

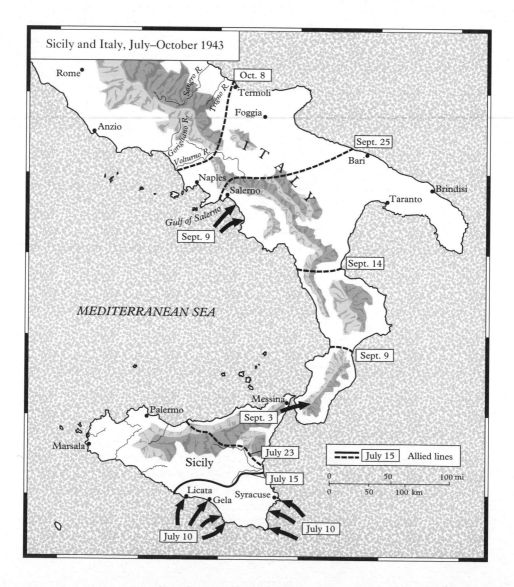

Sicily and Italy, July–October 1943

against Germany were obvious. At the Trident Conference in May 1943, the Americans accepted the strategic goal of eliminating Italy from the war but demanded that the forces involved consist only of those already in the Mediterranean. At Trident the Americans and British also agreed that planning begin for a cross-channel invasion in May 1944. The British, nevertheless, pressed for operations in the eastern Aegean and possibly in the Balkans. Finally, at the Teheran Conference in November 1943, Roosevelt, Churchill, and Stalin agreed to a cross-channel invasion—Operation "Overlord"—in spring 1944 in conjunction with an Anglo-American attack on southern France and a major offensive by the Soviets on the Eastern Front. This was the final blueprint for Allied strategy in Europe.

On July 10, 1943, the British Eighth Army under Montgomery and the U.S. Seventh Army under Major General George S. Patton stormed ashore on Sicily in Operation "Husky"—the largest amphibious assault in the war. Seven divisions made amphibious landings (compared to five divisions later at Normandy). The landings occurred on the southeast corner of the island, the British on the right, the Americans on the left. Montgomery, as the senior ground forces commander, had devised a straightforward plan for conquering Sicily; Eighth Army would drive up from the southeast corner of Sicily toward Messina, while Patton's army provided a flank guard. There seemed no reason why Montgomery could not execute his plan; only a small force of German and Italian troops defended the island. But the Germans proved as tenacious and combat-effective as usual; hilly and broken terrain aided their defensive efforts.

When Montgomery's attack slowed, Patton, who had no intention of acting as flank guard, raced west, captured Palermo, and then pushed east along the northern coast of the island. He got to Messina before Montgomery, but not before German ground forces escaped. Flak batteries on both sides of the straits of Messina protected this escape, while Allied air and naval units failed to intervene with sufficient vigor. In this operation as in everything he did, Patton projected flamboyance as well as leadership. But his political sensitivity was, unfortunately, considerably less than his military genius. He came close to ending his career by slapping two enlisted soldiers suffering from shell shock.

Whatever its failures, Husky gained considerable strategic and political advantages. It forced Hitler to shut down Citadel and confirmed his fears about the political stability of Mussolini's regime. On July 25, King Victor Emmanuel III dismissed Mussolini from office. Immediately thereafter, military police arrested the fallen dictator and whisked him away to a variety of secret locations (Luftwaffe paratroops and SS commandoes liberated him in September 1943, but he would perish at the hands of Italian partisans in April 1945). The king called on Marshal Pietro Badoglio, who had presided over the disasters of 1940, to get Italy out of the war.

By summer 1943, losses of manpower and equipment in Tunisia had destroyed the Wehrmacht's strategic reserves throughout the Mediterranean. Thoroughly distrustful of the Italians, Hitler understood the meaning of the coup against Mussolini; the new government would make a deal as soon as possible with the Allies—a deal that could place the British and Americans on the Alps and provide them bases in Italy at minimum cost. He immediately ordered the buildup of sizable forces under Rommel to intervene, while German units infiltrated to strategic locations throughout the peninsula. Hitler had every reason to worry. Though Badoglio reaffirmed Italy's loyalty, he immediately opened negotiations to switch sides. But Italy's new leaders failed to act decisively, and negotiations dragged into August and early September. By then the possibilities that Italy offered had almost slipped away.

On September 3, Eighth Army landed on the toe of Italy. Six days later an Anglo-American force under General Mark Clark in Operation "Avalanche" landed in the Gulf of Salerno, south of Naples, while the British Broadcasting Corporation, to Badoglio's horror, announced Italy's acceptance of an armistice. Italian dithering and incompetence, however, had convinced the Americans that a drop by the 82nd Airborne Division on Rome's airfields would result in disaster. The king, Badoglio, and other Italian leaders promptly decamped, leaving the army with no orders, and made their way south to Allied lines. The Wehrmacht disarmed the leaderless Italian military with minimum difficulty.

Meanwhile, Field Marshal Kesselring responded vigorously to the landings at Salerno. Well-organized counterattacks threatened to drive Clark's forces into the sea, while Montgomery's Eighth Army advanced at a snail's pace up the Italian toe. Supporting Allied naval and air forces prevented the Germans from exploiting their advantage. With the linkup of Clark and Montgomery's forces, the Germans began a slow retreat northward and eventually abandoned Naples. The Allied advance, however, turned into a nightmare as the Germans dug in on one ridge line after another. By late 1943 the advance had stalled seventy miles north of Salerno and eighty miles short of Rome. The only significant gain was Foggia and its airfields (opposite Salerno, on the eastern side of the peninsula). For the next year and a half the Allies fought their way slowly north over the peninsula and destroyed much of Italy in the process.

The East, 1944

Fall and Winter Disasters for the Wehrmacht

In October 1943 arrival of bad weather had ushered in a temporary slackening of fighting in the east. Army Group South lay battered and bleeding. Neither troops nor commanders had illusions about what was coming. Manstein, still the army group's commander, argued that the Red Army disposed of enormous reserves behind its front; on November 20, he warned OKH that in addition to the forty-four divisions and numerous armored brigades established in 1943, the Red Army had thirty-three infantry divisions and eleven tank and mechanized corps in reserve on the southern front. Only the provision of "sufficient and powerful reserves," he noted, would allow Army Group South to hold the line. He had no chance of getting such reserves given the grave state of German forces in other theaters;

Manstein's demands underline how woefully ignorant the German generals were of the Reich's strategic situation.

On Christmas Eve 1943, the Soviets launched the winter's offensive, aimed at regaining the rest of the Ukraine. South of the Pripet Marshes and west of Kiev, First Guards and First Tank armies under General N. F. Vatutin pushed Fourth Panzer Army back. Hitler again refused to authorize any retreats or to approve Manstein's request to withdraw Army Group South's right flank. By early January the Soviets had opened up a 110–mile gap between army groups Center and South. Though Army Group South's left was dissolving, Hitler refused to abandon the lower Dnieper so forces could be assembled to meet the growing emergency. As the situation became fluid, the Germans closed a small encirclement around a portion of First Tank Army and destroyed a sizable number of tanks and assault guns, while inflicting heavy casualties. But the Red Army trapped two German corps, over 56,000 troops, near Cherkassy, in the center of Army Group South. The Germans got 30,000 men out, but most had to swim to safety and were completely broken by the experience.

At the end of March 1944, Hitler finally had had enough of Manstein's streak of independence and relieved the field marshal. But Manstein's relief did not presage any fundamental changes in how the Germans fought on the Eastern Front. By this point Manstein's opponents were fully his equal, with a broader understanding of the logistic, intelligence, and deception needs for any successful operation. One must also recognize that there was little political or strategic disagreement between Manstein and Hitler, as the former's wholehearted cooperation in the murderous actions of the SS in 1941 and 1942 underlined.

Things did not go better in Army Group A along the Black Sea. The Soviets struck Sixth Army on January 10 and 11. When Hitler allowed a

Throughout the war the Germans had fewer trucks than the Allies and often used horse-drawn wagons to carry equipment and supplies.

withdrawal, the order came so late that Sixth Army abandoned much of its heavy artillery, engineering equipment, and even armored fighting vehicles. In mid-February the Soviets reorganized for a major effort to recapture the rest of the Ukraine before the spring thaw. By this point, Soviet mechanized forces enjoyed greater mobility than their German opponents. Using sturdy American trucks for logistical support, Soviet tanks maneuvered in alternating conditions of thaw, freeze, snow, and rain. Since the Germans had designed most of their vehicles for western European conditions, their trucks often broke down. For example, 24th Panzer Division lost 1,958 of its vehicles during the winter, more than half of its authorized number. Some German panzer divisions were reduced to using horse-drawn peasant carts for supply.

Over the next month and a half Soviet commanders concentrated on destroying the two enemy army groups in the Ukraine. Between the Pripet Marshes and Black Sea, the Red Army deployed from north to south First, Second, Third, and Fourth Ukrainian fronts, each about double the size of a German army. West of Kiev, First Ukrainian Front drove deep into German positions, and by late March First and Second Ukrainian fronts had encircled First Panzer Army and smashed across the Dniester River. Only a desperate counterattack extricated the encircled Germans. Meanwhile Third Ukrainian Front, having taken Nikopol, drove on to take Odessa and reach the Romanian border. Soviet advances lapped to the passes over the Carpathian Mountains leading into Hungary, but the Germans and Hungarians, aided by the spring thaw, blocked that route.

Elsewhere in the east the Red Army scored its first major advances outside of Army Group South since winter 1941–1942. In the north, the Germans still besieged Leningrad, although the Soviets had opened a corridor to the city. In late December 1943, Army Group North's commander, Field Marshal Georg von Küchler, almost convinced Hitler to authorize a withdrawal of approximately 150 miles to a newly fortified position, known as "Panther." However, Eighteenth Army's commander, Colonel General Georg Lindemann, argued that his forces could hold their well-fortified but exposed positions. Always willing to take the optimistic point of view, Hitler supported Lindemann. But the latter and his intelligence officers had missed extensive Soviet preparations for an offensive. With a three-to-one superiority, the Soviets attacked both sides of the besieging forces at Leningrad on January 14. Second Shock Army struck out from the Oranienbaum enclave west of Leningrad, while Forty-Second Army attacked south of the city. At the same time, heavy Soviet attacks put German positions around Novgorod (one hundred miles to the south) in mortal danger. When Küchler pressed Hitler to authorize a short pullback, the Führer reluctantly agreed, but the Germans could not disengage cleanly. By January 19 the Russians had surrounded substantial numbers of Germans at Novgorod. Though concerned about the fall of another important Russian city, Hitler finally authorized a breakout.

Meanwhile the situation remained desperate in front of Leningrad. Küchler begged for permission to fall all the way back to the Panther line. By the end of the month Eighteenth Army had disintegrated into three separate groups, all facing encirclement. On January 30, Hitler finally permitted Küchler to pull back about fifty miles. At that point he fired Küchler and replaced him with Colonel General Walter Model, who had gained a reputation as a great defensive expert, but who also remained a favorite of the Führer because of his fanaticism. Model immediately wired his new headquarters, "Not a single step backward."

Despite Model's optimism and the arrival of reinforcements, strong Soviet pressure forced Army Group North back to the Panther position on March 1. The Germans held in this position, which extended north and south of Lake Peipus. An early spring thaw covered the frozen lake with water and halted the Soviet advance.

One last disaster befell German forces in the spring. Since fall 1943, Seventeenth Army had clung to the Crimea. Despite the pleas of his staff and Marshal Antonescu, Hitler insisted that the peninsula, which he described as an "aircraft carrier aimed at the Romanian oil fields," hold to the last. On April 7, 1944, the new commander of Army Group A, Colonel General Ferdinand Schörner, inspected the Crimea defenses and declared them in excellent shape, so excellent that they could hold "for a long time." Schörner was one of a new breed of generals promoted by Hitler for their enthusiasm and fanaticism. His prediction proved one of the shortest lived of the war.

On April 8 the Soviets attacked the German and Romanian defenders on the peninsula. Schörner at last recognized that Seventeenth Army would have to retreat to Sevastopol and the sooner the better. Hitler, of course, refused to authorize a withdrawal. Only under intense pressure did he finally sanction retreat but then demanded Sevastopol be held indefinitely. Schörner argued for a total withdrawal from the Crimea; but Hitler marshaled counterarguments from the air force and navy that they could supply Sevastopol. In early May the Soviets broke through the city's defenses. Only at this point did Hitler authorize a pullout, but the navy, while under heavy air attack, botched the operation. Although enough ships were available to transport the troops only 38,000 out of 64,700 escaped. The original strength of Seventeenth Army had been 75,546 Germans and 45,887 Romanians.

Operation "Bagration"

At Teheran in November 1943, Stalin, Churchill, and Roosevelt approved a common strategy for the coming year: the Western Powers would land forces in France and open a second front, while the Soviets launched a great offensive to coincide with it. Roosevelt assured Stalin that the invasion would occur in spring 1944.

As the Soviets prepared for their offensive, they focused on the area north of the Pripet Marshes, the only substantial portion of Soviet territory still under German occupation, since much of the significant fighting since 1942 had occurred in the south. Consequently, as *Stavka* established priorities for summer 1944, the front opposite Army Group Center received the highest priority. Following an offensive against the Finns to fix German

attention, the Red Army would attack Army Group Center and advance to East Prussia, a distance of approximately 225 miles. After destroying Army Group Center, the Soviets would be well positioned for a move into the Balkans.

Code-named "Bagration," the upcoming operation against Army Group Center included two phases. In the first, Soviet forces would break through enemy defenses and envelop German forces at Vitebsk on the Dvina River and at Bobruisk on the Beresina River. They would then strike deeper and encircle German units east of Minsk. When Marshal Rokossovskii presented the plan to Stalin, he encountered strong doubts about the two-pronged envelopment of Bobruisk. Stalin approved the plans only after sending Rokossovskii out of the room twice to "think it over."

Preparations for Bagration began in the spring. Against Army Group Center's 700,000 soldiers, *Stavka* concentrated 1.2 million men on the front with another 1.3 million in reserve. It assembled 124 divisions, 4,000 tanks, 24,400 artillery pieces, and 5,300 aircraft. German intelligence picked up little information about the concentration; its estimates swallowed a superb Soviet deception plan that suggested another offensive against Army Group South. What few movements German intelligence picked up in the center, it dismissed as "merely a deception." This miscalculation of the situation resulted in a maldistribution of German forces. Army Group Center, defending a 488-mile front, possessed only thirty-eight divisions in the first line and five divisions in reserve; three Hungarian and five security divisions guarded its rear areas. By contrast, Army Group North Ukraine (previously Army Group South), defending a shorter front than Army Group Center, had thirty-five German and ten Hungarian divisions of which ten were panzer. Together the two southern German army groups contained eighteen panzer and panzer grenadier divisions.

But the greatest deficiency of Army Group Center lay in the slavish devotion of its commander, Field Marshal Ernst Busch, to Hitler's directives. Even in 1940, Busch had displayed a remarkable lack of imagination; by 1944 the war had entirely passed him by. Busch accepted Hitler's directive to establish "fortresses" around important centers and to hold them to the last man. He insisted on such a rigid defense that Ninth Army complained that it was "bound by orders to tactical measures which it cannot in good conscience accept and which in our own earlier victories were the causes of the enemy defeats."

By this point in the war, the qualitative as well as quantitative balance had swung against the Germans in the east. Soviet commanders down to the divisional level had mastered the conduct of the operational art; the *Stavka* could prepare, conduct, and exploit extraordinarily complex operations ranging hundreds of miles. Soviet deception entirely blinded German commanders as to Soviet operational intentions until the hammer blows fell. Once *Stavka* unleashed its forces, a skillful conduct of operations (sustained by an efficient and mobile support structure—largely due to American lend-lease trucks) enabled full exploitation of breakthroughs. Only at the tactical, small-unit level did German units enjoy some small advantage, but even here the Soviet quantitative edge gave German soldiers a sense of impending doom.

On June 22, 1944, the third anniversary of Barbarossa and two weeks after the landings in Normandy, Soviet armies attacked Army Group Center, which had its Third Panzer, Fourth, and Ninth armies deployed from Vitebsk to Bobruisk. After ripping through the Third Panzer Army's positions, Soviet spearheads closed around Vitebsk and trapped five German divisions. On the 24th, the next phase of Bagration began against Ninth Army; First Belorussian Front broke open its left flank. When Ninth Army requested permission to escape, the army group commander replied that "the army's mission was to hold every foot of ground." In fact, the speed of the Soviet offensive had already shattered Ninth Army and trapped its broken units in several small pockets around Bobruisk. At the last minute the OKH permitted a withdrawal, but again too late. The Soviets encircled two corps, 70,000 troops, and continued their drive toward Minsk. Positioned between Third Panzer and Ninth armies, Fourth Army tried to pull back, but the advancing units of Soviet armor were already closing the trap.

As the situation became increasingly confused, Hitler intervened and ordered Third Panzer, Fourth, and Ninth armies to hold east of Minsk, sixty miles behind their original positions. In fact, all three armies—or at least those units not yet captured, surrounded, or destroyed—were in desperate shape. By now OKH had finally concluded that the Soviets were launching an ambitious offensive, aimed at retaking Minsk. Hitler fired Busch, the army group commander, and replaced him with Model, but the latter confronted a catastrophic situation. On July 3, the Soviets captured Minsk amidst scenes of indescribable collapse and confusion that marked desperate German attempts to flee. In twelve days Army Group Center had lost twenty-five divisions; out of 165,000 soldiers Fourth Army alone had lost 130,000. The other armies in Army Group Center were in little better shape.

Still, OKH drew some comfort from its hope that the Soviet advance of 125 miles would cause the attackers to run out of supplies. Again the Germans were wrong. On July 8, Model reported that he could not hold a line 175 miles west of Bobruisk. A yawning chasm separated the remnants of Army Group Center from Army Group North. Model requested that Army Group North withdraw to the Riga-Dvinsk-Dvina River line, thereby shortening its front and freeing troops for use in the center. Hitler refused, this time because the Baltic coast was crucial to launching new U-boats and securing Swedish iron ore shipped through the Baltic. At the end of July the Soviet drive, having advanced some 200 miles, began to slow. The Soviets had finally outrun their supply system.

With German reserves drawn to the center, the Soviets attacked the flanks. In the south, Army Group North Ukraine lay exposed; by the end of July, Soviet forces had advanced sixty miles across a broad front. Likewise in the north, Soviet attacks unhinged Army Group North's flank and almost reached the Baltic.

Meanwhile, Soviet forces approached Warsaw. On July 30, elements of Second Tank Army reached within seven miles of the Polish capital; south of Warsaw Soviet units actually crossed the Vistula River. But at this point, short of fuel and with political concerns in mind, the Soviets stopped and refused to liberate the Polish capital. The Poles themselves had little desire for a Soviet liberation of Poland. Certainly, memories of Stalin's actions in September 1939, as well as the ferocious purges in eastern Poland in 1939 and 1940, left them none to eager to exchange one tyranny for another. Consequently, as the Red Army approached, the Poles rose in furious revolt in an attempt to liberate their capital before the Soviets arrived. Shortly before Soviet armor reached the outskirts of Warsaw, Stalin established his own Polish government, consisting of Communists obedient to him. The dictator certainly had no interest in helping anti-Communists establish themselves in Poland. Despite desperate Polish resistance, with Soviet forces totally quiescent, the Germans had little trouble crushing the rebellion.

An attempt on Hitler's life on July 20 added to the already difficult relations between the Führer and his officer corps. A small group of anti-Nazi officers placed a bomb in Hitler's daily conference. It exploded, killing a number of those present, but only slightly injuring Hitler. The SS quickly arrested the plotters and extinguished all hopes of a coup. General Guderian then became the army chief of staff and sought to rectify Germany's desperate situation by Nazi fanaticism and enthusiasm. Generals loyal to the regime, such as Guderian and Rundstedt, sat on courts of honor that stripped their comrades of rank and privilege before turning them over to Nazi "justice." Most conspirators suffered hideous deaths. Rommel was accused of cooperating with the conspiracy, but Hitler permitted him to commit suicide on October 14, 1944. Treachery and treason became Hitler's explanation for all Germany's defeats.

By early September, the Germans faced the Soviets with a patched together front. A message from the commander of Army Group North, Field Marshal Schörner, to a division commander suggests the kind of leadership that the German army had by 1944: "Major General Charles de Beaulieu is to be told that he is to restore his own and his division's honor by a courageous deed or I [the army commander] will chase him out in disgrace. Furthermore, he is to report by 2100 which commanders he has had shot or is having shot for cowardice."*

Collapse in the Balkans

In Romania the front had been quiet since April. Army Group South Ukraine had watched as a steady drain of its forces occurred. Its staff worried about the collapse of Marshal Antonescu's authority in Romania; defeats over the past two years and arrival of Soviet armies on the frontier had convinced most Romanians that they must abandon the disastrous German alliance. But commanders on the spot could convince neither Hitler nor OKH of the serious political situation since German experts in Bucharest reported all was well.

By early August the Germans had picked up indications that the quiet spell in the south would soon end. Given the catastrophes in the center and in Normandy, OKH could not reinforce Romania. On August 20, 1944, two Soviet fronts with ninety divisions, six tank and mechanized corps, and more than 900,000 troops attacked. By nightfall Soviet forces were in the open. The Romanians resisted at first but then refused to fight; Soviet spearheads were already encircling Sixth Army.

On the 23rd, worse news awaited the Germans. The young king, Michael, called Antonescu to the palace; as had happened with Mussolini, the king dismissed the marshal, arrested him, and dissolved the government. That night Michael announced that Romania would join the Allied nations and denounced the Treaty of Vienna, which had given Transylvania to Hungary. To free the German mission and overthrow the new government, Hitler authorized German air and ground forces to attack Bucharest.

---

*Earl F. Ziemke, *Stalingrad to Berlin: The German Defeat in the East* (Washington: Office of the Chief of Military History, 1968), p. 342.

However, fighting on the outskirts of Bucharest, as well as the bombing of the royal palace, only solidified support for the king.

As the Germans struggled to cope with political collapse, the military situation went from bad to worse. Romania's defection, followed by its declaration of war on August 25, placed every German unit in Romania at hazard. By the 27th, Army Group South Ukraine had collapsed. The Soviets cut Sixth Army into two separate pockets; in the debacle the Wehrmacht lost eighteen divisions and the headquarters of five corps. Moreover, the Romanians surrounded German forces in Bucharest, while at Ploesti they drove the 5th Flak Division from the oil refineries. Remnants of Army Group South Ukraine withdrew northwest and by September 15 had occupied positions along the spine of the Carpathian Mountains in a new line east of Budapest.

Bulgaria's defection followed on the heels of the Romanian collapse. The Bulgarians had never declared war on the USSR, and on September 2 they unilaterally ended their state of war with the Western Powers. But that was not enough for Stalin. On September 8 Third Ukrainian Front moved into Bulgaria, and the Bulgarians declared war on Germany. German forces in Greece and Macedonia were now in danger of isolation. Even Hitler recognized that there was no hope of holding the southern Balkans. A desperate retreat north began through the partisan-infested countryside of Yugoslavia. Yugoslav partisans harassed the retreating Germans but could not cut them off. The British, landing in Greece, pursued hesitantly, and Allied air power missed some substantial opportunities to interdict the escaping Germans. By mid-October most of the German forces had escaped from Greece and Macedonia.

But this temporary success did little to improve the situation. In early October the Hungarian leader, Admiral Miklos Horthy, signed an armistice with the Soviets. His government and the Hungarian army remained badly divided. Some Hungarians wanted to fight on, but many recognized Germany's hopeless position. Quick action by SS commanders overthrew Horthy's regime and installed a pro-Nazi puppet government. But Hungarian morale hit rock bottom as many senior generals, including the chief of staff, deserted. In some cases whole units went over to the Soviets.

Meanwhile the Red Army began a relentless push toward Budapest. The Germans, given their defeats elsewhere, lacked sufficient strength for a successful defense, while the Hungarians were on their last legs. In early November the Red Army fought its way into the suburbs of Budapest. By late December Soviet spearheads had closed around the city and surrounded four German and two Hungarian divisions. Hitler regarded Budapest as a symbol like Stalingrad, one that represented Germany's fanatical determination to see the war through to the end. While the Germans had made extensive preparations to withstand a siege, they did little to prepare for the needs of Budapest's one million civilians. Guderian, summing up the moral sensibilities of Hitler's military circle, commented that the requirements of the civilian population were immaterial.

★   ★   ★   ★

Events in the Mediterranean and on the Eastern Front represented a series of unmitigated disasters for the Germans from 1942 to 1944. By the winter of 1944 the Soviets had regained the Ukraine, and in the summer of 1944 they executed one of the most successful offensives of the war, Bagration, destroying all of Army Group Center and twenty-eight German divisions. In fall the Red Army liberated much of the Balkans and added that region to Stalin's empire. The Allies also made major gains in the Mediterranean, but they engaged considerably smaller German forces than the Soviets. By late 1943, British and American forces had driven Axis forces out of North Africa, captured Sicily, knocked Italy out of the war, and seized the air bases in southern Italy necessary to attack Romanian oil targets and Austria. Nevertheless, hard fighting remained before the entire Italian peninsula fell into Allied hands.

As the Allies pushed back Axis forces, the war attained new levels of scale and mechanization. At the battle of Kursk, the combatants employed about 7,000 tanks; in Operation Bagration, the Soviets committed 124 divisions and 4,000 tanks; in the landings on Sicily, the Allies launched an immense amphibious assault of seven divisions. On the Eastern Front, the Soviets overwhelmed the Germans with vast armies, supported by thousands of aircraft, while in North Africa, Sicily, and Italy, the Allies used enormous amounts of firepower to batter their way forward. As the toll of numerous battles reduced the Axis forces, the Germans slowly lost their qualitative edge, and the Allies became more proficient in planning and executing complicated and effective campaigns.

SUGGESTED READINGS

Bidwell, Shelford, and Dominick Graham. *Tug of War: The Battle for Italy, 1943–1945* (New York: St. Martin's Press, 1986).

Blumenson, Martin. *Kasserine Pass* (Boston: Houghton Mifflin, 1967).

———. *Mark Clark* (New York: Congdon & Weed, 1984).

———. *Masters of the Art of Command* (Boston: Houghton Mifflin, 1975).

Erickson, John. *The Road to Berlin* (Boulder, Col.: Westview Press, 1983).

———. *The Road to Stalingrad* (New York: Harper & Row, 1975).

Hardesty, Von. *Red Phoenix: The Rise of Soviet Air Power, 1941–1945* (Washington: Smithsonian Institution Press, 1982).

Howard, Michael. *The Mediterranean Strategy in the Second World War* (New York: Praeger, 1968).

von Mellenthin, Friedrich W. *Panzer Battles: A Study of the Employment of Armor in the Second World War*, trans. H. Betzler (Norman: University of Oklahoma Press, 1956).

Sajer, Guy. *The Forgotten Soldier*, trans. Lily Emmet (New York: Harper & Row, 1971).

Wray, Timothy A. *Standing Fast: German Defensive Doctrine on the Russian Front During World War II* (Fort Leavenworth: Combat Studies Institute, 1986).

Zhukov, Georgii K. *Marshal Zhukov's Greatest Battles,* trans. Theodore Shabad (New York: Harper & Row, 1969).

Ziemke, Earl F., and Magna E. Bauer, *Moscow to Stalingrad: Decision in the East* (Washington: Office of the Chief of Military History, 1987).

Ziemke, Earl F. *Stalingrad to Berlin: The German Defeat in the East* (Washington: Office of the Chief of Military History, 1968).

5

VICTORY IN EUROPE:
BRUTE FORCE IN THE AIR
AND ON THE GROUND

The Air War, 1944

The Campaign in the West, 1944

The Collapse of Germany

The battles on the periphery of Fortress Europe substantially wore down Germany's military forces. The Wehrmacht's battlefield excellence was no longer so sharply defined as in the earlier years of the war. Moreover, the overwhelming Allied quantitative superiority due to economic mobilization and vast resources provided a factor that no battlefield performance could match. In the west a sustained air battle began in February 1944 and continued for the next three months. When it was over, Allied air forces had broken the Luftwaffe and gained air superiority over the European continent. A successful amphibious landing on the beaches of Normandy immediately followed that success. From the east and west, Allied armies could now batter their way to and across the frontiers of the Reich.

Allied military operations, particularly those of Anglo-American forces, involved a close working of the services in a joint arena; air, sea, and land worked intimately to achieve larger purposes. Nowhere was this clearer than in Normandy and in the subsequent fighting and buildup. Naval and air forces got the ground forces ashore; naval support provided the great highway to the West's industrial might; and air power made the movement and supply of German troops a nightmare. In the end, infantry had to dig the Germans out of their positions in Normandy, hedgerow by hedgerow, but that infantry battle was possible due only to close interservice cooperation within the Allied forces.

The Air War, 1944

The Americans Defeat the Luftwaffe

Throughout fall 1943 and into early 1944, RAF's Bomber Command had waged a relentless campaign to destroy Berlin. But German night defenses recovered from the difficulties of summer 1943, and British losses mounted alarmingly. Nevertheless, as Bomber Command confronted defeat in its night offensive, the U.S. Eighth Air Force, supported by Fifteenth Air Force in Italy, returned to the attack. Not only had American bomber strength reached new levels, but now long-range escort fighters, in particular the P-51 Mustang, accompanied bomber formations all the way to targets deep in Germany. The P-51, the best piston-engine fighter of World War II, had out-standing aerial combat capabilities and the range with drop tanks even to reach Berlin.

In February 1944 the weather cleared sufficiently for Eighth Air Force to begin attacks on the German aircraft industry. The result was a massive battle of attrition that cost both sides heavily; the battle lasted until May when the German fighter force finally collapsed. Aiming to strangle production and deprive the Luftwaffe of its aircraft, the Americans initially attacked the factories manufacturing Luftwaffe fighters, but the raids failed to accomplish the objective. Despite savage pounding, the Germans raised

Due to flaws in doctrine and limitations in technology, Americans failed to develop an effective long-range day light escort fighter until early 1944. By May, however, fighters like the P-51 Mustang had won general air superiority over Europe.

fighter production by 55.9 percent during 1944, but only by shutting down production of other aircraft. The overall weight of airframes produced actually rose only 20 percent in 1944 and reflected a heavy emphasis on single-engine fighters. The new fighters also showed a marked decline in quality compared to earlier production runs.

Ironically, the offensive destroyed the Luftwaffe's air defenses, but in an entirely unforeseen fashion. The appearance of escort fighters deep in Germany represented a catastrophe for the Luftwaffe. The experience of one Bf 110 Group that scrambled twenty-one aircraft against B-17s in March was not atypical. In that incident the Germans shot down two B-17s but suffered heavily: four aircraft missing (three pilots bailed out), one crash-landing (pilot killed), another written off on landing, and three aircraft crashes on takeoff.

By early March, Eighth Air Force's new commander, Major General Doolittle, ordered his fighters to attack German airfields with low-level strikes. American fighter and bomber formations suffered heavy losses, but the Germans lost more heavily. Luftwaffe fighter-pilot losses reached an unsustainable level. In January the Germans lost 12.1 percent of their fighter pilots, killed, missing or wounded; in February, 17.9; in March, 21.7; in April, 20.1; and in May, 25 percent. From January to May the Luftwaffe averaged 2,283 pilots available in the fighter force; in that same period it lost 2,262 fighter pilots. In May 1944 the defenders cracked; the heavy losses that Allied bombers had been suffering dropped dramatically. From this point, while some daylight raids did suffer heavy losses, the Americans had won general air superiority over Europe.

Supporting the Invasion

In April, Allied air strategy changed direction. "Overlord," the invasion of the European continent, was finally ready. With achievement of air superiority over Europe, airmen had met the crucial precondition for a successful invasion. By the decision of the combined chiefs of staff, Overlord's supreme commander, General Dwight Eisenhower, commanded all air assets as of April 1, 1944. His chief deputy, RAF Marshal Sir Arthur Tedder, with advice from the scientist, Solly Zuckerman, had designed a plan to isolate Normandy by means of air interdiction. If successful, the air campaign would enable the Allies to win the logistic buildup once the battle began.

Eisenhower and Tedder ran into considerable opposition from Allied airmen. Lieutenant General Carl A. Spaatz, commander of U.S. Army Air Forces in England, argued for continuing the attack on the German aircraft industry. His planners, however, were already turning toward a new target, the German petroleum industry—which they believed represented the crucial weak link in the enemy's economy. Not surprisingly, Air Marshal Arthur Harris, commander of Bomber Command argued vociferously against air cooperation with Overlord. In particular, he worried disingenuously that attacks on French railroads would kill tens of thousands of innocent Frenchmen. Harris knew that Churchill desperately feared the postwar repercussions of such casualties.

Eisenhower and Tedder responded easily to the objections of American airmen: raids against German aircraft targets would continue, and in May attacks on oil targets would begin. Harris's claims were more difficult because of their political ramifications. However, Zuckerman discovered that Bomber Command based its estimates of French casualties on the pattern of night raids with many hundreds of bombers, when in fact French railway targets demanded attacks of no more than 100 to 200 bombers. Moreover, by this point British navigational devices were so accurate that Bomber Command could execute its attacks with great precision. The first tests showed that Bomber Command could hit targets even more accurately than Eighth Air Force. With his arguments disproved, Harris fell into line. Among the many night attacks, one on Vaires not only demolished the marshaling yard, but also caught trains from the 10th SS Panzer Division (*Frundsberg*) intermingled with a consignment of naval mines. When it was all over, the Germans collected identity disks from nearly 1,200 dead.

Out of the eighty most important transportation targets, Bomber Command attacked thirty-nine, Eighth Air Force, twenty-three, and tactical air forces, eighteen. Losses were heavy. Between April 1 and June 5, Allied air forces lost nearly 2,000 aircraft and 12,000 officers and enlisted men. But the attacks proved crucial. Beginning in early April, a precipitous drop in French railway traffic occurred. Attacks by fighter bombers on the Seine River bridges and trains further accelerated the decline. By late May, just prior to the attacks on the Seine bridges, rail traffic in France had dropped to 55 percent of January levels. By June 6, the destruction of the Seine bridges had reduced traffic levels to 30 percent, and by the end of July to 10 percent. By mid-June trains had virtually ceased to operate in western France. As the campaign progressed, Ultra intercepts and decrypts provided air commanders with crucial insights into the campaign's progress.

Air interdiction placed the Germans in an impossible situation. Since much of the Wehrmacht consisted of infantry divisions with horse-drawn equipment, the Germans depended on railroads to move reserves and supplies. Removal of that support made it difficult to redeploy forces once the invasion began. Destruction of the transportation network also forced German infantry to fight without adequate artillery support and even at times basic infantry supplies. Moreover, damage to roads and bridges made it difficult for motorized and mechanized units to reinforce the front. Thus air interdiction proved invaluable in winning the battle of France.

The Offensive Against the Petroleum Industry

Since 1939 the Germans had worried about petroleum. Romanian oil production was declining and difficult to get up the Danube River, and much of the Reich's oil came from synthetic plants that required great amounts of coal, the one natural resource Germany enjoyed in abundance. But the manufacture of synthetic fuels required refineries with miles of pipelines and production facilities, all vulnerable to air attack. In April 1944 a Luftwaffe staff officer warned that Germany's refineries and fuel plants lay within "the

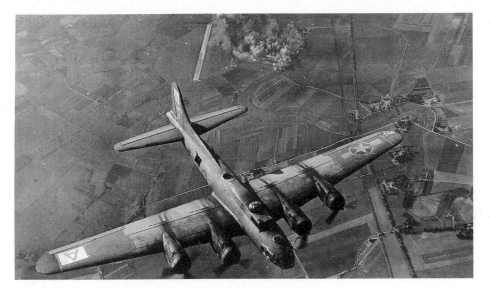

The Boeing B-17 Flying Fortress was the workhorse of the American strategic bombing campaign in Europe. The normal maximum radius of action for the B-17 and B-24 was 850 miles; this range could be extended with auxiliary fuel tanks or reduced bomb loads.

zone threatened by air attack," and he found it inexplicable that the Allies had not yet attacked the oil industry—a target that would jeopardize Germany's entire war effort.

One month later his warnings came true. Eisenhower released Eighth Air Force from invasion preparations to attack oil targets. On May 12,935 B-17s and B-24s attacked the major synthetic oil plants. American losses were heavy, forty-six bombers and twelve fighters. The results were encouraging but not decisive, for the plant at Leuna, although damaged, lost only 18 percent of capacity. Ultra, however, reported a major redistribution of Luftwaffe Flak units to protect the synthetic refineries; this report alerted Allied airmen to the seriousness with which the Germans viewed the attacks. Nine days later another Ultra message indicated that Allied air attacks on oil facilities, including those in Romania, had forced the German high command to reduce fuel allocations.

After feverish efforts to repair the damage, production had almost returned to normal by the end of May. On May 28–29, Eighth and Fifteenth air forces launched another series of attacks. In the two-day air battle, both sides suffered heavy losses. The Americans lost eighty-four bombers, but the Germans lost thirty-nine single-engine fighter pilots killed or missing (twenty-one more wounded) and a further thirty-three crew members of twin-engine fighters either killed or wounded. These two attacks combined with raids against the Romanian oil fields at Ploesti to reduce German petroleum production by 50 percent. Since the Germans had virtually no oil reserves, they faced a catastrophic situation.

The attacks in May were a prelude to devastating, follow-on raids in succeeding months. New attacks in mid-June knocked out 90 percent of aviation fuel production; by the end of July successive Allied raids had lowered aviation gas production by 98 percent. When Ultra detected German efforts to restore production, follow-on attacks wrecked the repair work and what little capacity remained.

The impact of these oil attacks on Germany's strategic situation was enormous. The raids severely restricted the Luftwaffe's frontline force in its ability to defend the Reich against strategic bombers. By mid-summer, Speer's desperate efforts to restore fighter production had borne bitter fruit. New aircraft were available in increasing numbers, but insufficient fuel grounded most of them. Furthermore, without fuel the Luftwaffe could no longer train new pilots. Thus the Luftwaffe, battered into desperate condition by its mauling in the spring, could not maintain the uneven contest.

Fuel shortages were no less serious for the army. Combat operations suffered immediately; training became impossible. The Ardennes offensive, launched in December 1944, had enough fuel to get panzer spearheads only to the Meuse River; the attackers hoped to advance the rest of the way to Antwerp by capturing Allied fuel dumps. In February 1945 the German defenders of Silesia possessed over 1,100 tanks. Nevertheless, the Soviets conquered much of the province in less than one week, because the defenders had virtually no fuel. The German soldier rarely, if ever, saw the Luftwaffe overhead; throughout 1944 and 1945 he was pounded on every front by enemy aircraft, while supplies, attacked by both day and night, reached him with decreasing frequency.

The Campaign in the West, 1944

Italy

At the end of 1943 a major reshuffling of Allied commanders took place between the Mediterranean and Britain. Eisenhower became the Supreme Commander Allied Forces Europe. In every respect, he was an inspired choice. He was a first-rate strategist and operational commander, but above all he possessed political gifts that allowed him to lead and work with a quarrelsome group of senior Allied commanders. A number of other commanders moved from the Mediterranean. Tedder became Eisenhower's deputy; Montgomery became the land force commander. Among other Americans, Patton, still on probation, and Lieutenant General Omar N. Bradley journeyed to London, while Spaatz and Doolittle assumed control of American air forces in Britain. The Italian campaign, however, was not over; it continued as a secondary theater as Allied forces fought their way up the Italian peninsula.

Late 1943 and early 1944 found Anglo-American forces in Italy in a disconcerting position. The drive of the 15th Army Group under General Sir Harold Alexander had stalled well short of Rome. In four months the Allies had advanced only seventy miles beyond Salerno. The Gustav Line, a German defensive position set in the rugged Apennines, proved impervious

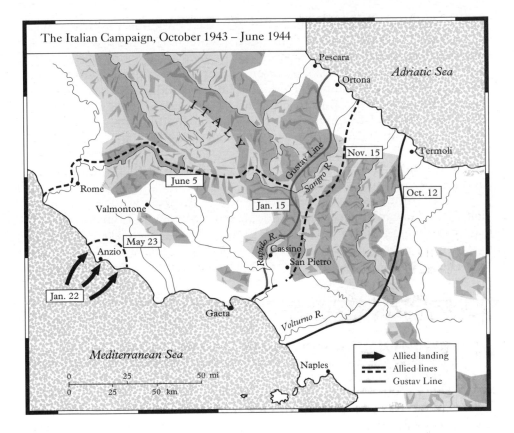

The Italian Campaign, October 1943 – June 1944

to attack. Frustrated, the Allies decided to make an amphibious landing south of Rome in coordination with another assault on the Gustav Line. They expected the amphibious assault to force the Germans to evacuate the Gustav Line and withdraw north of Rome. The target of the amphibious landing was the small town of Anzio, about sixty miles behind the Gustav Line. Chosen to command the landing was Major General John P. Lucas with his VI Corps. The attack was a combined operation with the British 1st and the American 3rd divisions making the initial landings. Assisting were commando and ranger units, a parachute regiment, and two tank battalions. Two more divisions were immediately available, U.S. 1st Armored and 45th Infantry divisions.

Unfortunately the landings in January 1944, known as Operation "Shingle," replayed the Suvla Bay fiasco of the 1915 British attack on Gallipoli. The first day went like clockwork; the landings at Anzio caught the Germans completely by surprise; the only Germans in the immediate vicinity were three drunken officers in a Volkswagen command vehicle who drove down the beach and into an LST. Within twenty-five miles of the beach were members of an engineer battalion who offered little or no resistance. By the end of the first day the Allies had landed 36,034 troops and over 3,000 vehicles. At the end of the second day VI Corps occupied a beachhead seven miles deep. The road to Rome lay open, and VI Corps was in a position to cut supply routes to the Gustav Line.

But before the invasion, Lucas expressed profound misgivings at its prospects. The Fifth Army commander, Lieutenant General Mark Clark, added to Lucas's caution by advising him not to stick his neck out. As a result, Lucas refused to exploit favorable circumstances and ordered his forces to remain inside the beachhead. The Allies did little more than consolidate their positions. But the Germans, never ones to waste time, reacted with dispatch, and by midnight on the day of landing, they had 20,000 troops closing in on Anzio. Within one week, they had concentrated elements from eight divisions and launched a series of counterattacks that nearly drove the Allies into the sea. Far from opening up the front, the Anzio landings soon represented a substantial liability.

Just prior to the Anzio landing, the Fifth Army attacked the lower half of the Gustav Line with a British, an American, and a French corps. As part of this operation, the U.S. 36th Infantry Division attacked across the Rapido River on January 20; its efforts failed miserably with almost 1,700 casualties. Neither this attack nor others broke German lines. Interdiction by Allied air forces also had little effect on the defenders; in some cases Allied air power even helped the Germans. At the abbey of Monte Casino, German paratroopers threw back every attack by Fifth Army; a major air raid on February 15 then destroyed the abbey completely. But in the scattered wreckage, German paratroopers waged an even more effective defense.

In May the balance of forces between the opposing sides finally reached the point where Allied air power, interdicting supplies from the north and pounding the front lines, combined with the overwhelming superiority of ground forces to break the deadlock. On May 11, the Allied offensive began. For three days attacks made little progress against stiff enemy resistance; but the ill-equipped Free French broke the stalemate by driving over the mountains where the Germans least expected an advance. Their success opened the Gustav Line to penetrations elsewhere. American forces at Anzio, now ably commanded by Major General Lucian K. Truscott, broke out of the beachhead, and German defenses collapsed. Truscott's VI Corps was positioned to trap many of the German defenders had it driven inland, but Clark ordered Truscott to turn north and capture Rome instead, which VI Corps did on June 5. Though Clark's capture of Rome grabbed the front pages of America's newspapers, much of the German Tenth Army escaped to fight another day.

Still, the Allies pushed the Germans northward until the front line stabilized on the Gothic Line north of Florence. In mid-August many of the U.S. and all of the Free French combat units moved off to participate in landings in southern France as part of Operation "Anvil" (later renamed "Dragoon"). The Italian theater again settled into stalemate. Some historians have claimed that Anvil prevented the Allies from driving through the Po River valley and on into the Alps and Austria. Such claims seem improbable. Not until the following April did the Allies finally break the deadlock and surge into Austria, but by that point the Wehrmacht was collapsing on every front.

What did the Italian theater contribute to victory? Through summer 1943 it proved an excellent training ground for Anglo-American forces.

The rough terrain of Italy restricted the mobility of the highly motorized American troops. In terrain where trucks could not move, mules provided valuable assistance in transporting weapons and supplies.

Moreover, the casualties the Allies inflicted on German ground and air forces in Tunisia and Sicily were a significant return on investment. After that point, however, Italy cost more than it gained. The skill and tenacity of German troops combined with difficult terrain and weather to make this a dismal theater indeed.

Northern France

In a speech to the French people in October 1940, Winston Churchill said: "Good night, then: sleep to gather strength for the morning. For the morning will come. Brightly will it shine on the brave and the true, kindly upon all who suffer for the cause, glorious upon the tombs of heroes. Thus will shine the dawn." Dawn came June 6, 1944, but only after immense preparations and a massive mobilization of manpower and resources in both Britain and the United States. The complexity of a cross-Channel invasion did not become fully apparent until after the Dieppe raid of August 1942. In that attack British commandoes and Canadian troops attempted to seize the French port of Dieppe. Anticipating less than 1,500 German defenders, they encountered three times that many, plus ample reserves, most of whom were third-line infantry. The Dieppe defeat suggested that an invading army could not gain a French port in the invasion's first days; an extremely powerful landing force would have to make the invasion over open beaches. In the end, the planners for Normandy had almost two years to absorb Dieppe's lessons, as well as those of other amphibious landings the Allies executed in the European and Pacific theaters. Consequently, the Normandy landing was perhaps the most thoroughly planned battle in the history of warfare.

A cross-Channel invasion presented enormous logistic difficulties. Not only men but also supplies would have to be down-loaded into landing craft and then moved to beaches in small boats for another unloading. Moreover, the northern French beaches fronted directly on the English Channel, which was famous for its rough and unpredictable seas. Consequently, the Allies required landing craft in far greater numbers than planners had initially envisaged. A worldwide shortage of such craft and demands from the Pacific created major hurdles. Only in 1944 did the Allies possess sufficient landing craft to make an invasion possible. Beyond landing craft, the planners decided to supply the beachhead through artificial harbors. In the first days of Overlord, Allied naval forces thus had the task of funneling hundreds of thousands of men and tons of equipment into France and of constructing two "Mulberry" artificial harbors, including breakwaters, piers, and landing facilities to speed the buildup.

The size of the invasion demanded general air superiority. During the Dieppe landing, the Luftwaffe had caused serious losses among landing

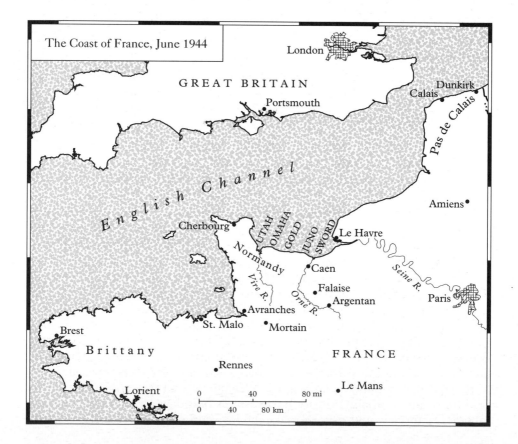

The Coast of France, June 1944

craft and naval vessels supporting the raid. But the victory of American air power over the Luftwaffe in spring 1944 removed that threat; the Luftwaffe would hardly get an aircraft over the crowded beaches of Normandy on June 6.

By summer 1943 planning was well underway; in November 1943 the planners received approval for the initial design for Overlord. They had rejected the easily accessible area around Pas de Calais, because that area was also obvious to the Germans, had received much of the effort to fortify the coast, and could be attacked from three different directions by German reserves. Instead the planners selected Normandy: it was farther removed from enemy reserves, the ocean could protect the invading force's western flank, and Allied air power could more easily isolate the battlefield from enemy reinforcements and resupply.

Logistic planning rested on a belief that once ashore the advance into France would be slow. Anticipating a methodical, rather than mobile campaign, the logisticians failed to prepare for swift movements that could consume vast quantities of gasoline. Exacerbating this miscalculation was the fact that through the end of July the battles in Normandy consumed more ammunition and less fuel than predicted. At the beginning of August, Allied logisticians increased ammunition allocations and decreased those of fuel—at precisely the moment when the campaign turned mobile.

By January the Allied high command was in place. Eisenhower commanded Supreme Headquarters Allied Expeditionary Forces, while Montgomery commanded 21st Army Group with responsibility for the landing. Under Montgomery was the British First Army (Lieutenant General Sir Miles C. Dempsey) and the U.S. First Army (Lieutenant General Bradley). Upon arrival in Britain, Eisenhower and Montgomery examined and rejected plans to land three divisions over the beaches and to drop one airborne division inland. They believed that such forces were inadequate to the task and that the initial landings would have to consist of five divisions, supported by three airborne divisions dropped inland.

The Allies would come ashore on five separate beaches; from east to west they were Sword, Juno, Gold, Omaha, and Utah. The British and Canadians would land on the three eastern beaches, the Americans on the two western beaches. On the eastern side, the British 6th Airborne would seize the Orne River bridges. On the other end of the front, the American 82nd and 101st Airborne would shield the westernmost beaches—the most exposed landing site. Above all, the Allies would have to get maximum men and equipment ashore before the Germans launched a strong counterstroke.

In the German high command, disunity and disharmony marked Nazi preparations. Field Marshal Rundstedt was in overall command in the west, but he lacked control over air and naval units and had only limited control of SS and parachute units. His chief subordinate was Rommel, who as commander of Army Group B, held responsibility for the immediate defense of western Europe. Above both hovered Hitler's disruptive influence; the Führer was determined to keep the levers for defending France firmly within his grasp. Consequently, neither Rundstedt nor Rommel had authority to move the mobile formations that made up the reserves. Moreover, they differed on how best to defend France. Rundstedt believed that German forces should conduct a mobile defense to inflict maximum casualties on the Allies; Rommel argued that superior Allied resources, air power, and manpower demanded that the Wehrmacht stop the invasion on the beaches. Should the Anglo-American force gain a foothold, he believed the war would be lost.

Rommel threw himself into the task of defending France with his usual energy. Under his inspiring leadership, German engineers laid millions of mines; beach defenses and obstacles sprouted; and "Rommel asparagus" (telephone poles with wire strung between them) spread across French fields to destroy Allied gliders. The construction of beach obstacles below the high-tide line forced the Allies to land at low tide; consequently, the landing had to take place between June 4 and 8, when low tide and dawn coincided.

The weather almost did not cooperate. After excellent weather in May, storms blew in from the Atlantic, and only on June 5 did conditions clear up sufficiently for Eisenhower to launch the invasion. However, the period of bad weather helped the Allies achieve tactical surprise. Rommel was in Germany visiting his wife, while the commander of Seventh Army and most of his corps and division commanders were away from their headquarters to participate in a war game.

Normandy

As dusk settled over airfields in England on June 5, paratroopers from three airborne divisions clambered aboard their aircraft. The first pathfinders were down in France before midnight. The British Sixth Airborne Division quickly seized the key bridges on the landing's eastern flank. The two American divisions were more dispersed on landing. In some areas heavy Flak greeted American transport aircraft; as a result troops from the 82nd and 101st divisions dropped all over western Normandy. But their spread confused the Germans, and the Americans achieved their purpose of preventing reinforcements from moving on Utah beach.

In the grey dawn of June 6, Allied troops came ashore on five different landing beaches. The assault went well on the British beaches and on Utah. Nevertheless, despite their gains, the British and Canadians failed to take full advantage of the situation. One Canadian battalion almost reached Caen but was ordered to pull back by the brigade commander because such a move was not in the plans. That night, the 12th SS Panzer Division (*Hitler Jugend*) moved into place, and the British and Canadians did not capture Caen for a month and a half. British official history attributed the failure to capture Caen on the first day to the unexpectedly high tide, congestion on the shore, strength of opposition, and a lack of urgency.

Only on Omaha did the Germans hold the attackers on the beach for a substantial period of time. Instead of encountering light defenses, the U.S. 1st Infantry Division, reinforced by elements of the 29th Infantry Division, ran head on into the 352nd Division, which had recently moved into the area. Because of strong currents and poor navigation, the Americans landed

American paratroopers prepare to jump from C-47 Dakota transport planes. Airborne forces in the enemy's rear areas in Sicily, Salerno, and Normandy confused and harassed the enemy and gave the Allies a greater chance of success.

on different parts of the beach than planned and then came under withering fire from well-placed Germans. Most of the special tanks that could supposedly "swim" sank in heavy swells, as did much of the artillery carried in amphibious trucks. For a time Bradley considered diverting follow-on forces from Omaha to other beaches. But small groups of soldiers began advancing under fire and somehow drove the Germans from the heights. By the end of the day infantry from the two divisions had pushed two miles inland, and bulldozers were clearing paths to the heights. By the morning of D+1, the Allies had over 177,000 troops ashore in four secure beachheads, and the buildup was already well underway.

The Allied success received considerable help from the Germans. As early as 0400 hours, German commanders on the scene requested release of the armor to launch a counterblow. But Hitler was asleep, and the OKW's chief of operations, General Alfred Jodl, refused to release the reserves or to wake the Führer. Not until late in the afternoon did the German high command allow 21st Panzer Division to attack, while other armored divisions were too far away from Normandy or released too late to participate in the first day's fighting.

Two distinct battles soon developed in Normandy, the British and Canadians fighting in the east, and the Americans in the west. Both efforts

While balloons provided protection against low-flying aircraft, an armada of ships poured thousands of men and tons of equipment and supplies onto the Normandy beaches.

involved a massive application of firepower, air power, and superior resources against the Germans. In the west, before driving south, the Americans were supposed to turn right, advance across and then up the Cotentin Peninsula to capture Cherbourg, but the port did not fall until June 27. To make matters worse, the Germans sabotaged the port facilities thoroughly, and Allied ships could not use its piers until August 7. In July the Allies had hoped to land some 725,000 tons of supplies but managed to land only 446,852. After capturing Cherbourg, the Americans concentrated on driving south and breaking through German defenses in western Normandy. Here they ran up against the worst of the *bocage* country and its thick hedgerows; virtually every field and village offered heavy cover for the defenders. Nevertheless, slowly, but inexorably, the Americans drove the Germans back.

On the eastern side, the British and Canadians fought in terrain more open and favorable than the hedgerow country. Dempsey, the British ground force commander, had his chances to make more substantial gains near Caen. On June 12, XXX Corps sensed a weakness in German positions. Seventh Armored Division got its lead brigade through German lines in undamaged condition. But upon reaching Villers-Bocage, the lead column consisting of tanks, soft-skinned vehicles, and supply trucks in peacetime formation came under fire on its flank from five Tiger tanks from the

501st SS Heavy Tank Battalion. In a one-sided action, the Tigers caught the British completely by surprise and destroyed almost the entire column. By the time the battle was over, the German tankers had destroyed twenty-five tanks and twenty-eight other armored vehicles and thrown 7th Armored back to its start line.

By July 1 the Allies held only a small portion of the area anticipated by Overlord planning. Caen remained in German hands. Seeking to capture that city, the British launched major offensives on July 8 and 18. Finally capturing Caen but failing to break through the enemy's positions, they drew German armor piecemeal into a battle of attrition that wore away the enemy's armored reserve.

Eisenhower identified three factors that made fighting in Normandy extremely difficult: "First, as always, the fighting quality of the German soldier; second, the nature of the country; third, the weather." The tired, weary, outnumbered, and outgunned German infantry displayed superior tactical skills and initiative compared to their opponents, and the terrain of the bocage country served only to exacerbate the imbalance. Operating in small units, they relied on an active defense and made limited counterattacks with local reserves and small groups of tanks. Soft ground limited the mobility of the highly mechanized Allied forces, and hedgerows divided the battlefield into numerous rectangular compartments that the Germans skillfully tied together. As for the weather, the amount of wind and rain in July exceeded that of any time in the past half-century and hampered air support and mobility. In the month of July, the U.S. First Army suffered about 40,000 casualties, 90 percent of whom were infantrymen. One American infantry regiment that entered combat shortly after D-day had only four officers remaining from its original complement in the third week of July.

As the Germans reinforced Normandy, extensive damage to the transportation system and road network made movement difficult. Allied fighter bombers dominated the daylight hours, while night movement was difficult. The French resistance added to German discomfiture by sniping and creating numerous obstacles. Units of 2nd SS Panzer Division (*Das Reich*) took nearly two weeks to arrive in Normandy from Limoges, a journey that should have taken two days. Along the way they committed a number of atrocities, the worst of which occurred at Oradour-sur-Glane and involved the murder of about 650 French civilians. The men were machine-gunned in open fields, and the women and children were burned to death in the village church.

As Allied forces poured into Normandy, German difficulties mounted. Ultra picked up the location of Panzer Group West's Headquarters, and an immediate strike by Allied tactical air destroyed the only headquarters in the west capable of coordinating movement of large panzer formations. The supply situation was catastrophic; only desperate measures kept the front lines from collapsing. Rommel was at his wits' end; on July 17 a fighter bomber attack badly wounded the field marshal and sent him home where Hitler would order him to commit suicide for participation in the July 20 assassination attempt. Hitler also relieved Rundstedt. In his case, in reply to Jodl's rhetorical question, "What shall we do?," the blunt old field marshal had replied: "End the war. What else can you do?" Rundstedt's replacement was Field Marshal Hans Günther von Kluge, one of Hitler's favorites. After taking over, Kluge told Rommel, "Even you will have to get used to obeying orders." After Rommel's wounding, Kluge also assumed command of Army Group B. The field marshal's experience since 1940 had been exclusively on the Eastern Front, so he had little idea of the immense superiority of Allied air power and its capabilities. He soon learned.

The Breakout

On July 25 the U.S. First Army launched Operation "Cobra," which sought to break through the German defenses at St. Lô. Major General J. Lawton Collins's VII Corps made the main attack with three infantry divisions leading and two armored and one motorized infantry divisions following. A massive bombing of German defenses was to precede the attack. On July 24, however, a major bombing went awry due to bad weather; American bombs killed twenty-five soldiers and wounded another 131. On the next day, under ideal conditions, 1,800 bombers from Eighth Air Force repeated the errors of the preceding day and dropped many bombs within American lines. This time, they killed 111 soldiers, including Lieutenant General

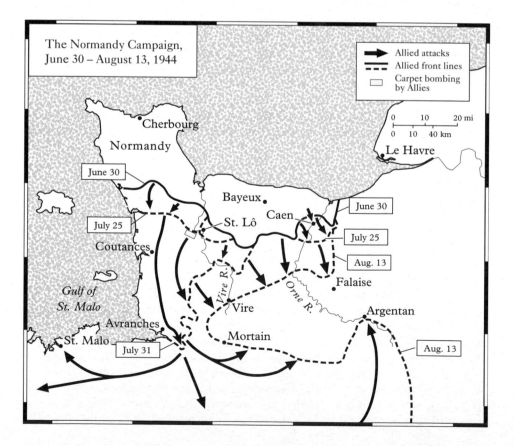

Lesley J. McNair, and wounded 490 others. The attack by the 30th Infantry Division went in anyway against the *Panzer Lehr* division. The Germans, though bloodied and battered, did not break at first. But on July 26 German resistance crumbled. VIII Corps, which was to the west of VII Corps, broke through the defenses on its front, and 4th Armored Division entered Coutances on the 28th and Avranches on the 30th. The swift advance of about thirty-five miles almost doubled the amount of terrain under Allied control.

As Cobra ended, key changes in command occurred. Under a barrage of protests from Montgomery, Eisenhower activated 12th Army Group under Bradley; with Bradley's promotion, Lieutenant General Courtney H. Hodges assumed command of First Army. Bradley in turn activated Patton's Third Army and released Patton from his role as a decoy. To trick the Germans into believing that a second invasion was coming at a location other than Normandy, the Allies had placed the flamboyant American in command of a nonexistent army group and allowed the Germans to collect information about its preparations for assaulting Pas de Calais.

On August 1, American forces poured through the bottleneck at Avranches. To secure the ports in Brittany, the first corps in Patton's Third Army turned west toward St. Malo, Brest, and Lorient. Concerned with logistical support, Overlord planners had aimed for Cherbourg to be turned over to the British as a supply base and for Brittany's ports to serve as a supply base for the Americans. To some, such as Major General John S. Wood, commander of the 4th Armored Division, the move toward the west was in the wrong direction, but the Allies remained concerned about gaining large port facilities. Recognizing the strategic importance of the ports, the Germans ordered them defended to the last man. After rushing through Avranches, 6th Armored Division raced almost 200 miles to reach Brest on August 6. Because Brest was well protected by several hills and streams, as well as numerous defensive positions, VIII Corps brought up three infantry divisions and amassed considerable ammunition reserves before it began a sustained attack on August 25, the day Paris fell. Brest finally fell on September 19, costing almost 10,000 American casualties. In retrospect, the costly siege of Brest seems wasteful and a blind adherence to plans that events had overtaken, especially since the Allies were unable to restore Brest to operating condition before the war ended.

As the area under Allied control expanded dramatically, Bradley decided on August 3, with Montgomery and Eisenhower's concurrence, to stop the movement west into Brittany and to turn American forces to the east. While the Canadian First, British Second, and U.S. First armies continued to battle the Germans in Normandy, three of the corps in Patton's Third Army raced south and then east, one corps driving south to seize Rennes (forty miles from Avranches) on August 3 and another corps driving southeast to seize LeMans (ninety miles from Avranches) on August 8.

Hitler recognized the threat posed by the breakthrough at Avranches. He ordered Kluge to pull the panzer divisions out of the battle against the British and concentrate on cutting off American forces rolling through Avranches. The target for their counterattack was the Norman village of

Mortain (twenty miles east of Avranches). Fortunately for the Allies, Ultra picked up enemy intentions, and Bradley placed strong forces on Mortain's dominating terrain to meet the attack. Moreover, American air power made German daylight movements a nightmare. The offensive failed to reach even its first objectives.

The counterattack at Mortain, however, placed German armor in danger of encirclement. With the Americans at LeMans and with the Canadians south of Caen, Fifth Panzer Army, Seventh Army, and Panzer Group Eberbach were in the middle of a rapidly closing pocket. Hitler reluctantly agreed to withdraw, but the escape exit from the pocket was narrow indeed. Neither Bradley nor Montgomery forced the closure of the pocket, or the "Falaise gap," as it became known. On orders from Bradley, Patton's forces halted at Argentan on August 13 to await the British and Canadians, driving from the north. The Canadian First Army drove south of Caen toward Falaise. On August 14, 800 heavy bombers attacked targets in front of the Canadians, but as at St. Lô, some bombs hit friendly troops, killing or wounding nearly 400. The next day the Canadians continued south but faced strong enemy resistance. At the end of the day on the 15th, they still remained two to three miles from Falaise. Meanwhile, Allied air strikes and artillery hit the mass of Germans fleeing the pocket.

Although the Germans lost more than 60,000 soldiers (killed or captured) and abandoned vast quantities of equipment in the Falaise pocket, large numbers of their best troops escaped. The loss of quantities of weapons did not create insurmountable problems, because German industry was producing vast amounts through Speer's effort. The Allies had let a golden opportunity slip through their fingers by the failure to close the Falaise-Argentan gap.

Advancing Toward the Rhine

The German collapse in France, nevertheless, was complete. Allied armies surged out across France in a wild drive toward the German frontier. On August 15, American and French troops landed in southern France in Operation Dragoon (previously known as Anvil), and German defenses collapsed as the Allies drove up the Rhône River valley. Paris fell on August 25; the Seine represented no obstacle. Unfortunately, the euphoria gripping Allied commanders and troops approaching the Reich turned into overconfidence and a belief that the war was won. The Allies correctly sensed the desperate state of the Wehrmacht, but their overconfidence carried with it seeds of failure.

As Allied forces approached the Seine, Eisenhower reconsidered his campaign strategy. The original plan had called for a halt on the Seine and buildup of supplies for three weeks before a resumption of the advance. Eisenhower knew that once a pursuit had begun, his forces should advance relentlessly, so he decided to press eastward as far as logistics would allow. But he had to decide whether to move on a broad front beyond the Seine River or whether to give priority to a single thrust into Germany.

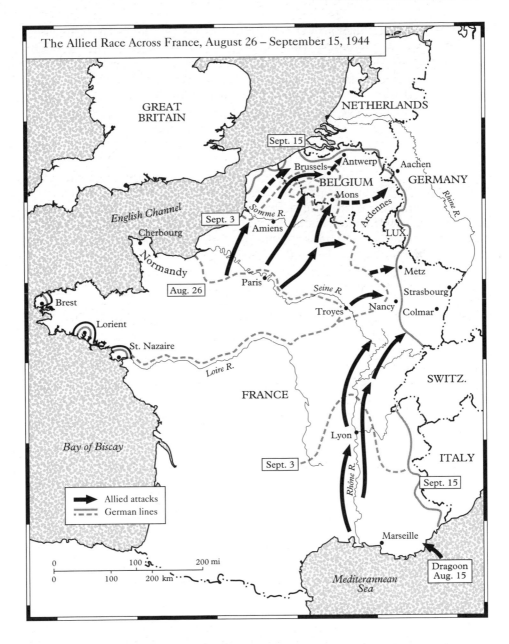

The Allied Race Across France, August 26 – September 15, 1944

The ensuing debate about "Broad Front" versus "Single Thrust" strategy revealed much jealousy and friction between Americans and British. Prior to crossing the Seine, the Allies had envisaged their advancing along two axes into Germany. The northern route went through Amiens, Mons, and Liège to the Ruhr industrial region; the southern one went through Reims, Metz, and the Saar to Frankfurt. On August 23, Montgomery proposed that the bulk of Allied divisions and supplies concentrate under his command for a single thrust along the northern route. On August 29, Eisenhower decided to adhere to the original plan but add weight to the north by having Hodges's First Army move along the northern, rather than southern axis. Montgomery would take Antwerp and drive toward the Ruhr, while Bradley's forces spread across the Ardennes—Hodges's First Army moving north, and Patton's Third Army toward Metz. The decision angered Bradley and Patton, for it weakened 12th Army Group and gave Third Army a low priority for gasoline supplies. On September 1, Eisenhower assumed control of the ground campaign, but not before calling a press conference in London and warmly praising Montgomery. Both 21st and 12th Army groups now reported directly to Supreme Headquarters, Allied Expeditionary Force (SHAEF). Eisenhower insisted that this was not a demotion for Montgomery, who was promoted to field marshal to assuage his ego.

Montgomery drove into Belgium, all the while complaining about shortages of supplies and fuel. He still was pressing for a single thrust—under his command. Arguing that insufficient logistical support existed for more then one major drive, he proposed that Bradley's forces should halt and that all logistic support go to 21st Army Group for the last, decisive blow against a tottering Wehrmacht. Although Montgomery received nearly 80 percent of the logistical support he requested, he missed a golden opportunity to shorten the war. On September 3 British forces captured Brussels; on September 4, 11th Armored Division seized Antwerp so quickly that the Germans could not destroy the port facilities. Everything fell into British hands in undamaged condition; only the opening of the Scheldt estuary stood between the Allies and the relief of their growing supply difficulties. But Montgomery, focusing his attention entirely on the Rhine, missed the logistic implications of Antwerp's capture. Furthermore, by capturing Antwerp, the British were in position to put the German Fifteenth Army in the bag. That sizable force had guarded Pas de Calais and was now fleeing up the coast. An advance of less than ten miles beyond Antwerp would have sealed off the Walcheren and South Beveland peninsula and bottled up Fifteenth Army. But Montgomery halted at Antwerp. Consequently Fifteenth Army, ferrying across the Scheldt at night, escaped to Walcheren Island and then back into Holland.

Montgomery's pause reflected his desire to tidy up the battlefield and bring his forces under tighter control. He proposed to Eisenhower an armored thrust, supported by British and American airborne forces, across Holland and the Rhine into the Reich. Eisenhower agreed to the operation which became known as "Market Garden." From its inception it proved to be badly thought out and, moreover, plagued by bad luck. Similar in conception to the German attack on Holland in May 1940, Montgomery's plan aimed for three airborne divisions to capture the bridges leading up to and over the Rhine. Then, his XXX Corps would drive through the Dutch countryside to the north German plain. The last, crucial bridge lay across the Rhine at Arnhem. Significantly, Montgomery's proposal meant that the Allies would not be able to clear the Scheldt estuary and therefore use Antwerp to relieve growing supply difficulties.

The British needed almost two weeks to get attacking forces ready. While preparations proceeded, the Germans replenished and reorganized their beaten units back into effective fighting formations. The pause also

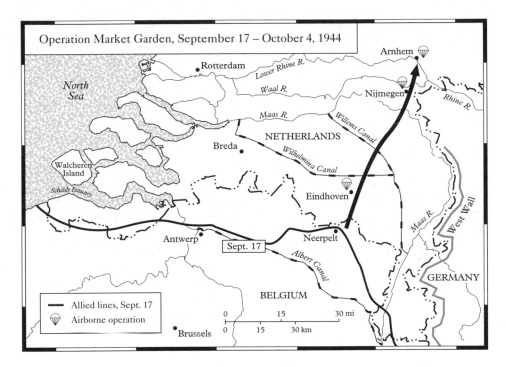

allowed a number of panzer divisions, including 9th and 10th SS Panzer, to withdraw for rest and refit; those two divisions went to southern Holland, while units from Fifteenth Army worked back into fighting trim in the same area. As early as September 5, Bletchley Park indicated that 9th and 10th SS Panzer were in the Arnhem area. Further Ultra decrypts, as well as intelligence from the Dutch underground, reinforced the first warning, but such intelligence made no impression on the British generals.

Montgomery and his airborne commander, Lieutenant General F. A. M. Browning, selected the inexperienced British 1st Airborne Division to capture the most difficult bridge at Arnhem. The more experienced American divisions, the 82nd and 101st, received the easier tasks of securing the bridges at Nijmegen and Eindhoven. Allied airmen then persuaded the inexperienced commanders of 1st Airborne to accept a drop zone six miles from their target because the flight path to the excellent drop zone immediately south of the bridge would expose aircraft to heavy antiaircraft fire.

Market Garden began on September 17 after extensive air attacks prepared the way. It went badly from the first; poor weather interfered with air reinforcements and supply. Despite stringent prohibitions, an American officer carried a complete set of the plans on board one of the attacking gliders; it crashed, killing him and the other occupants. Within hours, those plans were in the hands of General Kurt Student, commander of German paratroopers, who was in the area. The British 1st Airborne got only one battalion to the Arnhem bridge before the Germans sealed off the drop zone. In the south, XXX Corps advanced extremely slowly in its drive north to support the paratroopers; units from the German Fifteenth Army put up a tenacious resistance. Mud and water constrained XXX Corps' movement and forced armored vehicles to advance along a single road, an ideal killing zone for German antitank guns. Market Garden failed short of the Rhine. Though it opened a salient deep into German lines, XXX Corps never reached Arnhem, and the Allies failed to establish a bridgehead across the lower Rhine. Montgomery had prepared everything thoroughly but had wasted the most important commodity in war, time.

On September 22, Eisenhower directed Bradley to support Montgomery's operation with a drive toward Cologne. Bradley in turn ordered First Army to fight its way through the West Wall at Aachen. From October 13 to 21, some of the most bitter house-to-house fighting in the war occurred in that demolished city. As the Allied offensive slowed, it became apparent that the Germans had pulled off what Goebbels termed "the miracle of the west." The German West Wall and fighting around Arnhem, Aachen, and Metz brought the Allied offensive to a halt.

Logistic realities caught up with British and American forces who had outrun their supply system. Allied air power had wrecked the French railroad and road network in preparation for the invasion and breakout and had exacerbated the difficulty of moving Allied supplies. To shorten supply lines and ease the logistic situation, Montgomery had to open the Scheldt, but the Germans had had plenty of time to prepare defenses. Thus the failure to open the Scheldt in early September resulted in bitter and costly fighting. Not until mid-November did the Canadians finish the job. The first supply ship docked in Antwerp on November 28—nearly three months after the British had captured the port.

Weather added to Allied discomfort. British and Americans battered at weary German troops but could not break the deadlock. Swollen rivers and streams made movement difficult. The Germans hung on tenaciously in the hope that the Führer would deliver the promised miracle weapons. The widespread knowledge of the army's and Nazi Germany's criminal behavior throughout the war undoubtedly encouraged many Germans to resist to the bitter end. Moreover, the West Wall, constructed in 1938–1939 along the Reich's western frontier, provided the Wehrmacht with well-positioned defenses, although the Germans had moved most of its guns to the Atlantic Wall in 1943 and 1944.

In an attempt to move forward toward the Ruhr, Eisenhower assigned Bradley responsibility for the main effort. In mid-November the Ninth and First armies on Bradley's left launched an attack on a narrow front near Aachen in another attempt to break through the West Wall. Preceded by the heaviest close-air support bombing attack of the war, American troops encountered strong opposition, particularly in the Huertgen Forest. By early December they had advanced no more than twelve miles. Meanwhile, Patton fought his way beyond Metz. The French First Army, part of Lieutenant General Jacob M. Devers' 6th Army Group, failed to overcome strong German resistance around Colmar and created what became known as the Colmar Pocket west of the Rhine. Despite significant gains, the euphoria that had gripped Allied troops as they raced across France and Belgium had evaporated.

The Collapse of Germany

The Air Contribution

By December 1944 the Allied forces had battered the German army back to the Reich. Now the many pressures brought to bear on Germany worked in combination to broaden the effect of individual efforts. In early September 1944 control of Allied strategic bombing forces returned to the airmen. With the loss of its long-range warning network on the French coast and a sharp decline in oil production, the Luftwaffe could hardly wage an effective air defense. Moreover, Allied tactical air could also strike targets in Germany. The result was a three-pronged offensive by Allied air forces that contributed considerably to Nazi Germany's collapse.

Tedder argued strongly for a focused effort to destroy the German transportation system. His argument emphasized the Allied success in attacking French transportation. He received some support from airmen, but the strategic bombing barons had their own agenda. Harris obdurately clung to "area" bombing, but as most major railway stations lay in the center of German cities, he agreed to use them as aiming points. Spaatz still pushed for the oil campaign; nevertheless, when conditions did not permit precision bombing, he agreed to attack transportation targets. Much of the tactical air efforts also went into support for the transportation plan. The

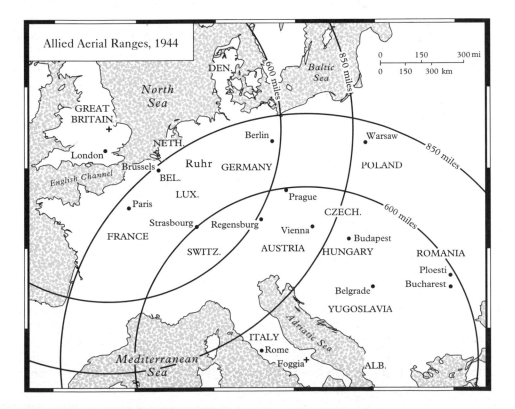

impact of such attacks on the Reich's rail and road system represented the single most effective use of air power in the war.

By early September 1944, air attacks against German transportation targets were well underway, and by October they were having considerable impact. For the week ending August 19, 1944, the German railroads had loaded and dispatched 899,091 cars; by the end of October that figure had fallen to 703,580 cars; by the end of December the total had fallen to 547,309 despite the demands of the Battle of the Bulge, the German winter counteroffensive. In that month, marshaling capacity of rail yards had declined to 40 percent of normal; in February 1945 it had fallen to 20 percent. The Battle of the Bulge indicated that attacks on transportation could not yet prevent the Germans from executing military operations. On the other hand, according to the Strategic Bombing Survey, these attacks "had reduced the available capacity for economic traffic in Germany to a point at which [the war economy] could not hope to sustain, over any period of time, a high level of military production." And, of course, the diversion of declining transport resources to supporting the Battle of the Bulge exacerbated the difficulties that German industry was already experiencing.

The steady decline of the transportation network gradually strangled the war economy by disorganizing and reducing the flow of raw materials and finished goods necessary for the production of weapons and munitions. Under such conditions neither planning nor production took place in an orderly fashion. The precipitous decline of coal transportation, essential to continued functioning of the economy, underlines the extent of the problem. In January 1944 the Essen division of the German railway system had loaded an average of 21,400 coal cars per day; by September that total had dropped to 12,000, of which only 3,400 were long-haul cars. By February 1945, Allied air attacks had cut the Ruhr off from the rest of Germany, while German railroads often had to confiscate what little coal they loaded just to keep locomotives running. The Ruhr was swimming in coal that it could no longer transport even to the industries in the region, much less to the rest of Germany.

The evidence suggests a general collapse of the war economy by mid-winter 1945. Since it was not a sudden and cataclysmic collapse, it remained difficult to discern even to those conducting the campaign. In July and August 1944 both the Eastern and Western fronts had suffered enormous defeats with great loss of equipment. Nevertheless, because German armaments production in summer 1944 remained at a relatively high level, the Wehrmacht reequipped the survivors and the new men (mostly boys) called upon to defend the frontier. There the Germans offered tough resistance and even launched the Ardennes offensive. However, beginning in January 1945 in the east, followed within a month and a half in the west, German armies again lost major battles, but this time neither on the Rhine nor on the Oder rivers were they able to reknit for a last stand. The collapse came because air attacks on the transportation network had successfully shut down the war economy, and the Wehrmacht no longer had the weapons, munitions, or petroleum necessary to fight. Even blind fanaticism could not maintain a struggle under such conditions.

Battle of the Bulge

The idea of counterattacking in the west had come to Hitler in early September 1944, even as his armies streamed back toward the German frontier. He believed that the Wehrmacht could still achieve a decisive battlefield victory that would drive the Western Powers from the war. Ever the gambler, he selected the Ardennes as the location of the main attack. The target would be Antwerp to destroy a vital logistic link for the Allies and to entrap much of the British army. But to get to Antwerp the Germans had to capture Allied fuel dumps, and the Wehrmacht possessed only enough petroleum to get to the Meuse.

On the Allied side, senior commanders remained optimistic despite German resistance on the frontier. Few could conceive that the enemy would be able to assemble the necessary resources for a major offensive. In early December, Eisenhower met with Montgomery and Bradley and outlined plans for an attack in early January 1945. The Allies would retain the broad-front strategy, but the main effort would be in the north. As Anglo-American armies prepared to launch another offensive, there were indications that the Germans were also preparing an attack. Even though the Wehrmacht faced desperate shortages of supplies, Ultra intercepts indicated major buildups of ammunition and fuel dumps opposite the Ardennes, the one place where the Allies were not attacking. But preoccupied with their own offensive and confident the Germans could not attack, Allied commanders

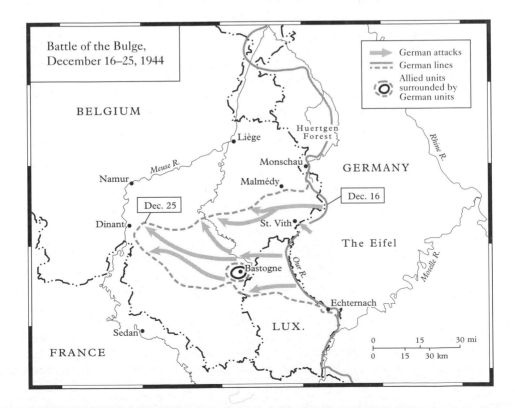

Battle of the Bulge, December 16–25, 1944

German attacks
German lines
Allied units surrounded by German units

BELGIUM

Huertgen Forest

Liège

Monschau

GERMANY

Meuse R.

Namur

Malmédy

Rhine R.

Dec. 16

Dec. 25

Dinant

St. Vith

The Eifel

Bastogne

Our R.

Moselle R.

Echternach

LUX.

Sedan

FRANCE

0   15   30 mi
0   15   30 km

missed the warnings. In late fall the vulnerability of the Ardennes increased with the insertion of inexperienced divisions into that quiet sector. Only the 82nd and 101st Airborne divisions were in reserve; the Allied high command had committed everything else to the front.

On December 16 the Germans struck between Monschau and Echternach along a fifty-mile front in the Ardennes. The weather cooperated by providing a heavy, thick blanket of clouds to obscure the battlefield and prevent the intervention of U.S. air power. Sixth SS Panzer Army attacked in the north but met stiff resistance on its right from the U.S. 99th and 2nd divisions, part of V Corps. Fifth Panzer Army to the south, however, broke through the U.S. 106th and 28th divisions. The Germans advanced rapidly, for the U.S. divisions were spread thinly across wide fronts and were inexperienced or weakened from previous fighting.

On the northern shoulder, the 99th and 2nd divisions held the critical Monschau and Eisenborn Ridge area and thereby denied use of its critical roads to the Germans. Because of the difficult terrain in the Ardennes, the main German advance was along secondary roads, but American troops offered strong resistance at several key road junctions, most notably St. Vith and Bastogne. At St. Vith, American soldiers blocked the vital road junction for six days. At Bastogne, a small armored detachment held the Germans long enough for the 101st Airborne Division to arrive. Though surrounded, the defenders at Bastogne refused to surrender. On the southern shoulder of the penetration, U.S. forces retreated, but as in the north, they eventually held. Thus strong defenses on the shoulders and at several critical road junctions limited the width of the German penetration and disrupted the enemy's advance.

The Allied high command responded more swiftly than the Germans had expected. Since the Germans had cut off Bradley's communications with the northern flank of the Bulge, Eisenhower turned the battle there over to Montgomery, while Bradley coordinated the battle in the south. Montgomery eventually brought in his XXX Corps to help strengthen the defenses.

In the south, Patton had his finest hour. His initial reaction when told of the attack in the Ardennes was to commit all his units in heavy fighting so that he would not lose any to the fighting farther north. When he recognized, however, that a full-scale enemy offensive had begun, he shifted units of Third Army on his own authority to counterattack the breakthrough from the south. He advised Eisenhower: "Hell, let's have the guts to let the sons of bitches go to Paris. Then we'll really cut 'em off and chew 'em up." When the weather failed to cooperate, he had his chaplain compose a particularly bloodthirsty prayer. On December 23, the weather cleared, and Allied tactical and strategic air forces pounded the Germans throughout the Ardennes. Patton decorated his chaplain.

By Christmas Eve elements of Fifth Panzer Army had reached within three miles of Dinant and the Meuse River, an advance of about sixty-five miles, but that was as far as they got. Along the way Waffen SS troops under Lieutenant Colonel Jochen Peiper massacred American prisoners near Malmédy; the SS troops also murdered Belgian civilians as they advanced.

News of the atrocities and the presence of Germans in American uniforms and vehicles created considerable turmoil; sentries energetically questioned unknown Americans passing through their position about who played first base for the Cubs or how many home runs Babe Ruth had hit in 1927.

As Allied units attacked the northern and southern flanks of the Bulge, Allied aircraft raked the exposed German units. On December 26, Patton's 4th Armored Division made contact with the defenders of Bastogne. By mid-January Allied counterattacks had pushed the Germans back, and the bulge had disappeared. Hitler's desperate gamble had gained the Reich nothing. Instead he had wasted the Wehrmacht's mobile reserves and lost 100,000 men, and the Allies were on the western frontier of Germany with their forces poised for the final campaign and with their logistic base steadily improving.

Collapse in the East

The German offensive in the Ardennes led the Western Powers to request the Soviets to launch their long-expected winter offensive. The Red Army had preparations well in hand. On January 12, 1945, it struck along the Vistula; the number of forces was totally in the Soviets' favor, for the Germans had bled off most of their reserves for the Ardennes offensive. What little remained went to Hungary to fight around Budapest. The Soviets launched two concurrent offensives. The first, on the central portion of the front, saw the First Belorussian and First Ukrainian fronts break out between Warsaw and the Carpathian Mountains. They intended to drive through central Poland into Germany to the Oder River. The second, north of Warsaw, resulted in the Second and Third Belorussian fronts striking East Prussia and Pomerania. Up to now the Red Army's watchword in its conduct of operations had been "liberation"; now it was "vengeance." Soviet troops entered German territory fully encouraged to pay the Germans back for their momentous crimes in the Soviet Union.

The offensive on the central portion of the front opened with the First Ukrainian Front's attack, which hit seven weak German divisions with nearly five armies, two tank armies, and over 1,000 tanks. Within a day it had opened a forty-mile hole through which its troops and tanks poured into Silesia and raced toward the Oder River. On January 14, the First Belorussian Front launched its attack; within a day it had broken through German lines north of Warsaw. Guderian warned Hitler that Soviet attacks had shattered Army Group Center and that weakened German forces could not halt the Red Army unless reinforced. Hitler released some forces from the west but promptly shipped them off to Budapest.

By January 17, the Soviets had taken Warsaw and were approaching Cracow. Hitler sent Field Marshal Schörner to restore the situation and blamed the OKH for Warsaw's fall. After having three OKH staff officers arrested, he ordered that henceforth no command be given that could not be countermanded from above. Schörner brought unwarranted optimism and a fanatical belief in Naziism to a hopeless situation. By January 19, Army

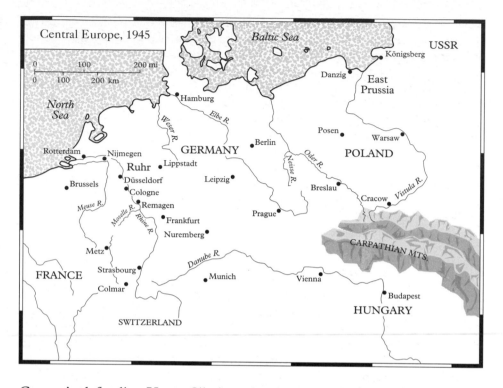

Central Europe, 1945

Group A, defending Upper Silesia and central Poland, had lost contact with Army Group Center. Soviet forces had ripped Army Group A's front to shreds; only logistical limitations could halt their advance. In Hitler's headquarters, the Führer appointed Heinrich Himmler to restore the front on the Oder. As commander of Army Group Vistula, Himmler's mission was to maintain an open corridor to East Prussia and prevent breakthroughs to Danzig and Posen. But his experience as the head of the SS did not translate into battlefield competence.

Before Himmler arrived to take command, the dam broke. Soviet forces attacked German units protecting East Prussia. Though Hitler had diverted divisions from East Prussia to central Poland, he refused permission for any withdrawals; German defenses again unraveled. On January 24 the Soviets reached the coast west of Danzig and the mouth of the Vistula; this advance isolated East Prussia from the rest of Germany. On the 25th the Soviets drove past Posen.

By early February 1945 the Soviets had pushed 200 miles west of Warsaw. Their leading units rested on the Oder within forty miles of Berlin; they had surrounded large German garrisons in Posen and Breslau. Though on the brink of final collapse, the Germans pulled themselves together for a final stand in front of Berlin. Not surprisingly the Soviets themselves were experiencing logistical difficulties, given the distances they had covered. In February and March, the Red Army cleaned up East Prussia, except for Königsberg and a small coastal strip. As the main body of the Russians closed on the Oder-Neisse line (the eventual Polish-German boundary), they did not resume their offensive toward Berlin. Perhaps close to the wolf's lair, they did not want any failures to dampen their triumph at war's end. Since Western ground forces still remained on the west bank of the Rhine, there seemed little need for haste.

Despite what subsequently happened to the Germans, many found it hard to sympathize with them, since they had committed such horrible crimes in the east. Nevertheless, a terrible revenge fell on eastern Germany, as Soviet troops began systematically looting and raping the territories they conquered. Soviet soldiers, often in a drunken stupor, murdered tens of thousands of civilians. Estimates of civilian casualties are as high as 3,000,000. Whatever the total, it represented the hideousness of the ideological war unleashed by the Nazis on June 22, 1941.

Collapse in the West

Meanwhile, German defenses in the west unraveled at a fast rate during January and February 1945. In the south Devers's 6th Army Group reduced the Colmar Pocket in the first week of February, while in the north and center, Allied units began closing in on the Rhine. By early March British and American units had battered their way into the Rhineland. By March 11, 21st Army Group held the Rhine between Düsseldorf and Nijmegen. Eisenhower planned on encircling the Ruhr by having Montgomery make the major crossing of the Rhine north of the Ruhr, and having Bradley make secondary crossings to the south with First and Third armies. Montgomery ordered a pause to prepare the massive assault across the Rhine, but the Americans moved more quickly.

In early March Third Army cracked German defenses in the Eifel (northeast of Luxembourg) and in three days reached the Rhine. Hodges's First Army did even better: on March 7, 9th Armored Division reached the Rhine at the moment that the Germans were blowing up the Ludendorff railroad bridge at Remagen. German engineers had placed their charges too evenly on the bridge supports. After pressing the plunger, the appalled defenders watched with amazement as the bridge, with much smoke and noise, rose several feet in the air and then settled back on its pilings. U.S. infantrymen rushed the bridge and then seized the cliffs overlooking the river. They now commanded the approaches and reinforcements surged across.

Hodges, with Bradley's support, rushed a large number of units across without fully informing SHAEF, for fear that the Allied high command might not recognize the opportunity. Eisenhower's operations officer lived up to expectations. He told Bradley: "Sure, you've got a bridge, Brad, but what good is it going to do you. You are not going anyplace down there at Remagen. It just doesn't fit into the plan."* But Eisenhower proved more flexible, allowing Hodges and Bradley to push strong forces over the Rhine.

An enraged Hitler ordered an immediate search for traitors. With no reserves, the Nazi army could do little to contain a growing American

---

*Omar N. Bradley, *A Soldier's Story* (New York: Holt, 1951), p. 500.

bridgehead. The Luftwaffe launched a number of sorties against the bridge and even fired off V-2s, while the navy floated mines and frogmen downriver in desperate efforts to cut the cord across the Rhine. Eventually the bridge collapsed, but by then the Americans had pontoon bridges and four divisions across the Rhine.

To the south Patton moved down the Rhine valley and in cooperation with Seventh Army cleaned up the left bank. To Goebbels' outrage German civilians greeted the Americans everywhere with white bed sheets displayed from windows; there was no fanatical resistance in the Rhineland. Not to be outdone by Hodges's accomplishment at Remagen, Patton threw a bridge across the Rhine at Oppenheim on March 22 and rushed everybody he could across the river. That day, in reference to Montgomery's coming assault across the Rhine on March 24, Patton's briefing officer reported: "Without benefit of aerial bombing, ground smoke, artillery preparation, and airborne assistance, Third Army at 2200 hours, Thursday, March 22, crossed the Rhine River." The rapid advance of the U.S. First, Third, and Seventh armies through the Rhineland had killed, wounded, or captured 225,000 Germans at a cost of 5,000 casualties.

After two weeks of intense preparations, Montgomery was finally ready to launch his blow. Against five ill-equipped, weakly manned divisions holding a thirty-mile front, the British used an artillery bombardment of 3,300 guns, Allied strategic and tactical air forces, and two airborne divisions. The weight of the offensive initially slowed its forward movement, but the British soon broke out into the open. The combined effect of Mont-

Allied forces made rapid progress in Germany. Many towns decked themselves in white flags whereas others offered only token resistance.

gomery's advance and the Americans' advance south of the Ruhr placed the Germans in a hopeless position. The exploitation occurred at an even faster pace than in the Normandy breakout. On April 1, the U.S. 2nd Armored Division from the north met First Army's 3rd Armored Division at Lippstadt, seventy-five miles east of the Rhine, thereby encircling the Ruhr. Within the wreckage of Germany's industrial heart lay Field Marshal Model's Army Group B. Nothing remained in western Germany except a few pockets of fanatical Nazis to hinder Anglo-American forces.

The Allied advance followed political realities as well as operational concerns. Since the political agreements at Yalta had already placed the area around Berlin within the Soviet sphere, it made little sense for Allied soldiers to die capturing territory that would end up under Soviet control. Consequently, Allied troops halted along the Elbe River. In the south the Red Army had already reached Vienna's outskirts; it made equal sense not to reach for what was within Soviet grasp. Only by seizing Prague could the Western Allies perhaps have made a difference in the postwar settlement, but Eisenhower halted Patton's Third Army before it reached the Czech capital.

One last act remained. As Anglo-American forces rampaged through western and central Germany, the Red Army launched its forces on Berlin. The Germans had no prospect for delaying the coming blow. Their Ninth Army, defending the capital, consisted of fourteen understrength divisions; Third Panzer Army on its left flank had eleven divisions. In total, the Germans possessed 754 tanks, 344 artillery pieces, and 900–1,000 antiaircraft guns. Their opponents, First and Second Belorussian fronts, disposed of 110 infantry divisions, eleven tank and mechanized corps, and eleven artillery divisions (4,106 tanks and self-propelled guns, and 23,576 artillery pieces).

The main Soviet offensive across the Oder came on April 16. Despite initial difficulties and fanatical resistance, the Soviets by April 20 had won the battle of Berlin. On the 21st, Soviet artillery shells began falling on the German capital. In the bizarre atmosphere of his bunker, Hitler maneuvered nonexistent units on his battle maps, but there was no hope of relief. On April 25, Soviet and American units met on the Elbe and cut Germany in half. On the afternoon of April 30, Adolf Hitler, having just married his mistress Eva Braun, committed suicide; he was soon followed by Goebbels and his family. The nightmare in Europe was finally over.

*   *   *   *

The collapse of Germany reflected a war waged by one major industrial power against three of the world's other major industrial powers, including one that by itself could outproduce most of the world. Allied air had brought Germany's transportation network to a halt by winter 1945, which in turn caused the collapse of war production, while the destruction of petroleum facilities grounded much of the Luftwaffe and robbed the German army of its mobility. On the Eastern and Western fronts, Allied superiority wrecked the German Army. Hitler's strategic and operational direction of the war made a bad situation worse, but his fanatical will drove the German nation to fight to the end. Nevertheless, the Wehrmacht's competence at tactical and operational levels mitigated some of Hitler's decisions and prevented Allied thrusts from breaking into Germany until 1945.

The battles in Europe in the last year of the war reflected the narrowing of the gap between German battlefield performance and the performance of the opposing armies. The steadily improving tactical and operational capabilities of Allied forces was, of course, substantially aided by their overwhelming superiority in numbers and firepower. The invasion of Normandy, the expansion of the beachheads, and the breakout and surge across western Europe demonstrated the Allies' improved ability to join infantry, tanks, and artillery into effective combined arms teams and to use air power to extend the performance of their ground forces. Particularly noteworthy was the capacity of Allied forces to work together in a joint environment in which the services complemented the capabilities of each other. Combined with the advantages of superior intelligence and deception on a massive scale, these capabilities had placed the Germans in a hopeless situation.

SUGGESTED READINGS

Ambrose, Stephen E. *The Supreme Commander: The War Years of General Dwight D. Eisenhower* (Garden City, N.Y.: Doubleday, 1970).

Bennett, Ralph. *Ultra in the West: The Normandy Campaign, 1944–45* (New York: Scribner, 1979).

Blumenson, Martin. *Breakout and Pursuit* (Washington: Office of the Chief of Military History, 1961).Bradley, Omar N. *A Soldier's Story* (New York: Holt, 1951).

Eisenhower, Dwight D. *Crusade in Europe* (Garden City, N.Y.: Doubleday, 1948).

Harrison, Gordon A. *Cross-Channel Attack* (Washington: Office of the Chief of Military History, 1951).

Hastings, Max. *Overlord: D-Day and the Battle for Normandy* (New York: Simon and Schuster, 1984).

Hechler, Ken. *The Bridge at Remagen* (New York: Ballantine, 1957).

MacDonald, Charles B. *The Mighty Endeavor: American Armed Forces in the European Theater in World War II* (New York: Oxford University Press, 1969).

———. *Time for Trumpets: The Untold Story of the Battle of the Bulge* (New York: Morrow, 1984).

Montgomery, Bernard L. *The Memoirs of Field-Marshal the Viscount Montgomery of Alamein* (New York: World, 1958).

Patton, George S. *War as I Knew It* (Boston: Houghton Mifflin, 1947).

Pogue, Forrest C. *The Supreme Command* (Washington: Office of the Chief of Military History, 1954).

Ryan, Cornelius. *A Bridge Too Far* (New York: Simon and Schuster, 1974).

Weigley, Russell F. *Eisenhower's Lieutenants: The Campaign in France and Germany, 1944–1945* (Bloomington: Indiana University Press, 1981).

Wilmot, Chester. *The Struggle for Europe* (New York: Harper, 1952).

Ziemke, Earl F. *Stalingrad to Berlin: The German Defeat in the East* (Washington: Office of the Chief of Military History, 1968).

6

VICTORY IN THE PACIFIC: NAVAL AND AMPHIBIOUS WAR ON THE OPERATIONAL LEVEL

The Americans committed large forces to the Pacific even though U.S. grand strategy was one of "Germany first." No matter how appealing such an approach might be in strategic terms, the strategy of "Germany first" flew in the face of the fundamental political reality that it was Japan against whom the American public directed its anger. The strategy also encountered the military reality that a major invasion of the European continent could not have occurred before spring 1944. Thus throughout the war, Japan received a higher priority in terms of the commitment of U.S. military forces than the grand strategy seemingly dictated. Many of the debates about strategy focused less on strategic objectives and courses of action than on the allocation of scarce resources. In the end it worked out, but there were times when American strategy and operations in the Pacific possessed a distinctly ad hoc nature.

173

The war in the Pacific differed greatly from most other wars in the twentieth century. After the battle of Midway in early June 1942 halted the tide of Japanese victory, U.S. commanders in the Pacific possessed only the slimmest of resources; the move against Guadalcanal with one marine division underlined this fact. Though the Americans initially could do little more than defend the sea lines of communication to Australia, the mobilization of manpower and industrial production eventually allowed them to take the offensive. Partially due to interservice rivalries, U.S. forces made two great drives—one from the south Pacific, one across the central Pacific—to destroy Japanese military power. As the Americans confronted their Pacific enemies, the number of naval battles and ships sunk exceeded the combined totals of all other twentieth-century conflicts. Nonetheless, the Americans combined air, land, and sea forces in an unprecedented manner for giant leaps across the ocean. In the end the war in the Pacific concluded the same way it had begun, by air attack, but the explosion of two atomic bombs over Japan heralded the unleashing of new levels of destructive power.

The South Pacific, August 1942–December 1943

The Allied moves against Guadalcanal in August 1942 and into New Guinea in October–November occurred because of the strategic requirement to protect sea lines of communication to Australia. Although American leaders gave Europe first priority, they could not permit the Japanese to consolidate their position in the Pacific. Moreover, public opinion in the United States, still outraged by Pearl Harbor, demanded revenge. The South Pacific saw a series of inconclusive air and naval battles that collectively turned the tide against Japan. There were no decisive victories, but American naval, air, and ground forces emerged from these battles in greater strength, whereas the opposite occurred with the Japanese. Above all, the growing American superiority reflected the awesome industrial capabilities of the United States.

Guadalcanal

In August 1942, U.S. Marines found themselves haphazardly deposited on Guadalcanal. The naval disaster at Savo Island forced the transport fleet to leave, and marines ashore received only half the equipment they required. Fortunately for the Americans, the Japanese had almost completed the airfield on the island; within two weeks the U.S. Navy Seabees had completed it, and fast destroyers brought in fuel, bombs, and ground crewmen. Soon marine aircraft arrived, and from that point on American air reigned over the Solomon Islands. Japanese arrogance and miscalculations also aided the Americans considerably. The Imperial high command, misled by Savo Island, believed the American attack against Guadalcanal was nothing more than a raid; the Japanese army estimated that a reinforced regiment would suffice to regain the airfield on Guadalcanal. Consequently the Japanese launched an ill-prepared countermove on August 21; the marines almost wiped out the attackers in a night of savage fighting. That defeat finally woke up the Japanese high command to the seriousness of the threat; both sides rushed to build up forces on Guadalcanal—the Japanese at night, the Americans by day. Meanwhile a series of naval and air battles swirled around Guadalcanal. On August 24, in the battle of the eastern Solomons, the Americans sank the small carrier, *Ryujo*; the U.S. carrier *Enterprise* in turn received three bomb hits that put it out of action.

By the end of August, the Japanese had built their forces up to 6,000 men. In a series of ferocious attacks on September 13, they came close to breaking through to Henderson Field, but the marines held. The attackers lost 50 percent of their men; the marines lost nearly 20 percent. In early October the U.S. Navy slipped the 164th Regiment of the Americal Division into Guadalcanal. The Japanese by now had over one division ashore and prepared a three-pronged attack on the defensive perimeter despite insufficient artillery. The attacks on October 23–26 came in disjointed fashion. The main attack hit the south side of the perimeter which one marine battalion, reinforced by a battalion from the 164th, held. Throughout two nights of fierce fighting, the well-entrenched Americans beat off the attack. Nearly 3,500 Japanese died in the unsuccessful attempts. The line on Guadalcanal had held.

When American marines landed on Guadalcanal on August 7, 1942, 75-mm pack howitzers came ashore with the assault battalions to provide fire support. Heavier 105-mm howitzers landed later in the day.

From September through November, naval battles continued in furious but indecisive fashion. The Japanese sank carrier *Wasp* and badly damaged carrier *Saratoga* and new battleship *North Carolina*. Off Cape Esperance, northwest of Guadalcanal, American cruisers and destroyers bested their Japanese opponent for the first time at night on October 11–12; their success was largely a result of radar and of Japanese confusion rather than of improvement in U.S. tactical skill. As the Japanese attacks against Henderson Field failed in late October, another inconclusive naval clash occurred north of Guadalcanal. In the battle of the Santa Cruz Islands, 350 miles east of Guadalcanal, the Japanese sank carrier *Hornet* and again damaged *Enterprise*; in turn, American aircraft damaged two Japanese cruisers. Though the U.S. Navy had suffered heavier losses, both sides pulled back.

Recognizing the need for new leadership, Nimitz fired the naval commander of the South Pacific who had originally objected to the campaign in the Solomons and who had become exhausted and indecisive from the strain. His replacement was Vice Admiral William F. "Bull" Halsey, an aggressive combat sailor. As he told the marine commander on Guadalcanal, Major General Alexander A. Vandegrift: "Go on back. I'll promise you everything I've got."

By now the Japanese were not only slipping reinforcements down the Solomons by night but were also bombarding Henderson Field with heavy cruisers and battleships. In November they attempted to land large numbers of reinforcements on Guadalcanal. They began their effort on the night of November 12–13 with an attack against American ships off Guadalcanal and an attempt to land troops on the island by transports. The Americans suffered heavily but forced the enemy to turn back. They badly damaged battleship *Hiei*, and U.S. aircraft sank it the next day. The Japanese returned on November 14, but the Americans sank seven of eleven troop transports. A clash of battleships, one of the few in the entire war, also took place: on the American side battleships *South Dakota* and *Washington*; on the Japanese side, *Kirishima*. Although the Japanese had to scuttle the badly damaged *Kirishima*, they beached four transports on Guadalcanal. Thereafter they risked no more capital ships in the Solomons campaign. The Japanese attempted to send reinforcements by troop transports on December 3, 7, and 11, but heavy losses forced them to abandon the effort to reinforce Guadalcanal.

By early January 1943 the situation completely favored the Americans. The 2nd Marine Division had replaced the 1st, while the 25th Division and the remainder of the Americal Division had arrived. Under the command of Lieutenant General Alexander M. Patch, the Americans drove west to push the Japanese off the island. The Japanese conceded defeat, however, and pulled off 11,000 weary, beaten troops in the first week of February 1943. Of 60,000 American marines and soldiers who fought on Guadalcanal, 1,600 died and 4,200 were wounded; of 36,000 Japanese, 15,000 were killed or missing, 9,000 died of disease, and 1,000 were captured. The air and naval contest had also ended in an American victory; there the results were even more decisive. Air battles over the Solomons cost the Japanese 1,000 naval aircraft and a further 1,500 in defending New

Guinea and Rabaul. The fighting cost the Japanese navy nearly half its fighter pilots and an even greater percentage of dive bomber and torpedo crews; those losses, combined with Midway, undermined the Japanese navy's capacity to fight a naval air battle on anything approaching equal terms with its American opponents.

Papua

The American victory in the battle of the Coral Sea in May 1942 momentarily halted the drive on Port Moresby in New Guinea, and victory at Midway in June swung the initiative tentatively to the Americans. The Japanese, however, did not abandon their hopes of seizing Port Moresby and thereby threatening Allied lines to Australia. On July 21 they landed 11,000 troops on New Guinea and marched south over the mountains toward Port Moresby. After the Japanese got within twenty miles of their goal in mid-September, Australian forces drove the enemy back to the northeast coast where the Japanese established a defensive perimeter. They intended to renew their offensive once they had beaten the Americans on Guadalcanal.

Since MacArthur believed the best way to defend Australia was to control New Guinea, he reacted strongly. In October and early November, the Australian 7th Division and the American 32nd Division moved across from Australia to Port Moresby and on to the northeast coast of Papua (the easternmost extension of New Guinea). When the 32nd Division attacked Buna on November 19, it discovered the Japanese solidly dug in, surrounded by a huge swamp. Without heavy artillery, flamethrowers, or tanks, American attacks gained little. Unwilling to tolerate delays, MacArthur sent Lieutenant General Robert L. Eichelberger to remedy the situation.

While the Australians attacked Japanese forces west of Buna, Eichelberger replaced the 32nd Division's commander and swiftly improved the supply situation and combat power of his forces. In addition to providing better food and ensuring that his soldiers rested, Eichelberger obtained tanks to support the infantry and developed more effective methods for capturing enemy bunkers. Thirty-two days after his arrival, Buna fell. One month later Australians and Americans captured Sanananda, three miles northwest of Buna and the strongest Japanese position in Papua. The Allies had learned important lessons about reducing Japanese defensive positions, but the cost was heavy—8,500 casualties, over 3,500 dead. Nonetheless, the Allies had held at Guadalcanal and driven the Japanese from Port Moresby; they now held the initiative.

Operation "Cartwheel"

These successes raised the question of what to do next. At the Casablanca Conference in January 1943, the Americans lost most of the strategic arguments, but the Combined Chiefs of Staff agreed to retain the initiative in the Pacific. Admittedly, this decision reflected political realities; it also reflected the fact that the great fleet the U.S. Navy was assembling could

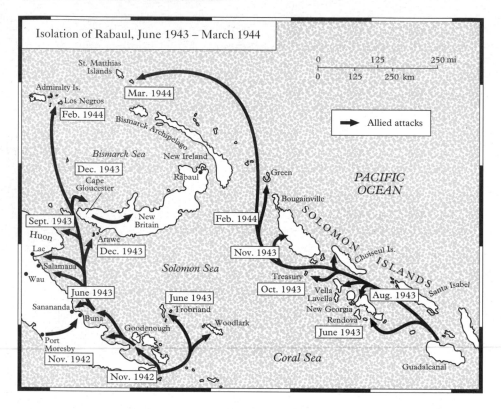

Isolation of Rabaul, June 1943 – March 1944

serve no other purpose. The Combined Chiefs of Staff, however, did not envisage a full-scale offensive against Japan until after Germany's defeat.

Soon after Casablanca, the issue of unity of command in the Pacific arose. The army favored MacArthur, the navy Nimitz. Washington had not yet reached a decision when representatives of the Pacific commanders gathered in the U.S. capital. There, MacArthur's chief of staff asked for much larger forces for a drive on Rabaul: no less than five additional divisions and 1,800 aircraft. Appalled at the magnitude of MacArthur's request, the Joint Chiefs of Staff concluded that there were not enough planes, ships, or divisions available in the Pacific to capture Rabaul in 1943. In March they postponed plans to seize Rabaul and accepted MacArthur's new proposal for a two-pronged drive converging on the Japanese base. With MacArthur in overall command of Operation "Cartwheel," Halsey would advance up the Solomons as far as Bougainville, while forces under MacArthur would move along the coast of New Guinea before attacking the western end of the island of New Britain. Whether or not to attack Rabaul on the eastern end of New Britain would depend on the availability of additional forces.

Operation Cartwheel established a model that Pacific commanders would use for the rest of the war. The Americans would advance by great bounds due to their air superiority, hit the Japanese at weak spots, seize existing airfields and ports, and then use their newly acquired bases to support the next leap forward.

Air Power

Air power played a key role in Cartwheel, as well as subsequent Pacific operations. Much of the Allied effort aimed to cut Japanese lines of communication—the air, sea, and land routes over which troops and equipment moved—and to prevent Japanese reinforcement or escape. In August 1942, MacArthur had received a new air commander, Major General George C. Kenney. Kenney may have been the premier airman of World War II; he was certainly the best in the Pacific. Unlike many other airmen, he was no ideologue; he understood the need to adapt military forces to actual conditions and to use air power to accomplish overall theater objectives. Kenney took over a weak organization: combat crews were discouraged and dispirited, maintenance was in shambles, and supply channels were inefficient and incompetent. He gave his air units a thorough housecleaning and relieved no fewer than five generals and an even larger number of colonels. But Kenney made his greatest contribution in air tactics and operations. High-level bombing of ships had thus far killed mostly fish, and Kenney determined to change his forces' tactical approach. Among other improvements, he retrained medium bomber crews and modified their aircraft to attack at low level. B-25s now carried eight .50-caliber machine guns in their noses and six 100-pound bombs that could be skipped into targets.

Meanwhile the Japanese replied to the increasing American threat in the South Pacific by moving forces from as far away as China to the theater. They placed their Eighth Army at Rabaul, Seventeenth Army in the Solomons, and Eighteenth Army in New Guinea and New Britain. In April 1943, they moved the 51st Division from Rabaul to New Guinea; eight transports and eight destroyers provided sea lift. Nearly one hundred fighters were to provide continuous cover for the convoy as it rounded New Britain. "Magic" (the breaking of Japanese codes) picked up Japanese plans. Forewarned of enemy intentions, Kenney studied past experience with Japanese convoys. These assessments along with further Magic intelligence allowed U.S. aircraft to strike with devastating effectiveness. Japanese fighters looked for high-altitude bombers; instead, B-25s attacked at low level from head on. Machine-gun fire and fragmentation bombs rained death on crowded transport decks, while 100-pound bombs skipped into the enemy ships. In one day's air attacks, Kenney's aircraft sank all the transports and four destroyers; the Japanese lost about 3,000 soldiers and most of the 51st Division's staff. Besides demonstrating Kenney's skills, the battle of the Bismarck Sea represented a decisive success for land-based air against naval power.

The Japanese concentrated much of their land-based air at Rabaul and Wewak (an island off the north-central coast of New Guinea). To halt erosion of the Japanese situation, Admiral Yamamoto Isoroku launched a series of massive air raids—the "I" operation—against New Guinea and Guadalcanal in April 1943. The raids achieved little. Moreover, by utilizing Magic the Allies learned of a visit by Yamamoto to the theater and shot down his aircraft. Despite Japanese opposition, Kenney built air bases in

New Guinea, gained air superiority above MacArthur's ground forces, and attacked the Japanese bases. American raids not only destroyed one hundred enemy aircraft on the ground at Wewak on August 17 but also wrecked the enemy's base and supply organization. Consequently the Japanese no longer could shuttle air units back and forth within the theater.

A deteriorating operational situation led the Japanese to undertake desperate remedial measures. The navy committed its new carrier pilots to defend Rabaul's airfield; code name for the counterattack was "RO." A series of savage air battles occurred over Rabaul and New Britain in October and November. Again there was no clear winner; both sides suffered heavy losses, while claiming even heavier ones for their opponents. But in the end, the Americans could replace crews and aircraft without difficulty; the Japanese, their naval air units decimated by the fighting, lost the full combat value of their carriers for the remainder of the war.

The Amphibious Campaign

By early summer 1943, MacArthur and Halsey had begun Operation Cartwheel. The arrival of additional landing craft made movement and commitment of amphibious forces far easier. Specially designed craft such as the Landing Ship Tank (LST), Amphibious Tractor (Amtrac), and Landing Craft Infantry (LCI) moved men and equipment from ship to shore. Halsey's forces had more new craft than MacArthur's forces did in the southwest Pacific, but MacArthur had an Engineer Amphibious Brigade, which carried troops and equipment to shore and organized the beachhead. Such support left the landing troops free to fight the battle.

Halsey's first amphibious strike went against the Munda airfield on New Georgia, which threatened Guadalcanal. Landing on a small, nearby island in late June, about 32,000 soldiers and 1,700 marines moved to New Georgia but took several weeks to dislodge the Japanese from the dense jungle. The next target was Kolombangara with 12,000 Japanese troops in strong defenses. Instead of attacking the enemy force directly, Halsey skipped Kolombangara and landed on the next island, Vella Lavella, where there were no Japanese. Though enemy land-based air posed some risk, the move caught the Japanese off guard. They had no choice but to evacuate the isolated troops on Kolombangara.

MacArthur's forces achieved similar success in New Guinea. Late in January a small contingent of Australian forces repulsed an attack on Wau (about 150 miles northwest of Buna). Allied reinforcements arrived by air, while Kenney's destruction of enemy transports carrying the 51st Division halted Japanese reinforcements. In late June, Allied forces landed on the New Guinea coast east of Wau. On September 5, the 503rd Parachute Regiment dropped on the airfield at Nadzab (fifty miles north of Wau); Kenney's transports then flew in the Australian 7th Division. Combined with another amphibious assault, this vertical envelopment forced the Japanese to abandon strongly held positions at Salamaua and Lae on the coast. A few weeks later the Allies grabbed the Huon Peninsula north of Salamaua and Lae.

The peninsula lay just west of New Britain, which had Rabaul on its eastern tip. Taking advantage of the favorable situation, Kenney's aircraft dropped 685 tons of bombs on Rabaul in October.

Halsey now moved against Bougainville; on November 1, 1943, 3rd Marine Division landed at Empress Augusta Bay. In eight hours both troops and equipment were ashore, a considerable improvement over Guadalcanal. Offshore, the navy, with radar's assistance, fought the Japanese on even terms at night. Staying outside the range of "Long Lance" torpedoes, American ships blasted Japanese light cruisers and destroyers that had come from Rabaul to attack the transports. The Japanese responded by sending a larger naval force to reinforce Rabaul and attack the Allied naval forces near Bougainville. On November 5, violating previous practice, Halsey sent almost one hundred carrier aircraft against Japanese ships anchored at Rabaul. The raid damaged six cruisers and two destroyers and ended the enemy threat to Empress Augusta Bay. Meanwhile the 37th Infantry Division with a New Zealand brigade arrived to assist the 3rd Marine Division in clearing Bougainville, a task not completed until the war's end. As the Allies expanded control over the island, they built an airfield that placed them in an even better position to attack Rabaul.

In mid-December, the 112th Cavalry Regiment landed on the south coast of New Britain. Two weeks later the 1st Marine Division landed at Cape Gloucester on New Britain's western tip. These landings effectively neutralized Rabaul. MacArthur saw no need to undertake a costly assault on the fortified port; the Americans could leave the Japanese to wither on the vine and move to more distant and significant targets. After mid-February 1944 no Japanese warships remained in Rabaul, and no aircraft rose from Rabaul to challenge Allied bombers.

The island-hopping campaign was underway. The Americans, where possible, now avoided Japanese strong points and struck deep into the Japanese island empire. The carriers or land-based aircraft provided air superiority to suppress enemy ground-based air in the area and to fend off enemy naval forces. The amphibious forces, army or marine, would then capture the base, and Allied logistical forces would move up to support the next jump. Without aircraft and cut off from support, the isolated Japanese posed no threat to the Allied advance.

The Submarine Campaign

While two great American drives pushed up the Solomons and New Guinea and across the central Pacific, the U.S. Navy waged one of the most effective campaigns of World War II—one that brought the Japanese to the brink of collapse. That campaign was the submarine offensive against enemy commerce. Before the war, the Japanese had recognized that commercial shipping would play a crucial role in bringing raw materials from the "Greater East Asia Co-Prosperity Sphere" to keep the war economy functioning.

Therefore, in their prewar buildup they expended considerable resources on modernizing their merchant fleet.

Ironically, the Japanese made virtually no preparations to defend commercial shipping. In fall 1941 only two junior staff officers in the naval high command were responsible for protecting the entire Japanese merchant fleet from enemy submarines. The title for their area of responsibility was "rear area" defense; within their sphere lay not only antisubmarine warfare but also antimining and antiaircraft operations. One officer with the derogatory title of "staff officer for training" was responsible for all commercial shipping along the Honshu coast and from Tokyo to Iwo Jima. Despite the obvious success of German submarines against British shipping in the Atlantic, the Japanese failed to provide escorts for merchant shipping at the onset of war. Not until six months after Pearl Harbor did they establish an escort fleet at Formosa, but it consisted of only eight destroyers.

At the beginning of the war the U.S. Navy could not take advantage of such weaknesses. It possessed excellent submarines with enough range and load capacity to operate in the wide expanses of the Pacific, but most submarine commanders were overage and lacked a killer instinct. It took the war's first year to create a cadre of younger, more aggressive skippers. But the problem was not just one of leadership; American torpedoes simply failed to work. The magnetic device designed to make them explode underneath enemy ships rarely functioned because the navy had tested torpedoes inadequately before the war. The navy's Bureau of Ordnance refused to believe reports coming from the Pacific about defects and blamed misses on the submarine commanders. When the evidence finally became too overwhelming to deny, another equally serious defect cropped up: the contact firing pin, designed to explode the torpedo by direct hit, was too delicate; direct hits jammed the firing mechanisms without an explosion. Not until July 1943 was the second problem recognized at Pearl Harbor, and not until September 1943 did U.S. submarines finally have effective torpedoes.

The failure of U.S. boats in their attacks on merchant shipping lulled the Japanese into a false sense of security; they waited until March 1943 to establish a second escort fleet. Even then their escorts numbered only sixteen destroyers, five coast-defense frigates, and five torpedo boats. In no fashion could they handle the storm that now broke. In September 1943 the Japanese lost a record 172,082 tons of merchant shipping; by November that total had climbed to 265,068 tons. Magic and other signals intelligence revealed the routing of Japanese merchant vessels; consequently U.S. submarines easily intercepted enemy shipping. In 1944, American submarines formed wolf packs in response to increasing use of convoys by the Japanese. The slaughter continued; in 1944 the submarine offensive sank more tonnage than the Japanese had lost in the entire 1941–1943 period. By the end of 1944, American submarines had sunk half the Japanese merchant fleet and two-thirds of their tanker fleet. Movement of oil from the Dutch East Indies stopped; shipments of raw material to the Home Islands slowed to a trickle.

Overall, American submarines sank 1,113 merchant vessels over 500 tons, a total of 5,320,000 gross tons. In addition they sank 201 naval vessels, including battleship *Kongo* and supercarrier *Shinano*. The total naval tonnage sunk reached 577,000 tons. All of this cost the U.S. Navy only fifty-two submarines. Considering that American losses included 22 percent of the sailors in the submarine force (the highest casualty rate of any branch), one should not minimize the cost, but the succes of the submarine campaign more than repaid the investment in resources and manpower.

Advance Across the Central Pacific, November 1943–February 1944

In May 1943 at the Trident Conference in Washington, the Combined Chiefs of Staff set long-range objectives for the defeat of Japan: while the Allies would continue to pursue a strategy of Germany first, they would maintain relentless pressure on Japan. The first aim would be to cut the Japanese Empire off from the raw materials of Southeast Asia; the second to launch a strategic bombing campaign against Japan; and the third to invade Japan and break its military power. To achieve these goals the Allies planned to build upon British efforts in Burma, American successes in the South Pacific, and Chinese military power in East Asia for a final offensive against the Home Islands of Japan.

But Admiral King had his own conception. Beginning in January 1943 he pressed for a drive across the Central Pacific by naval forces. This drive would move toward Japan over the coral atolls scattered across the

Admiral Ernest J. King believed, as a distinguished naval historian has explained, that "what was good for the Navy was good for the United States, and indeed the world." Never a seeker of publicity, he was an enormously talented officer who had a firm grasp of naval strategy and tactics.

Pacific. During the same period, MacArthur proposed an advance across the South Pacific via New Guinea and the Philippines. While King emphasized the advantages of leaping vast distances across the Pacific, MacArthur emphasized Allied obligations to the Filipinos, the advantages of maintaining pressure against an already retreating enemy, and the possibility of a renewed Japanese threat to Australia. Even Nimitz had qualms about two Pacific drives. In the end the American chiefs of staff performed a delicate balancing act; King would get his way, but the drive across the central Pacific would move first against the Gilbert Islands and then advance toward the Philippines, as would MacArthur. The move against the Gilberts and then the Philippines would leave considerable sea lift for MacArthur's forces.

Sea Power

While Halsey's and MacArthur's successes in Cartwheel were wearing away Japanese ground and air power, the naval balance swung drastically in favor of the Americans. The first Essex-class fleet carriers arrived at Pearl Harbor; at 27,000 tons, with a top speed of thirty-two knots and one hundred aircraft, they represented a major increase in naval air power. American industry was producing them at the rate of nearly one a month. At the same time the Independence-class light carriers of 11,000 tons with a similar speed and a capacity of fifty aircraft were also arriving. By autumn 1943, Fifth Fleet under Admiral Raymond A. Spruance had grown to six fleet carriers, five light carriers, five new and seven old battleships, nine heavy and five light cruisers, and fifty-six destroyers—all of which required an enormous support system of tankers, supply ships, and tenders. The carriers, moreover, possessed the F6F Hellcat fighter, which finally gave navy pilots a fighter superior to the Zero. All of this reflected design and production decisions made in the late 1930s and early 1940s. The new carriers provided the navy the capability to advance across the central Pacific toward Japan.

One of the great triumphs of the Pacific war was the fact that the U.S. fleet remained at sea on a constant basis with only individual ships returning for refit and with Halsey's and Spruance's headquarters rotating command. While Halsey's headquarters, Third Fleet, was commanding at sea, Spruance's headquarters, Fifth Fleet, would be in Pearl Harbor planning the next operations; and when Spruance and his headquarters went to sea, Halsey and his headquarters returned to Pearl.

No matter who commanded, a vast armada of supply ships sustained the fleet across the immense distances of the central Pacific. The unsung story of the drive across the central Pacific was the logistic support for that fleet, a fleet that quite literally never returned to its bases. It represented a triumph that no other nation could match. In a manner not anticipated in the 1920s and 1930s, the fleet could exist by itself in enemy waters for indefinite periods of time; it required anchorage only for resupply and refit, but more often than not the former took place while ships were underway in the open ocean. Island bases provided only the logistic structure from which the fleet drew its sustenance.

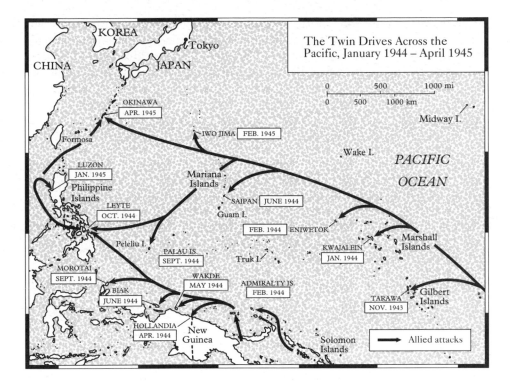

In October 1943 Nimitz created two mobile service squadrons. By the end of the year three squadrons contained thirteen large fleet oilers, innumerable stores and ammunition ships, and a whole host of smaller repair barges and tugs. These squadrons enabled the American attack fleet to cut its ties with the shore. Individual ships, of course, returned to port for overhaul and refitting, but the fleet remained at sea. The attack on the Mariana Islands in June–July 1944 suggests the immensity of the logistical operations. Some 535 combat and auxiliary ships carried 127,571 troops to island targets 1,000 miles from Eniwetok and 3,500 miles from Pearl Harbor; they then executed a massive set of landings *and* fought a series of great naval and air battles to protect the landings. By 1945 logistic capabilities of the U.S. fleet had reached an undreamed of extent. On July 21–22, for example, Task Force 38, after completing a series of air strikes on Tokyo, replenished at sea less than 450 miles from the Japanese capital. In less than two days supply ships transferred 6,369 tons of ammunition, 379,157 barrels of oil, 1,635 tons of stores and provisions, and 99 replacement aircraft. The Japanese had no chance against such capabilities.

Tarawa

The first target of King's Central Pacific drive was the coral atoll of Tarawa. The assault on Tarawa on November 21, 1943, was a costly but necessary learning experience for American amphibious forces. The preinvasion bombardment was too short, lasting only two-and-one-half hours. It stunned the enemy but failed to impair fighting capacity. Unfortunately for the attacking marines, the planners had underestimated enemy defenses. Equipped with 200 artillery pieces, including some 8-inch guns removed from the British defenses at Singapore, 5,000 Japanese troops defended Tarawa. As the landing craft moved toward shore, communications problems caused the bombardment to lift too early. Advancing in Amtracs, the first of three waves of marines reached the shore safely, but low tide prevented following landing craft from crossing the barrier reef. Some marines had to leave their landing craft 700 yards short of the beach; Japanese defenders slaughtered them as they waded ashore and pinned others into a narrow beachhead less than 300 yards deep. At the end of the first day the marines had 5,000 men on Tarawa, but 1,500 were dead or wounded. In the end, however, superior American firepower destroyed the defenders. When it was over only seventeen Japanese soldiers had survived, while the marines had lost 1,000 dead and 2,000 wounded.

As the marines suffered heavy casualties on Tarawa, the army's 165th Regimental Combat Team and 105th Infantry Regiment landed on Makin in the Gilberts. There the Japanese possessed fewer troops and virtually no heavy weapons. Nevertheless, the soldiers took four days to reduce the garrison. While their deliberate, careful approach kept the casualty rate low, naval support had to remain overly long on station. As a result, a Japanese submarine got in among the invasion fleet and sank escort carrier *Liscome Bay*, killing nearly 650 sailors. With control of Tarawa and Makin, the Americans had control of the Gilberts; the Marshalls were the next target.

Kwajalein and Eniwetok

Almost immediately after Tarawa, American naval leaders debated where to strike next in the advance across the central Pacific. Previous plans had called for a two-step operation aimed at two atolls at the eastern edge of the Marshalls, followed by seizure of Kwajalein in the chain's center. But Nimitz believed the Japanese had strengthened the eastern Marshalls and preferred Kwajalein as the next target. Spruance and Admiral Richmond Kelly Turner, commander of amphibious forces, argued that an attack on Kwajalein would expose U.S. forces to enemy air attacks from bypassed positions in the eastern Marshalls. When Nimitz insisted on moving directly on Kwajalein, Spruance received permission to seize an unoccupied atoll in the eastern Marshalls to provide a protected anchorage.

Accompanied by Task Force 58 with twelve carriers and 650 aircraft, the amphibians attacked the Marshalls at the end of January 1944. Although the defenders possessed formidable defenses, more than three-quarters of the 8,000 Japanese defenders were supply and administrative rather than combat troops. Moreover, the Americans had thoroughly studied Tarawa and other recent landings and succeeded in overcoming many problems that had occurred in earlier operations. Some improvements included a more

A battleship fires salvos onto a beach as Amtracs loaded with infantry move forward for the amphibious assault.

thorough reconnaissance of beaches and reefs, more extensive naval support fire, and enhanced communications between those landing and those supporting. Following three days of bombardment, the 4th Marine Division and the army's 7th Division captured Kwajalein at a fraction of Tarawa's cost in lives.

Success at Kwajalein led to a move within a month against Eniwetok, an atoll west of the Marshalls, while at the same time fast carriers neutralized Truk, 750 miles farther to the west. In a series of heavy blows, they destroyed 200 enemy aircraft, damaged the island's airfields, and then sank fifteen naval vessels and twenty-four cargo vessels and tankers. This ended Japanese use of Truk as an operating base and effectively isolated Eniwetok. On February 19, 1944, marines and soldiers hit the beaches at Eniwetok. Though a strong Japanese garrison occupied the island, the enemy had not prepared extensive defenses; and incessant air attacks hindered what efforts they did make before the invasion. Nevertheless, fighting was heavy but not nearly as heavy as might have occurred had the Japanese had time to strengthen their positions. Consequently the decision to attack Eniwetok in February 1944 rather than May saved a large number of American lives. By seizing Eniwetok the Americans had moved nearly one thousand miles from Tarawa. The Mariana Islands were next; once there, the Americans could begin aerial bombardment of Japan.

Continuing the Two Drives Across the Pacific, 1944–1945

By early 1944, relations between the army and navy were so delicate that the Joint Chiefs gave no clear priority to either drive across the Pacific. Their strongest guidance was that "due weight should be given to the fact that operations in the Central Pacific promise more rapid advance." At the Quadrant Conference at Quebec in August 1943, the British expressed concern about the twin drives and suggested that the Americans halt MacArthur. When King and Marshall defended the U.S. approach by arguing that the drives were mutually supporting, the British responded that they were also mutually competing.

MacArthur's Advance in the Southwest Pacific

While the Central Pacific thrust picked up speed, MacArthur's drive also accelerated. By avoiding enemy strong points and moving forward in leaps, he sought to advance the fighter-escorted bomber line until it could cover an invasion of the Philippines. In February 1944, Kenney reported that there was no sign of major Japanese units in the Admiralty Islands, 400 miles west of Rabaul. Anxious to complete his isolation of Rabaul and to accelerate the advance, MacArthur accompanied 1,000 assault troops from the 1st Cavalry Division to the Admiralties and landed on February 29. The attackers hit Los Negros Island, held by a Japanese garrison nearly four times U.S. strength. Fortunately for MacArthur, the enemy had deployed to protect the other side of the island. By the time the Japanese had reorganized, American destroyers had brought in 1,500 additional cavalrymen and 400 Seabees. Japanese counterattacks failed. By mid-March another brigade had landed, and the islands were securely in American hands.

MacArthur's risky but successful stroke encouraged another move. It also focused Washington's attention on the Southwest Pacific; thus MacArthur found support to strike at Hollandia, far up the coast of New Guinea. The new target, 580 miles from American bases, was barely within range of Kenney's fighters, but the capture of Hollandia would isolate 40,000 enemy troops and provide American control of three Japanese-built airstrips. Nimitz offered support from fleet carriers, but Kenney argued that his fighters could achieve air superiority by themselves. They did.

In mid-April the landing force departed from the Admiralty Islands. The main attack targeted Hollandia and a smaller force targeted Aitape (125 miles to the east of Hollandia) on the coast of New Guinea. The Japanese had 11,000 men in the Hollandia area, but few were combat troops. Achieving surprise, two infantry divisions under Eichelberger landed on April 22. By the 26th the Americans held all three airfields. The landing by a regiment at Aitape also achieved surprise. The Allies poured in additional troops, however, when they learned that the Japanese Eighteenth Army was moving west toward Aitape. After about a month's intense fighting and a loss of nearly 9,000 soldiers, the Eighteenth Army withdrew.

In late May, MacArthur's forces seized Wakde (150 miles west of Hollandia) off the coast of New Guinea, and a small beachhead on New Guinea to protect the island. On May 27 the Americans struck Biak (325 miles west of Hollandia). Both Wakde and Biak had airfields, but from Biak American aircraft could reach the Philippines.

At this point the Japanese were expecting to fight a major naval battle in the Central Pacific, but they recognized the threat posed by American land-based bombers on their southern flank. Consequently the Imperial navy assembled powerful amphibious and naval forces and moved against Biak in late May, but false reports about sizable Allied naval forces near the island convinced them to withdraw. After assembling an even larger force, including battleships *Musashi* and *Yamato*, the Japanese again prepared to move. Just before they could move, however, the Japanese received word of Spruance's strike against the Marianas in the Central Pacific. They immediately called off the attack on Biak, set in motion "A-GO," code name for a decisive fleet operation, and prepared for a battle in the Central Pacific. These events point out the risks as well as the benefits of having two Pacific drives. Had the attack on Biak begun earlier or had Spruance moved later, the Japanese might well have dealt MacArthur a serious blow—one that could have set the Pacific advance back by a number of months. Such an event would have also given Japanese morale an enormous boost.

Saipan

In the Central Pacific, the next objective was Saipan in the Marianas, one thousand miles west of Eniwetok. Even Nimitz doubted the wisdom of the move, for all the protecting air power would come off carriers. Aware of the impending landing in Normandy, King made clear that the fleet must reach for the Marianas and gain a significant victory. Only 1,200 miles from Japan, Saipan was the closest major island in the Marianas to the Home Islands; the new American superbomber, the B-29, could strike Japan from airfields located there. Along with Saipan, the Americans planned to seize Guam and Tinian as well. Protection for landing forces consisted of Spruance's Fifth Fleet. The attack force for Saipan included the marines' 2nd and 4th divisions and the army's 27th Infantry Division. After taking Saipan that force would assault Tinian. To the south 3rd Marine Division and 77th Infantry Division attacked Guam. On Saipan itself, the Japanese had 32,000 troops, but they had not completed their defenses. Again the Americans had moved faster than their enemy expected.

Overall commander at Saipan was the marine amphibious expert, Lieutenant General Holland M. Smith, referred to behind his back as "Howling Mad" Smith. The plan called for landing two marine divisions in the southwest corner of the island. New lightly armored amphibian tractors were to drive deep into the beachhead. A two-day bombardment by battleships, cruisers, and destroyers, as well as air strikes, preceded the landing.

The bombardment, however, had not concentrated sufficiently on the immediate beachhead and had been too brief; heavy enemy fire and rough terrain prevented the amphibians from driving inland. By nightfall, June 15, 1944, the Americans had 20,000 troops ashore, but the beachhead was 1,000 yards deep, half the distance anticipated by planners. Within two days, Smith brought in the 27th Division to reinforce the marines. That division had moved too slowly at Makin Island and Eniwetok, and on Saipan with a marine division on each flank, its performance was again marginal. At this point, Holland Smith did what MacArthur and Eisenhower regularly did in their theaters: he relieved the division commander. The result, however, was a cause célèbre, one that caused unnecessary bad blood between army and marine corps.

Outside the 27th Division and one or two other anomalies, army and marine divisions performed similarly in the Pacific. The divisions in the Pacific had an advantage over those in the European theaters, for once committed to the battle, army divisions in Europe remained in sustained, unremitting combat, in which replacements had to be integrated directly on the battle front. In the Pacific, fighting for the most part involved sharp bitter engagements over Japanese-held islands where casualties were usually high. But substantial periods of noncombat usually followed, during which units could adapt to new conditions, retrain their combat personnel on the basis of lessons learned in the last campaign, and integrate replacements in a coherent and effective fashion. The result was a steady and impressive improvement in the combat effectiveness of army and marine units in the Pacific.

By early July, the Americans had pushed the Japanese to the northern tip of Saipan. From there the enemy launched the largest banzai attack of the war. When the battle was over, the Americans had suffered 14,000 casualties, while most of the 32,000 Japanese were dead. To add to the tragedy, many Japanese civilians committed suicide or were killed by their own troops to avoid falling into American hands.

On July 24, 4th Marine Division attacked Tinian. The marines hit the narrow beaches opposite Saipan (within artillery range) where the Japanese did not expect a landing. Within eight days Tinian and its valuable airfields were in American hands. Meanwhile, 3rd Marine Division and the army's 77th Infantry Division took Guam. Here soldiers and marines got along without difficulty; the 77th, although never before in combat, was an exceptionally well-trained outfit, and its performance was every bit as good as its more-experienced marine counterpart. By early August the Americans had secured the island. Within several months, B-29s would begin the great aerial bombardment of Japan.

Battle of the Philippine Sea

As noted earlier, the American advance on the Marianas and the landing on Saipan caused the Japanese to halt their move against Biak and send the First Mobile Fleet of nine carriers, five battleships, thirteen cruisers, twenty-eight destroyers, and over 400 aircraft to fight a decisive battle in the Central

Pacific. In the subsequent battle of the Philippine Sea from June 19–21, the Americans enjoyed numerous advantages: their pilots were more experienced; their aircraft were superior; and they outnumbered the Japanese in almost every category. While the Japanese counted 222 fighters and almost 200 bombers, the Americans possessed 500 fighters and over 400 bombers. Enemy aircraft were superior only in range, but that superiority came from a lack of self-sealing fuel tanks and armored protection. Nevertheless, Japanese carriers could launch aircraft against American carriers while remaining outside the reach of U.S. aircraft from those carriers.

The battle of the Philippine Sea occurred after Spruance held his fleet between the Japanese and the American forces attacking Saipan and refused to sail west in search of the enemy. On the afternoon of June 18 the Japanese spotted the Americans. On the next morning they launched heavy air attacks but had to fight their way through a dense screen of F6F Hellcats, and then through heavy antiaircraft fire from American fast battleships before reaching the carriers. Relying on radar, American naval pilots intercepted and destroyed four successive waves of attacking aircraft; less than one hundred enemy aircraft survived out of 373. The Americans lost only twenty-nine aircraft; the pilots nicknamed their victory the "Great Marianas Turkey Shoot." Late that afternoon, American reconnaissance aircraft located the enemy carriers. Although the Japanese were almost out of range, the commander of Task Force 58, Vice Admiral Mark A. Mitscher, launched his aircraft and sank one carrier and damaged three others; U.S. submarines had already sunk two enemy carriers. Much of the Japanese fleet escaped, but it had lost the bulk of its trained aviators. As a result, enemy carriers had entirely lost their combat effectiveness.

The performance of American carriers in the battle of the Philippine Sea deserves note. No fewer than five subdivisions of Task Force 58 operated in close coordination, four containing fast carriers and fast battleships. Each carrier group contained between three and four carriers, fifteen fleet and light carriers altogether, while the fast battleship group possessed no fewer than six battleships. This conglomeration of capital ships, all completed and manned since Pearl Harbor, worked in close cooperation to provide the combat air patrols to shield the fleet, to cover the carriers with antiaircraft gunnery, and eventually to attack the Imperial fleet as it approached. In every respect the American performance reflected not only an awesome projection of military power across Pacific distances but an organizational triumph of impressive magnitude.

The Invasion of the Philippines

During summer 1944, the Americans squabbled over their next major target. King advocated a continuation of "island hopping" by seizing a foothold on Mindanao in the southern Philippines and then making a long leap to Formosa and the China coast; not surprisingly, MacArthur disagreed and argued that the United States could not leave the Filipino people under Japanese control. By and large, naval commanders in the Pacific supported MacArthur.

In September a raid by aircraft from Halsey's carriers suggested (wrongly) that the Japanese lacked strong forces in the Philippines. Halsey recommended cancellation of a number of secondary operations and a direct attack on the Philippines. Nimitz approved, moved the invasion to an earlier date, and canceled secondary attacks—except one. In September, following a three-day bombardment, the 1st Marine Division landed on Peleliu in the Palau Islands; this time, however, the Japanese had withdrawn from the beaches and established strong defenses inland. The marines that made the amphibious assault suffered more than 40 percent casualties, the highest casualty rate of any assault in the war. A joint force of soldiers and marines finally secured the island at the end of November but lost over 1,000 dead and 5,000 wounded. Unfortunately the island proved of little use in the invasion of the Philippines. Peleliu was probably Nimitz's worst mistake.

Leyte

Meanwhile, American planning and preparations proceeded for a landing on Leyte in the central Philippines as a stepping stone to Luzon, the main island in the northern Philippines, which included both Manila and the Bataan Peninsula. The invasion of the Philippines married the two Pacific drives. MacArthur's staff would control ground fighting, while his air commander, General Kenney, would be responsible for land-based air. Rear Admiral Thomas C. Kinkaid's Seventh Fleet, which had older battleships, would provide direct support. Finally, Halsey's Third Fleet with its fast carriers and new battleships would provide long-distance cover.

In early October 1944, Halsey's ships moved between the Philippines and Formosa, and a huge air battle took place. When it ended, American naval air had destroyed much of the enemy's land-based and naval air in the area. Inexperienced Japanese crews gave wildly optimistic but false reports of the damage inflicted on American ships. Meanwhile the Imperial navy returned its carriers to Japan for repairs and pilot training; the "Marianas Turkey Shoot" and Halsey's raids in October had stripped Japanese carriers of their air crews. The remainder of the fleet moved to Lingga Roads, near Singapore. Although the Japanese would have preferred to concentrate their fleet in home waters, the loss of tankers to American submarines forced the surface fleet to remain close to Borneo's oil.

The Imperial navy, nevertheless, prepared for a decisive battle. As usual, the Japanese drew an excessively complex plan, code-named "Sho-1," which was the Philippine variation of its overall defense plan called "Sho." Four separate task forces would move against the Americans: the carriers would sortie from the Home Islands and draw the American carriers away from the landings; the Japanese surface fleet, including super battleships, would move through San Bernadino Strait (south of Luzon) and attack the landing forces; a smaller task force would move through Surigao Strait (south of Leyte); and finally, another small force of destroyers and cruisers from the Home Islands would also move through Surigao Strait. For once the complex plan came dangerously close to success.

On October 20, MacArthur attacked Leyte. Under the command of Lieutenant General Walter Krueger, Sixth Army struck the northeast coast of Leyte. After the 6th Ranger Battalion cleared several off-shore islands, X Corps (1st Cavalry and 24th Infantry divisions) landed near Palo, while XXIV Corps (96th Infantry and 7th Infantry divisions) landed ten miles to the south. In the face of moderate Japanese opposition American infantry fought their way inland.

The Japanese responded immediately. On October 23 two U.S. submarines reported the main Japanese fleet north of Borneo; the Americans

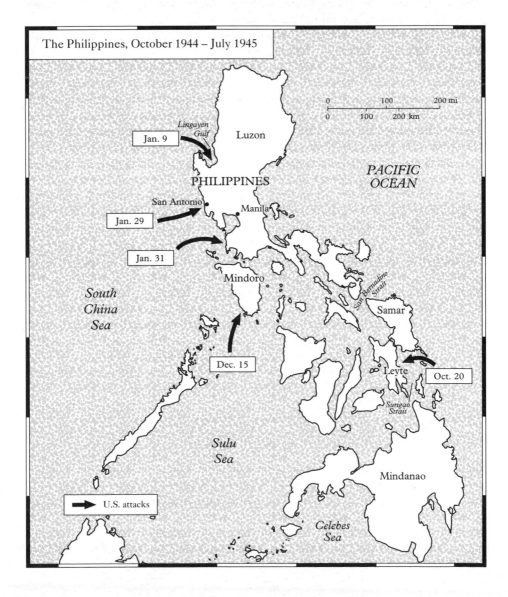

then attacked and sank two heavy cruisers and badly damaged another. Admiral Kurita Takeo, commander of the main San Bernadino task force, was using one of the heavy cruisers, the *Atago*, as his flagship. He transferred his flag to battleship *Yamato*, but the sinking clearly unnerved him at the start of the battle.

On the morning of October 24, the battle of Leyte Gulf moved into high gear. Japanese aircraft, based in the Philippines, found Halsey's fleet and launched a series of attacks. Hellcats destroyed most of the attackers, but one enemy aircraft got through to hit carrier *Princeton*, which eventually had to be scuttled. Meanwhile, Halsey's aircraft found Kurita's battle fleet west of San Bernadino Strait and sank super battleship *Musashi*. Although most of Kurita's force escaped serious damage, the admiral lost his nerve and turned back. American pilots reported his move but considerably exaggerated the damage they had inflicted on his other ships.

Now began a series of miscalculations that nearly resulted in disaster. Halsey had finally picked up the Japanese carriers to the north. Satisfied that he had taken care of Kurita, he moved to the north and took with him all the carriers and fast battleships. He left nothing behind to guard San Bernadino Strait and failed to inform other naval commanders. Meanwhile, the Japanese naval high command communicated its displeasure to Kurita about his retreat, and Kurita reversed course to the east toward the unguarded San Bernadino Strait.

The first contact between surface fleets came on the night of October 24–25 in Surigao Strait. Two Japanese task forces entered the strait separately, but battleships from the Seventh Fleet crossed the enemy "T" and sank all of the enemy except one destroyer. Shortly after dawn on the 25th, escort carriers supporting landings off Leyte suddenly spotted Kurita's force of heavy cruisers and battleships. Kurita had passed unopposed through San Bernadino Strait and turned south toward the invasion fleet where only a few destroyers and escort carriers stood in his way. Weak American forces desperately harried the Japanese and even sank three heavy cruisers, but if the Japanese steamed on, there was no chance of stopping them. Under continuous attack from American aircraft and weary after the pounding of the previous days, however, Kurita turned back. That ended the naval battle, although it did considerable harm to Halsey's reputation.

But attacks on the American fleet protecting the Leyte invasion had not ended. On that same day, the Japanese delivered the first *kamikaze* (divine wind) attacks. Though the suicidal pilots managed to damage some American ships and sink escort carrier *St. Lô*, their attacks marked the end of the battle of Leyte Gulf.

As the invasion of Leyte proceeded, the Japanese made other responses. Reinforcements arrived through early December and more than tripled the forces defending the island to about 55,000 troops and elements of five divisions. To achieve this level of reinforcement the Japanese stripped their forces from other islands, including Luzon and Okinawa. American air power, unfortunately, failed to interfere with the reinforcement because of the battering that the kamikaze attacks were giving the escort carriers. Moreover, it took a considerable period to construct air bases for the army's

On October 25, 1944, a bomb dropped by a plane from the USS *Essex* hit the *Ise*, a Japanese battleship to which flight decks had been added.

Fifth Air Force on Leyte. Following the arrival of the Japanese reinforcements, the operation became much more difficult for the Americans.

Krueger's objective was the port of Ormoc on the western coast of Leyte through which the Japanese had shipped reinforcements onto the island. Fearing the possibility of an enemy landing in his rear, Krueger moved slowly until the arrival of additional American forces. With the arrival of the 7th Infantry, 11th Airborne, and 32nd Infantry divisions, the Americans pressed forward. Nevertheless, the Japanese had used the time to strengthen their defenses along the mountains that extended north to south through the center part of the island. On December 7, the 77th Division landed just south of Ormoc and three days later captured the city. At about the same time the Japanese made a combined ground and airborne attack against the airfield at Burauen in the center of the island. After the seizure of Ormoc, however, Japanese resistance collapsed, and on Christmas Day the Americans seized the last port on the island. The Leyte campaign had cost the Japanese dearly; in addition to losing most of five divisions, their naval and air losses had doomed their other forces in the Philippines.

Luzon

Early January 1945 saw MacArthur finally in a position to redeem his pledge to return to the heart of the Philippines: Luzon. This campaign was the largest of the Pacific war with two armies (ten divisions and five regimental combat teams) fighting their way across a battle-scarred landscape. None-theless the campaign would still see Japanese forces in the field when the emperor finally surrendered in August 1945. For his amphibious landing, MacArthur selected the beaches of Lingayen Gulf on the western coast of Luzon; that location offered him access to the best road and railroad network in the islands as well as to Manila and its port facilities.

Had the Japanese attempted to defend Manila and Bataan as MacArthur had in December 1941, they would have suffered an even quicker defeat. But they did not. The Japanese commander in the Philip-pines, General Yamashita Tomoyuki, who had gained a brilliant victory over the British in Malaya and Singapore early in the war, yielded the main cities, particularly Manila, as well as the coastal lowlands, in favor of a prolonged resistance in the mountainous region of northern Luzon.

In early January 1945 the American invasion fleet sailed against Luzon. From the first, kamikazes subjected it to savage attacks; the U.S. Navy had no fewer than twenty-five ships sunk or damaged by these suicide attacks. Despite the kamikazes, Krueger's Sixth Army made an amphibious assault on January 9 against the beaches of Lingayen Gulf with four infantry divisions and a regimental combat team. Within several days the Americans had 175,000 men ashore. Facing only light opposition, Krueger's forces advanced south more than forty miles within two weeks.

Despite dense jungle and difficult terrain, American infantry relied on tanks for support. Tanks often destroyed enemy pillboxes and strong points or covered enemy positions with fire as American infantry advanced.

On January 29 the Americans made the first of two landings intended to keep the Japanese off balance. As part of Eichelberger's Eighth Army, XI Corps landed near San Antonio, sixty-five miles northwest of Manila. Two days later a regiment of 11th Airborne Division made an amphibious landing forty miles southwest of Manila. On February 3 another regiment of 11th Airborne made a parachute landing twenty miles inland. On that same day the first units from the landing at Lingayen Gulf reached Manila. Despite Yamashita's order to abandon the capital city without a fight, Japanese marines, not under his command, fought to retain the city. The resulting month-long battle wrecked Manila almost as completely as Warsaw. As many as 100,000 Filipino civilians died in the carnage.

Meanwhile, American forces rapidly liberated Bataan and Corregidor, names that still resonated from the dark days of the war. MacArthur also set in motion reconquest of the remaining Philippine Islands; in a month and a half, Eighth Army under Eichelberger made almost forty amphibious landings and swiftly liberated the remaining islands. The subsequent campaign in the mountains of northern Luzon, however, proved to be almost as difficult as the fighting in Manila. Yamashita dug his forces in and fought a skillful delaying action against the Americans. Despite severely pounding their Japanese opponents, MacArthur's forces never succeeded in breaking Yamashita's hold on the northern mountains. The end of the war would find the Japanese still tenaciously holding on, but by that time the fighting had passed well beyond the Philippines to the very gates of Japan.

The Final Campaigns

Iwo Jima

In fall 1944, B-29s began operations against Japan from the Marianas; by January 1945 the bombers were suffering heavy losses without achieving significant results. One reason was that Japanese radar on Iwo Jima (midway between the Marianas and Japan) provided the Home Islands with advance warning of impending attacks. Intending to halt this early warning, the Joint Chiefs ordered Nimitz to seize Iwo Jima. Planners also recognized that airfields on the island could provide emergency landing strips for damaged B-29s returning from Japan.

The Japanese recognized the danger; from June 1944 they had prepared to meet an American landing. The garrison commander, Lieutenant General Kuribayashi Tadamichi, utilizing already existing caves, turned Iwo Jima into a fortress with deep redoubts. As on Peleliu, the Japanese launched no suicide charges and did not attempt to hold the Americans on the beaches; instead, Kuribayashi chose to allow the attackers to come ashore and then to impose the highest possible casualties on them. The geography of the island helped the defenders. The Japanese placed their main defenses in a volcanic peak, Mt. Suribachi, which overlooked the entire island and provided an excellent view of the landing beaches.

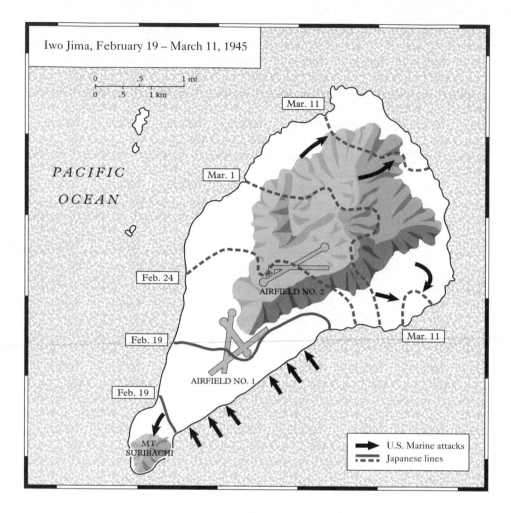

Iwo Jima, February 19 – March 11, 1945

PACIFIC

OCEAN

Mar. 11

Mar. 1

Feb. 24

AIRFIELD NO. 2

Feb. 19

Mar. 11

AIRFIELD NO. 1

Feb. 19

MT. SURIBACHI

→ U.S. Marine attacks
- - - - Japanese lines

Major General Harry Schmidt's V Amphibious Corps received the mission to take Iwo Jima. With the 3rd, 4th, and 5th Marine divisions, the corps was the largest force the marines had ever assembled. Though Schmidt requested a ten-day bombardment, Spruance agreed to only three days with a possible fourth. Instead of supporting the marines, Spruance used his carriers for an attack on Japanese aircraft factories; one suspects that the navy wanted to show what naval air could accomplish in comparison with the failures that B-29s had thus far encountered. On February 19, 4th and 5th Marine divisions stormed ashore after a four-day bombardment. They initially encountered light enemy fire, but soon a virtual storm swept up and down the beaches. Among the nearly 30,000 marines who had reached shore by evening, casualties were heavy, especially from artillery dug into the caves of Mt. Suribachi. The conquest of the flatter terrain was relatively easy, but the attack on Japanese troops dug in on the sides of the volcano was a nightmare. After four days of heavy fighting some marines worked their way to Suribachi's summit and planted the American flag. However, not until the end of March did the marines end Japanese resistance on Iwo Jima. The casualty bill was horrendous: 6,821 marines dead; nearly 20,000 wounded. Few Japanese from a garrison of 21,000 survived. Admiral Nimitz best described the sacrifice of the marines: "Among the Americans who served on Iwo Island, uncommon valor was a common virtue."

Okinawa

Barely had the fighting on Iwo Jima subsided when the next major amphibious assault began. This time the target was Okinawa, an obvious jumping-off position for the invasion of Japan. Defending the island was Lieutenant General Ushijima Mitsuru's Thirty-Second Army with over 70,000 troops. Ushijima recognized that he did not possess sufficient troops to defend the whole island; therefore he determined to fight for the southern portion to inflict maximum casualties on invading Americans. He also hoped that kamikazes would damage supporting naval forces sufficiently to reduce air and gunfire support. The attacking American Tenth Army, under Lieutenant General Simon Bolivar Buckner, Jr., attacked with a corps of two marine divisions and another of two army divisions. Two additional army divisions remained in reserve. Offshore no fewer than forty fleet and light carriers, eighteen battleships, and nearly 200 destroyers bolstered the landing force.

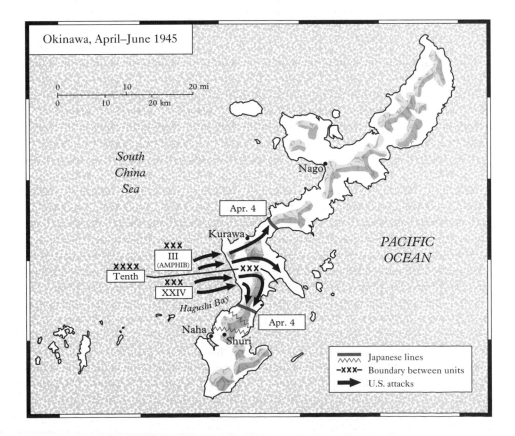

On April 1 the armada reached Okinawa and began landing soldiers and marines on the west coast of the narrow, long island. About 50,000 Americans landed the first day; by the second they had reached the east coast. While III Amphibious Corps turned north, XXIV Corps turned south. On April 6 the invasion fleet came under intense attack from kamikazes flying from Japan. On that day alone, 700 enemy aircraft—over half of them suicide aircraft—attacked the American fleet. Nine other kamikaze attacks, altogether numbering over 1,000 aircraft, hit the fleet standing off Okinawa in succeeding weeks. These ferocious attacks sank thirty ships, damaged 368 vessels, killed 5,000 American sailors, and injured a further 5,000.

On Okinawa, the marines cleared the northern half of the island in two weeks. But when XXIV Corps closed on Japanese defenses in the south, the killing began. The 96th Infantry Division ran into the main Japanese defenses first; soon three infantry divisions battered at the enemy's elaborate defenses. Some staff officers urged Buckner to use his reserve to make an amphibious assault and take Japanese defenses in the rear. Buckner believed such a landing would be difficult and costly and continued attacking straight ahead. As the Americans pressed forward, the Japanese launched two counterattacks, one of which cost them nearly 6,000 dead.

The Americans fought their way through the Machinato Line and then encountered the even stronger Shuri Line, which consisted of a web of mutually supporting strong points with artillery and mortars firing from caves. It was probably the strongest defensive position encountered by the Americans in the Pacific. But they continued pressing forward. By the end of June 1945, the U.S. Tenth Army had destroyed the Japanese Tenth Army of 70,000 troops. At least 80,000 Japanese civilians died in the fighting. The U.S. Army and Marines lost nearly 7,000 dead, with total American casualties (including the navy) 65,631 killed or wounded. Okinawa provided a frightening forecast of the coming invasion of the Home Islands.

Strategic Bombing

Strategic bombing attacks on Japan had begun in June 1944 with B-29s flying from bases in China, yet the problems in supplying that force from India over the Himalaya mountains presented insurmountable difficulties. Moreover, the Japanese army in China launched an offensive and took out the air bases, as Chinese nationalist forces proved incapable of serious resistance. But as Chinese bases fell, air bases in the Marianas (Saipan and Tinian) became available to the B-29s.

The bombing from the Marianas initially reflected the precision bombing doctrine with which U.S. Army Air Forces had entered the conflict. However, both weather and the nature of Japanese industry made such a campaign a dubious proposition. Much of the enemy's production occurred in small decentralized factories, the location of which was almost impossible to identify. In February 1945 a new commander, Major General Curtis E. LeMay, decided to launch incendiary raids on Japanese cities instead of precision attacks. Two high-altitude raids against Kobe and Tokyo proved encouraging.

Then LeMay changed the pattern of American bombing. The B-29s, now stripped of armor and defensive armament, attacked with incendiaries at night and at low altitude. In effect these attacks were indistinguishable from those of RAF's Bomber Command against Germany's cities. On March 8 the B-29s again struck Tokyo. Though attacking individually, LeMay's aircraft concentrated their bombs in the center of the capital; within minutes they had started a great firestorm. Japanese defenses were as incapable of stopping the attacking planes as the firefighting units were incapable of stopping the fires. By morning 83,000 Japanese had died, while a further 41,000 were injured; the attack burned out the center of Tokyo.

American bombers then proceeded to destroy Japanese cities, one after another. By July they had gutted the major industrial cities. Hundreds of thousands were dead, millions homeless. To add insult to injury, B-29s dropped mines and closed down Japanese shipping in the inland sea.

By summer 1945, Japan was prostrate. Industry was entirely isolated from the raw materials of Southeast Asia; cities were burning deserts; the Imperial navy no longer existed; and the tide of enemy conquest had reached Okinawa. Only the army remained intact, but much of it remained in China. If the Americans chose not to invade but rather to blockade the Home Islands, millions of Japanese would face starvation in the near future.

With this catastrophic military situation, one would expect the Japanese to seek an end to the war. They did not. They prepared, instead, to make a last-ditch stand. Some Japanese officers argued that such resistance would force Americans to concede more favorable terms. But most looked on further resistance as a matter of honor. A few Japanese, particularly in the foreign ministry, hoped to escape a final cataclysm; the Japanese did put out feelers to the Soviets, but Stalin had no interest in helping, since he had his own desiderata in the Far East. Moreover, even those interested in getting out of the war were generally unrealistic in the terms that they proposed.

Meanwhile, the Japanese military had arranged a deadly reception for the Americans. As a staff officer indicated after the war:

> We expected an allied invasion of southern Kyushu and a later invasion of the Tokyo plain. The entire army and naval air forces had volunteered for an all out Kamikaze defense, and each had from four to five thousand planes. Five thousand pilots were available with 3,000 in training. We planned to send over waves from 3–400 at a rate of one wave per hour. On the basis of Leyte and Okinawa we expected about one out of four planes to hit a ship.

The naval staff estimated that these attacks would damage somewhere between 30 and 50 percent of the attacking fleet. In addition there were nearly half a million regular troops in Kyushu, plus innumerable local militiamen. Finally the Japanese had packed hundreds of suicide speed boats with high explosives.

As the Japanese expected, the Americans planned to come ashore on southern Kyushu. In Operation "Olympic," Sixth Army with eleven army and marine divisions (650,000 troops) would execute the landing. The first wave would consist of three separate landings of three divisions each. To ensure availability of adequate forces, a steady flow of veterans from Europe began moving across the Pacific. Some senior officers in Washington estimated the conquest of Japan would double American casualties in the war, thus far approximately 700,000; even the much lower figures favored by some historians interested in minimizing the contribution of the atomic bomb would have represented a terrible price. What the Japanese casualties, civilian as well as military, would have been is unimaginable.

At this point the atomic bomb made its appearance. As the result of a warning from Albert Einstein to President Roosevelt, the Americans had started a major atomic weapons development program in the early 1940s. Code-named the "Manhattan Project," the program received vast resources from the U.S. government throughout the war. Nevertheless, U.S. scientists, aided by scientists from other nations, did not solve the intractable scientific and engineering problems until summer 1945. A successful testing at Alamogordo in New Mexico in July 1945 proved that atomic weapons had a good chance of working.

The new American president, Harry S Truman, then confronted the question of whether to use this terrible new weapon against the Japanese. Truman had learned about the A-bomb project only after succeeding to the presidency upon Roosevelt's death. In World War I he had served as an artilleryman on the Western Front and consequently had a real appreciation of the sharp end of combat. Some scientists argued against using the bomb; others argued that the Japanese should receive a warning or a demonstration of the new weapon.

In the end, Truman, influenced by the potential carnage of an invasion, decided to drop the bomb. On August 6, 1945, three B-29s flew over Hiroshima; the small size of the formation occasioned no fear among the Japanese. Over 90,000 people died in a flash brighter than the sun; three days later the Red Army rolled across the Manchurian frontier from Siberia and rampaged through Japanese defenses on the mainland of Asia. That same day another B-29 dropped the second atomic weapon on Nagasaki; another 35,000 Japanese died.

Amazingly, even after Hiroshima, the Imperial government still did not seek peace. The Japanese military had questioned whether the Americans really had such a weapon; then when incontrovertible evidence came in about Hiroshima, they claimed that the enemy could possess only one such weapon. The second bomb convincingly undermined that argument, but the Japanese cabinet remained deadlocked on whether to surrender. The deadlock, however, allowed Emperor Hirohito to take matters into his own hands. He ordered his advisors to surrender on American terms if he could retain a ceremonial position. Hirohito's decision was immensely courageous; for several weeks it was unclear whether the military, particularly the junior officers, would obey his command. In the end most did, and on

The second atomic bomb was dropped on Nagasaki on August 9, 1945. The fire-bombing of Tokyo in March 1945 killed and injured more Japanese and destroyed more square miles of urban area than either of the atomic bombs on Hiroshima and Nagasaki.

September 2, 1945, representatives of the Imperial government signed the surrender on the decks of the battleship *Missouri*. The six-year conflict was finally over.

World War II

On the decks of the *Missouri* in September 1945, World War II came to an end. By any criterion it was the most destructive conflict in human history, and the damage it had caused extended from one end of the globe to the other. Only North and South America had escaped the full impact of the fighting. Almost immediately after the war, the Cold War—overshadowed by the threat of atomic war—began. Consequently, World War II did not provide an enduring peace, yet it did see the destruction of one of the world's most pernicious and dangerous tyrannies, Adolf Hitler's Third Reich, as well as the destruction of Benito Mussolini's Fascist government and the Japanese Imperial government. Those accomplishments alone justified the war.

In the larger framework of military history, World War II was the most fluid of all major wars. Aircraft and tanks, as well as concepts for using them, restored mobility to land warfare. Gliders, parachutes, and airborne units greatly increased the reach of armies. More capable aircraft lifted larger bomb loads and flew greater distances, thereby exposing unconquered nations to sustained attack. Aircraft carriers and carrier-based planes permanently enlarged the dimensions of war at sea. Equipment and techniques for replenishing ships at sea allowed fleets to remain nearly permanently at sea and gave fleets almost unlimited range. Landing craft became large and seaworthy enough to sustain highly ambitious amphibious operations across open beaches. Improvements in sonar, submarines, and antisubmarine weapons and doctrine intensified the struggle for sea lanes. Radar helped airmen and sailors see beyond the horizon to find and destroy enemy forces. Improved communications permitted commanders to be better informed and to move units and equipment to critical areas. Altogether these developments ensured that air, land, and sea campaigns remained mobile.

Other developments gave the war a different character from previous conflicts. The Allies' ability to intercept and decode radio transmissions—Ultra and Magic—gave intelligence a timely and important effect on operations and provided the Allies significant advantages. In both the Atlantic and the Pacific, successful campaigns required an unprecedented interdependence of air, land, and sea forces—never before had large armies been transported over such great distances and landed on hostile shores with support from aircraft and warships. Waging war on a global scale also required unparalleled harnessing of men, women, machines, and raw materials. Ultimately it was the superiority of the Allies' production that gave them a decisive advantage.

World War II, nevertheless, represented an evolutionary change in the nature of warfare. Many key developments in the war that seemed revolutionary were in fact a continuation and an amplification of developments that had occurred in World War I. For example, the seemingly "revolutionary" operational employment of tanks by the Germans in 1940 in fact represented the fruition of tactical and operational concepts developed by the Germans in the latter part of World War I. Even strategic bombing, which carried the war directly to the enemy's homeland, had appeared in the last war, as had the relentless campaigns that American and German submarines executed against the commerce of their opponents. Developments did result, however, in substantially improved methods and equipment. One has only to compare the awkward armored attacks of 1918 with those of 1940, or the amateurish landings at Gallipoli in 1915 with those of 1945 to recognize the improved performance.

What was truly different about World War II was the unparalleled destruction it wrought, particularly on civilians and their possessions. Much of the devastation originated in Nazi Germany's fight for an ideology that aimed at destroying the liberal heritage of the nineteenth century and replacing it with a monstrous polity based on race. The Holocaust and the German crimes against the people of eastern and southeastern Europe were a direct result of the Nazi crusade. When the Soviets brought their own communist ideology to bear on the Eastern Front, the scene was set for an unrestrained and merciless war. The Allies added to the slaughter with strategic bombing, their air forces unleashing the whirlwind that the Axis had sowed at Rotterdam, London, Belgrade, and hundreds of other places. Raids by hundreds of bombers against German and Japanese cities killed and injured hundreds of thousands of civilians.

Adding to the devastation, the explosion of atomic bombs at Hiroshima and Nagasaki represented a true technological and philosophical revolution in war. These two explosions suggested that a war between powers possessing the bomb might lead to the annihilation not only of the opponents, but of humankind itself. By its development, the atomic bomb increased humanity's destructive power so greatly that it constricted warfare and ushered in an age where war between the Great Powers became unlikely.

The war also significantly affected political boundaries after 1945; the course of military events in the last months of the war in Europe and Asia largely established the borders between the new superpowers, the United States and Soviet Union. Soviet strategy and operations in the last years of the war had deliberately aimed at assuring firm control over much of Europe. The Yalta Conference in February 1945 occurred at a moment when Soviet forces were almost on the Oder River, a short hop from Berlin, while Anglo-American troops were barely breaking through the frontier defenses of western Germany. The resulting division seemed favorable to the West at the time, and the subsequent surge of Western forces almost to Berlin should not obscure the grim military realities of February 1945. In the Pacific the outcome reflected the consequences of military events. Since the destruction of Japanese military forces had resulted almost exclusively from American operations, the occupation of Japan became a U.S. concern and brought sweeping political and social change. On the continent of Asia, however, the hasty intervention of the Soviet Union ensured that Manchuria and northern Korea would fall into the hands of political movements favorable to the Soviets. The scene was set for future confrontations between the new superpowers.

The war also had an unexpected and crucial effect on the colonial powers and their dominions. The fall of France in 1940 loosened its control over its possessions in Africa and Southeast Asia, and the stunning successes of Japanese arms in 1941 and early 1942 against British and other colonial regimes further undermined their credibility in Asia and the Pacific. As a result, the dismantling of the great Western colonial empires began during the war and accelerated thereafter. In some cases that process was accomplished in a peaceful fashion (India and other British possessions being the foremost examples), but in other cases (Indochina and Algeria in particular), the process of decolonization proved extraordinarily costly and painful. In the long term, the war brought an abrupt end to Western political domination of Asia.

The settlement of World War II, nevertheless, proved to be surprisingly durable despite the Soviet-American confrontation in the Cold War. Conflicts would occur on the periphery and on occasion threaten cataclysmic war. But such a war never occurred. In that sense, World War II represented an enormous political and strategic success for the victors.

SUGGESTED READINGS

Appleman, Roy E., et al. *Okinawa: The Last Battle* (Washington: Office of the Chief of Military History, 1948).

Barbey, Daniel E. *MacArthur's Amphibious Navy: Seventh Amphibious Force Operations, 1943–1945* (Annapolis: Naval Institute Press, 1969).

Blair, Clay. *Silent Victory: The U.S. Submarine War Against Japan* (Philadelphia: Lippincott, 1975).

Buell, Thomas B. *The Quiet Warrior: A Biography of Admiral Raymond A. Spruance* (Boston: Little, Brown, 1974).

Cook, Charles. *The Battle of Cape Esperance: Strategic Encounter at Guadalcanal* (New York: Crowell, 1968).

Crane, Conrad C. *Bombs, Cities, and Civilians: American Airpower Strategy in World War II* (Lawrence, Kans.: University Press of Kansas, 1993).

Dower, John W. *War Without Mercy: Race and Power in the Pacific War* (New York: Pantheon Books, 1986).

Eichelberger, Robert L. *Our Jungle Road to Tokyo* (New York: Viking Press, 1950).

Frank, Richard B. *Guadalcanal* (New York: Random House, 1990).

Isely, Jeter A., and Philip A. Crowl. *The U.S. Marines and Amphibious Warfare* (Princeton, N.J.: Princeton University Press, 1951).

James, D. Clayton. *The Years of MacArthur,* 2 vols. (Boston: Houghton Mifflin, 1970).

Krueger, Walter. *Down Under to Nippon: The Story of the Sixth Army in World War II* (Washington: Combat Forces Press, 1953).

Lewin, Ronald. *The American Magic: Codes, Ciphers, and the Defeat of Japan* (New York: Farrar Straus Giroux, 1982).

Morison, Samuel Eliot. *The Two-Ocean War: A Short History of the United States Navy in the Second World War* (Boston: Little, Brown, 1963).

Potter, Elmer B. *Bull Halsey: A Biography* (Annapolis: Naval Institute Press, 1985).

————. *Nimitz* (Annapolis: Naval Institute Press, 1976).

Inoguchi Rikihei, and Nakajima Tadachi with Roger Pineau. *The Divine Wind: Japan's Kamikaze Force in World War II* (Annapolis: Naval Institute Press, 1958).

Roscoe, Theodore. *United States Submarine Operations in World War II* (Annapolis: Naval Institute Press, 1949).

Slim, William S. *Defeat into Victory* (London: Cassell, 1956).

Smith, Robert R. *The Approach to the Philippines* (Washington: Office of the Chief of Military History, 1953).

————. *Triumph in the Philippines* (Washington: Office of the Chief of Military History, 1963).

Spector, Ronald H. *Eagle Against the Sun: The War with Japan* (New York: The Free Press, 1985).

Thorne, Christopher G. *The Issue of War: States, Societies, and the Coming of the Far Eastern Conflict of 1941–1945* (New York: Oxford University Press, 1985).

PHOTOGRAPH CREDITS

Index